THE *KALĀM* COSMOLOGIC

LIBRARY OF PHILOSOPHY AND RELIGION

General Editor: John Hick, H. G. Wood Professor of
Theology,
University of Birmingham

This new series of books will explore contemporary religious understandings of man and the universe. The books will be contributions to various aspects of the continuing dialogues between religion and philosophy, between scepticism and faith, and between the different religions and ideologies. The authors will represent a correspondingly wide range of viewpoints. Some of the books in the series will be written for the general educated public and others for a more specialised philosophical or theological readership.

THE *KALĀM* COSMOLOGICAL ARGUMENT

William Lane Craig

Wipf and Stock Publishers
EUGENE, OREGON

Wipf and Stock Publishers
199 West 8th Avenue, Suite 3
Eugene, Oregon 97401

The Kalam Cosmological Argument
By Craig, William L.
Copyright©1979 by Craig, William Lane
ISBN: 1-57910-438-X
Publication date 5/24/2000
Previously published by The Macmillan Press LTD., 1979

TO
MY WIFE JAN
IN
LOVE AND APPRECIATION

Contents

Preface

Does God exist? Most people today would probably regard this question as having great existential import, but as one to which rational arguments are irrelevant. But historically, this has not been the case. Ever since Plato, great thinkers have, until recently, regarded this as an issue central to rational philosophical inquiry, and they sought to prove or to disprove to the best of their ability that God exists. In this book, I seek to examine one particular proof for the existence of God: the *kalām* cosmological argument. Although its roots go even further back, the *kalām* argument as a proof for God's existence originated in the minds of medieval Arabic theologians, who bequeathed it to the West, where it became the centre of a hotly disputed controversy. Great minds on both sides were ranged against each other: al-Ghāzāli versus ibn Rushd, Saadia versus Maimonides, Bonaventure versus Aquinas. The central issue in this entire debate was whether the temporal series of past events could be actually infinite. Proponents of the *kalām* argument contended that it could not and that the universe therefore had an absolute beginning; but since the universe could not have sprung into existence uncaused out of nothing, there must exist a Creator of the universe, or God. In the first part of this book, I exposit the *kalām* arguments of al-Kindi, Saadia, and al-Ghāzāli, whose proofs for the existence of God constitute exemplary models of the historical *kalām* cosmological argument. In the book's second part, I attempt to assess the worth of the argument in light of modern developments in philosophy, theology, mathematics, and science. Here we confront some of the most baffling and, at the same time, exciting problems that have ever stretched the human mind: the nature of infinity, the beginning of time, the origin and destiny of the universe, the existence and nature of God.

I would like to thank John Hick and Anthony Kenny for their reading of the text. I also wish to thank my wife Jan for her partnership in this enterprise, especially in the production of the typescript.

I especially thank Mr Hugh Andersen and Mr and Mrs F. C. Andersen of the Andersen Foundation of the Baywood Corporation for their generous grant that made this research possible.

WILLIAM LANE CRAIG

Albertville, France

PART I

Historical Statements of the *Kalām* Cosmological Argument

Introduction

Probably no chapter in the history of the cosmological argument is as significant—or as universally ignored—as that of the Arabic theologians and philosophers. Although we find in them the origin and development of two of the most important versions of the cosmological argument, namely the argument from temporal regress and the argument from contingency, the contribution of these Islamic thinkers is virtually ignored in western anthologies and books on the subject.[1] Furthermore, until quite recently the only articles on them had to be ferreted out of esoteric orientalist or Near Eastern journals. A paucity of English translations of primary sources exists; moreover, those works that have been translated are often available only through obscure publishing houses in far off places, making it all the more difficult to obtain material. These obstacles notwithstanding, anyone desiring a basic knowledge of the history of the cosmological argument cannot afford to overlook the contribution of these Muslim theologians and philosophers.

Most philosophers today probably have a passing knowledge of the principal Arabic philosophers, having read a chapter on Islamic philosophy in a secondary source such as Copleston's *History*.[2] If so, then they are aware that the Muslim philosophers may be divided into two groups, the eastern and the western, the former encompassing the Middle Eastern nations and whose most famous representative is Avicenna (ībn Sīnā), the latter centred in Muslim Spain and whose most well-known thinker is Averroes (ibn Rushd). The eastern group flourished from about the ninth to the twelfth centuries, while the western group, enjoying in Spain a culture vastly superior to that of medieval Christian Europe, arose about the tenth century and reached its height in the second half of the twelfth.

For our purposes, however, there is a much more significant distinction within Muslim thought than that between eastern and western. Muslim thought on the cosmological argument may be divided into two schools, each of which contributed one of the proofs: *kalām*, which developed various forms of the argument from temporal regress, and *falsafa*, which originated the argument from contingency, from possible and necessary being. *Kalām* may be simply defined as 'natural theology' or philosophical theism, while *falsafa* is the Arabic word used to denote philosophy, a new intruder into Islamic culture.[3]

Taken literally, *kalām* is simply the Arabic word for 'speech'.[4] It came to denote the statement of points of theological doctrine, and was later used to mean the statement of an intellectual position or the argument upholding such a statement. Ultimately, *kalām* became the name of the whole movement within Arabic thought that might best be called Arabic scholasticism.[5] A scholastic theologian, or a practioner of *kalām*, was called a *mutakallim*. Richard Walzer described them as 'dialectical or speculative theologians' and noted that they are methodologically distinct from the philosophers in that they 'take the truth of Islam as their starting point'.[6] The original *mutakallimūn* were the Mu'tazilites. This school of Islamic theology came into being through controversies involving the interpretation (*ta'wīl*) of the *Qur'ān* in its anthropomorphic descriptions of God and denial of free will. The Mu'tazilites denied literal interpretation of these *Qur'ānic* passages and affirmed man's free will, while the orthodox traditionalists adhered to literalism and determinism. Thus involved as they were in speculative theology, the Mu'tazilites soon confronted Greek philosophical thought and the challenge it posed to faith. Rather than adopt the traditionalist attitude that one knows his faith to be true without knowing *how* it can be true, the Mu'tazilites chose to defend the faith by the use of reason and thus to render their beliefs intellectually respectable. The defence of the faith was taken up by Abū al-Hudhayl al-'Allāf (d. 840/50), who in so doing, introduced into Islamic theology many of the

Greek metaphysical notions that were to characterise later *kalām*. According to Peters, the Mu'tazilite debt to Greek philosophy is best seen in their belief in the autonomy of human reason and in their metaphysical atomism.[7] With regard to the first, they maintained that man could come to know God through reason alone, unaided by revelation. With regard to the second, the Mu'tazilites adopted the metaphysics of substance and accidents, but with an atomist twist, for they identified substance with the atoms of which everything is constituted.[8] Not all the *mutakallimūn* were atomists, but all did agree on the nature of the accidents, that the accidents could not endure for two instants of time. Therefore, the atoms were radically contingent and had to be continuously re-created by God in every successive instant.[9] The theological motive behind this was to make God not only the creator of the world but its constant ground of being as well.[10]

W. D. Ross has commented that the advantage of the Aristotelian distinction of actuality and potency is that it conceives of change as a continuous process instead of a catastrophic re-creation of new states of being after former states of being.[11] In opting for a metaphysics of atoms and accidents which are continually being re-created by God, the Islamic theologians necessarily had to reject Aristotle's actuality/potency distinction and its attendant analysis of causality. For Aristotle, causation occurs when an actual being actualises some potency. But the *mutakallimūn*, with their metaphysics of atoms and accidents, could allow no such action of one being upon another.[12] Any change in being could not be due to the atoms, for they do not endure through time. Change would occur only when God re-created the atoms in new states of being at each successive instant.[13] Thus, the metaphysics of atoms and accidents inevitably led the Islamic theologians to deny the presence of any secondary causality in the world. God is the only cause there is, and everything that occurs is the result of His direct action in re-creating the atoms in different states of instantaneous being. Later *mutakallimūn*, such as al-Ghāzāli, argued fervently against the notion of secondary causality, contending that all we perceive is the succession of events, not any causal connection between them.[14] In this he has often been compared to David Hume, who denied that we perceive any necessary connection between events, which are given to us in atomic, separated sense impressions.[15] This comparison, however, can be very misleading. For Ghāzāli actually did not believe in secondary causality at all, God being the prime and only cause of all that takes place.[16] Hume, on the other hand, firmly *believed* in secondary causality, denying only that one could *prove* its existence or necessity.[17] The position of Ghāzāli and the *mutakallimūn* is much more akin to the occasionalism of Nicolas Malebranche than to the scepticism of Hume.[18] In the evolution of Islamic occasionalism, this resulted in a denial of man's free will on the part of the most rigid theologians. Fakhry notes that the metaphysical system of the *mutakallimūn* was therefore just as responsible as the doctrine of the *Qur'ān* for the fatalism that characterises the religion of Islam.[19] But this is to jump ahead a few centuries to the culmination of *kalām*. The Mu'tazilites, as we have seen, adhered to the notion of man's free will, so naturally many felt quite uncomfortable with the incipient determinism implicit in the repudiation of secondary causality which was necessitated by their metaphysical atomism. Therefore, some of them sought to modify the nature of the accidents in order to allow man the responsibility for his acts.[20] Apparently, however, the Mu'tazilites could not unravel this self-contradiction, and their successors whole-heartedly embraced the determinism which they so earnestly wished to avoid.

Bound as it was to political considerations, the fortunes of Islamic theology changed with the Caliphs. Thus, the Mu'tazilites dominated the theological world of Islam from about 833-48, when in that year the Caliph al-Mutawakkil repudiated Mu'tazilitism. The forces of traditionalism, led by Ahmad ibn Hanbal (d. 855), sought to restore conservative orthodoxy with a vengeance, severely repressing the Mu'tazilites. In 912, Abū al-Hasan 'Ali al-Ash'ari announced his defection from the Mu'tazilite cause and became the pioneer of a movement that took middle ground between the Hanbalites and the Mu'tazilites.[21] The Ash'arites and Hanbalites vied for power for over a century until the ascendancy of the Seljuk regime in 1055. This guaranteed the victory of the Ash'arites, and in 1063 the Caliph promulgated an edict of toleration, thus giving the Ash'arites the freedom necessary for the propagation of their doctrines. Very little is known about the development of *kalām* from the time of al-Ash'ari to that of al-Ghāzāli. Ash'aritism eventually came to be identified as Islamic orthodoxy. The term *mutakallim*, which had earlier denoted a Muʻtazilite, was now used to designate an Ashʻarite as opposed to a Ḥanbalite traditionalist. *Kalām* had become the argumentative theism employed by the Ashʻarites to defend moderate orthodoxy. Although the Muʻtazilite threat to orthodoxy was met successfully by the Ashʻarites, during the years that followed a much more ominous threat arose in the brilliant intellect of ibn Sīnā and the philosophy he propounded. This threat was also met, in this instance by Ghāzāli, whose philosophical theism marks a high point of *kalām*. But though *kalām* was to triumph over *falsafa* in the end, it was itself shaped by its opponent. For in every contest with *falsafa*, *kalām* itself became more imbued with the leaven of philosophy. Hence, Peters remarks,

> When the polemic finally abated Islam found that the experience of al-Ashʻari had been repeated: *falsafah* as such was further weakened, but in its place stood the scholastic *kalām*, faithful in principle to the revelation of the *Qurʼān*, but unmistakeably the product, in shape and procedure, of the Hellenic tradition in philosophy, orthodox and at the same time Aristotelian.[22]

What were the principle arguments employed by the *mutakallimūn*, both Muʻtazilite and Ashʻarite, for the existence of God?[23] Certainly the major thrust of the *kalām* arguments for divine existence was the demonstration that the universe is a created thing. Fakhry rightly calls this 'the classical argument for the existence of God in Islam',[24] and its development in the hands of the *mutakallimūn* forms one half of the legacy that the Arabs gave to the history of the cosmological argument, the other half being contributed by the philosophers. Al-Alousī lists six arguments employed by the exponents of *kalām* to prove the temporality of the world.[25] (1) The argument from the contrary nature of the simple bodies: the basic elements of the universe (earth, air, etc.) and their elementary qualities (hot and cold, light and heavy, etc.) are mutually opposed, yet in the world we find them combined; such combination requires a cause, which is the Creator. (2) The argument from experience: *creatio ex nihilo* is not unlike our experience, for in change the old form of the being vanishes, while a new form appears *ex nihilo*.

(3) The argument from the finitude of motion, time, and temporal objects: motion cannot be from eternity, for an infinite temporal regress of motions is impossible, since finite parts can never add up to an infinite whole; therefore, the world and motion must have had a beginning. Or again, motion cannot be from eternity, for an infinite temporal regress of motions is impossible, since an infinite cannot be traversed. Or again, if at any given point in time, an infinite series has transpired, then at an earlier given point only a finite series has transpired; but the one point is separated from the other by a finite interval; therefore, the whole time series must be finite and created. (4) The argument from the finitude of the world: since the world is composed of finite parts, it is finite; everything finite is temporal; therefore, the world must be temporal, that is, have had a beginning and been created. (5) The argument from contingency: the world does not have to exist; therefore, there must be something that determines it to exist. (6) The argument from temporality: bodies cannot be devoid of accidents, which are temporal; whatever cannot exist without the temporal is temporal; therefore, the whole world is temporal and must have been created.

The first and second arguments are primitive and not nearly so influential as the remaining four. There is general agreement that the third and fourth arguments stem from the last great champion of *creatio ex nihilo* in the pre-Islamic era, the Alexandrian commentator and Christian theologian John Philoponus (d. 580?), known in the Arab world as Yahyā al-Nahwī. Hardly a household word, Philoponus's name is nonetheless well known among Islamicists as the source of much of the *kalām* argumentation against the Aristotelian conception of the eternity of the world. Philoponus's *Contra Aristotelem*, in which he refutes the philosopher's proofs for the eternity of the universe, has been lost, but quotations of the work are cited in Simplicius's commentaries on Aristotle's *On the Heavens* and *Physics*.[26] Fortunately, a similar work of Philoponus's against the Neoplatonist Proclus has been preserved.[27] That the Islamic theologians knew of his works is evident from their bibliographical references.[28] These also give indication that the Arabs knew of a shorter treatise by Philoponus on the creation of the world.[29] Davidson provides this convenient summary of Philoponus's arguments:

A. Proof of the generation of the universe from the finiteness of the power contained within it: . . .

. . . First supporting argument: The heavens are composed of matter and form. Consequently they are not self-sufficient, and what is not self-sufficient does not have infinite power . . . .

Second supporting argument: The nature of matter is such that matter cannot retain any form indefinitely. Therefore, nothing composed of matter and form can be indestructible. . . .

Third supporting argument: The heavens are composite. Whatever is composite contains the grounds of its dissolution and therefore does not contain infinite power. . . .

The fourth supporting argument . . . any mass can be divided into minimal particles, and those particles can be shown to have finite power. . . .

B. Proofs of the generation of the universe from the impossibility of eternal motion:

First argument: If the universe were eternal, the generation of any object in the sublunar world would be preceded by an infinite series of generations. But an infinite cannot be traversed. Therefore, if the universe were eternal, none of the objects presently existing in the sublunar world could ever have been generated. . . .

Second argument: The eternity of the universe would imply an infinite number of past motions that is continually being increased. But an infinite cannot be added to. . . .

Third argument: The number of the revolutions of the heavenly bodies are multiples of one another, and therefore eternity would imply infinite numbers of past motions in varying multiples. But infinite numbers cannot be multiplied. . . .[30]

Anxious as they were to vindicate the *Qur'ānic* doctrine of creation, the denial of which they considered tantamount to atheism, the *mutakallimūn* eagerly employed Philoponus's arguments in various versions.[31] The first set of the above proofs corresponds with the fourth argument listed by al-Alousī, the argument from the finitude of the world. The second set of proofs correlates with the third argument, the proofs from time and motion. The fifth and sixth *kalām* arguments for the temporality of the universe are based on the atomism of the *mutakallimūn*.

The universe as a whole is contingent and temporal and needs God to sustain it in time instant by instant.

The overriding aim of these proofs is to demonstrate that the world had a beginning at a point of time. Having demonstrated the temporality of the world, the theologian may then ask why it exists. To account for the existence of the world the *mutakallimūn* invoked the *principle of determination*.

> With the temporality of the world as a premiss, the Mutakallims proceeded to prove that the world being created (ḥadīth) must necessarily have a Creator (muḥdith), by recourse to the so-called 'principle of determination'. In its barest form, this principle meant that since prior to the existence of the universe it was equally possible for it to be or not-to-be, a determinant (murajjiḥ) whereby the possibility of being could prevail over the possibility of not-being was required; and this 'determinant' . . . was God.[32]

Now this raises an extremely interesting and intricate problem: just what did the *mutakallimūn* mean by the principle of determination? It appears to be a genuine anticipation of Leibniz and his celebrated principle of sufficient reason. But what makes the question so perplexing is that the principle of the Islamic thinkers seems to involve the same sort of ambiguity as the principle invoked by Leibniz. That is to say, it is not at all clear whether the *mutakallimūn* mean by 'determinant' a *cause* or a *reason*. In other words, are they arguing that the equal possibility of the world's existing or not existing necessitates an efficient cause which creates the world in being or a sufficient reason, that is, a rationale, for the world's existence? The problem is complicated by the fact that the Muslim thinkers, again like Leibniz himself, do not always use the word in one sense only, but employ 'determinant' to mean 'cause' on one occasion and 'reason' on another. For example, Ghāzāli uses the two terms *murajjiḥ* and *takhsīs* in three different senses, according to Simon Van Den Bergh:

> In the argument given by Ghazali we find the term   مرجح
> ('determining principle', or more literally 'what causes to incline'; the Greek word is τὸ ἐπικλῖνον . . .), which is used by the Muslim theologians in their proof . . . for the existence

of God: the possible existence of the world needs for its actual existence a مرجح , a determining principle which cannot itself have a cause, for an infinite series of causes is impossible.

. . . The confusion lies in the term مخصص ('differentiating principle'), which can mean as used by Ghazali (like مرجح *praeponderans*, determining principle or principle giving preponderance) (1) a principle which, determining or choosing without any motive one of two *similar objects*, establishes a distinction between them through this choice, (2) a principle which determines or chooses, without the motive being known, the existence of one or two opposites which seem *equally purposeful*, (3) the dissimilarity which is the motive for the choice.[33]

In the above enumeration, (1) and (2) would be classed as efficient causes, while (3) would be a sufficient reason. The question is, in which sense do the *mutakallimūn* take 'determinant' when discussing the origin of the world? To answer this question we must examine the basis of the principle itself.[34] From information provided by al-Ash'ari, it appears that the Mu'tazilites used the word 'cause' ('*illa*) in at least two senses: (1) that which necessarily accompanies its effect, (2) that which is free and precedes its effect. God could only be called a cause in the second sense. But from the end of the third century A.H., the term '*illa* came to be used exclusively in the first sense. The term *sabab* was reserved for cause in the second sense. Thus, al-Suyūtī states, '. . . that which necessitates is called '*illa* and that which permits is called *sabab*.'[35] Thus arose the problem of God as the 'perfect cause' ('*illa tāmma*). For if God is the perfect cause, then either His effects must be eternal or He must never act, for if He came to effect something at some point in time, He would not then be perfect and all-sufficient. Thus, the world must be eternal or it could never exist. It is in this context that the principle of determination arises. Al-Alousī explains,

As to the idea of the determining principle (*al-murajih*); this arises out of the problem of the perfect cause, and its content is in brief that God is eternally perfect, and His will encompasses all potential objects; but why then does His will specify

that the world shall be created at one particular time, rather
than bring about its existence from eternity? Clearly there
must be a temporal determinant (*murajih*) responsible for
the activation of the will at one particular time. But all
times are equivalent in respect of God's ability to create
the world; either God must create the world in eternity,
in which case there is no need for a determinant; or God
did not create the world in eternity, but created it after
the passage of ages, in which case a temporal determinant
is necessary.[36]

Employed in this sense, the principle demands a sufficient reason
as to why God created when He did. The *mutakallimūn* were
divided in their response; for example, al-Khaīyāt attempted
to give a reason by saying that God knew which time would
be most conducive to the good of man, but al-Ash'ari repudiated
the principle by stating that God's will acts freely without
need of motive or object.[37] The school of Ash'ari was more
influential, and Ghāzāli follows his lead in this. According to
Ghāzāli, the principle of determination in the sense of sufficient
reason is simply invalid with regard to God. Hence, we find
him putting the principle of determination into the mouths
of his objectors.[38] Then he commences an elaborate two-step
refutation: (1) the world is willed from eternity to appear
at a particular time, and (2) that the world began in time
is demonstrable through the cosmological argument from temporal regress.[39] The second step is Ghāzāli's proof for God
which we shall examine later, but a word on his first contention
will aid us in dealing with the present conundrum. Ghāzāli's
first point is a clear repudiation of the notion of perfect cause.
God is not the 'cause' of the world in the sense that a cause
is that which necessarily accompanies its effect. But God is
a cause in the second sense mentioned above, a free agent
that precedes its effect.[40] Thus, the effect (the universe) need
not follow upon the heels of the cause (God), but can appear
a finite number of years ago when God willed from eternity
that it should. As to the riddle of why God did not choose
to create sooner, Ghāzāli, like Ash'ari, responds that God's
will needs no determinant to choose; rather, 'Will is an attribute
of which the function—rather, nature—is to distinguish something from its like'.[41] He illustrates this by imagining a man

confronted with two delectable, absolutely identical dates, of which he may choose one to eat. If the will cannot distinguish like from like, then 'the excited man will keep fondly and helplessly gazing on for ever, and will not be able to take either date by mere will or choice which is devoid of purpose'.[42] But the absurdity of this is self-evident. For it is of the very nature of will to simply choose, even when the options are identical. Thus, Ghāzāli rejects the use of the principle of determination in the sense of sufficient reason.

But as Van Den Bergh noted, Ghāzāli does use the principle in two other senses, each of which is akin to efficient causality. Thus, he would agree that the equal possibility of the world's existing or not existing requires a determinant to achieve its existence; but this determinant is not a reason, but a cause, and the cause is God Himself. This corresponds to Van Den Bergh's sense (1) of 'differentiating principle'. Sense (2) arises when one asks why *this* world rather than another?[43] This is the problem of specification, which arises out of the principle of determination, as al-Alousī explains,

> . . . by this was meant the specification by the creator that the world should possess the various properties, dimensions, etc. that it has, rather than others which it might equally have had. This question is closely related to that of determination but it differs from it in the fact that the possibilities from which the specification is made are not alike, . . . as in the case of occasions for creation.[44]

This problem also bedevilled the *mutakallimūn*, and the answer given to this problem is the same as that given to the question of the differentiating principle. God specifies what the world shall be like without the necessity of motivating reasons. Thus, according to Ghāzāli, God is the cause of both the world and all its particular specifications.[45] Certain aspects of the world—such as whether the spheres should rotate east to west or *vice versa* or where the poles of the spheres should be placed—have no sufficient reason why they are that particular way. God simply specified them in that way without a sufficient reason. There is no principle of specification immanent in the structure of the spheres themselves that demands that they should exist in the particular way they do; as Davidson points out, 'To refute Ghazālī, it would be necessary to show that a *rational* purpose is in fact served by the movements of the heavens in their present directions and by the present locations of the poles. . . .'[46] The only principle of specification that exists is God himself as he specifies without sufficient reasons.

To summarise, then: there are three applications of the principle of determination. (1) When the *mutakallimūn* demand a determinant for the world's existence, they are demanding an agent who chooses to create the world. (2) When it is asked what differentiating principle caused God to create at one moment rather than another, the answer is that no such principle exists. (3) And when it is asked what is the principle of specification that caused God to create this world rather than another, the answer is simply His will. Thus, we have separated out three principles—the principle of determination, the principle of differentiation, and the principle of specification—but in the Arab writers themselves, the principles are often used interchangeably.

Only the first principle, however, plays a direct role in the cosmological argument. This becomes quite evident when we consider the *kalām* proof for God. Ghazālī's statement of the proof makes it clear that he is demanding a determining agent who is the cause of the world:

It is an axiom of reason that all that comes to be must have a cause to bring it about. The world has come to be. *Ergo* the world must have a cause to bring it about. The proposition that 'What comes to be must have a cause' is obvious, for everything that takes place occupies a certain span of time, yet it is conceivable that it come about earlier or later. Its confinement to the particular time span it actually fills demands some determinant to select the time.[47]

Therefore, it seems that despite similarities the principle of determination is not the Leibnizian principle of sufficient reason. Rather the principle of determination in its application to the problem of the origin of the world demands an efficient cause of the existence of the universe.

But this does not mean that the principle of determination is simply the principle of efficient causality. For the cause of the world to which the argument concludes is conceived by the

Muslim thinkers to be, not just the mechanically operating, necessary and sufficient condition for the production of an effect, but a personal agent who by an act of will chooses which equally possible alternative will be realised. God is the *sabab* of the world, but not its *'illa*. Otherwise, the universe would exist from eternity. Goodman defines 'determinant' as 'selecting agent' and remarks that

> The notion of God as a Determinant, although related to that of God as Actualizor (and . . . as Creator, or even as prime mover), is conceptually distinct, and its development as an argument for divine existence may well be Islamic.[48]

Thus, when the *mutakallimūn* demand a determinant for the world's existence, they are demanding an agent who chooses to create the world.

This survey of the *kalām* arguments for the existence of God will serve as a basis for a more detailed analysis of the cosmological arguments of three of the *kalām* argument's greatest proponents: al-Kindi, al-Ghāzāli, and the Jewish thinker Saadia ben Joseph. But I would also like to say a word about that second great movement within Islamic thought: *falsafa*. Walzer has described Islamic philosophy as

> . . . that trend of Muslim thought which continues the type of Greek philosophy which the later Neoplatonists had created: a blend of Aristotelian and Platonic views as understood by philosophers in the later centuries of the Roman Empire.[49]

In these philosophers we find a strange blend of Plotinus and Aristotle, an amalgam aptly described as a 'synthesis of Neoplatonic metaphysics, natural science, and mysticism: Plotinus enriched by Galen and Proclus'.[50] For Arabic philosophy sprang out of the translation movement, which imported Greek philosophy ready-made to the Arabs; as Peters so nicely puts it, 'There was no Arab Thales pondering the possibility of reducing all things to the principle of sand.'[51] Rather Arabic thought was shaped by the Hellenism mediated to it through Syria. Syrian converts to Christianity at Antioch, Edessa, and other seats of learning, after having learned Greek to read the New Testament, turned to classical studies to provide an underpinning for their theological discussion.[52] When Islam superseded Christianity, the translation of Greek works into Syriac and Arabic was encouraged by the Caliphs, thus preserving in the Muslim world what was lost in the West, until the Arabs should return it again via the Jews. The translation movement had disadvantages that were to have a marked impact upon Arabic philosophy. For example, the famous *Theology of Aristotle* was actually a translation of Plotinus's *Enneads* 4–6, wrongly ascribed to the Stagirite. And the *Liber de causis* was actually excerpted from Proclus's *Elements of Theology*. The Arabs firmly believed that Aristotle and Plato were in agreement on the one true philosophy, which is understandable when one realises that they were under the impression that these Neoplatonic works were authored by Aristotle himself.

Perhaps the most marked aspect of Plotinian influence on the Arabic philosophers is in their emanationism. God is the One from which emanate all multiplicity and matter. But reflecting Aristotelian influence, they did not want their First Principle to be beyond Being, for metaphysics is the study of Being as Being and of the One as well. Thus, they brought the One into Being, and brought the world out of the One in a series of successive emanations, which correspond to the system of Aristotelian spheres. In order to avoid a pantheism inimical to Islam, they sought to make the One a necessary being in whom essence and existence are not distinct, whereas in all other beings such a distinction holds. Nevertheless, the universe is in a sense necessary, for it emanates inevitably from the One. Thus, what the Arabic philosophers gave with one hand, they took back with the other, and this produced a system of continual tension. Arnaldez remarks,

> Thus, this *falsafa* unites seemingly contradictory concepts of the universe; on the one hand there is a First Principle in whose unity are rooted both the essences and the existences of all beings, and in consequence a continuity is postulated between the Being and beings, which is not interrupted by any creative act; on the other hand, there is an absolute discontinuity between the modes of being of the Principle and of that which proceeds from the Principle. Thus it is possible to speak of a cosmological continuity between the

universe and its source (theory of emanation), tending to a form of monism, and of an ontological discontinuity between the necessary and possible, tending to re-establish the absolute transcendence of God. Furthermore, the possible beings, in whom essence is distinct from existence, are only possible if considered in themselves. But they are necessary if considered in relation to the Principle: granted a Being necessary *on its own account*, everything else is necessary *because of it*. . . . Hence, we return to monism.[53]

As for the philosophers themselves, they may be distinguished from their theological counterparts, the *mutakallimūn*, in several ways: (1) their more systematic use of more technical terms derived from Greek philosophy; (2) their whole-hearted endorsement of Aristotelian logic; (3) their study of the natural sciences, such as astronomy, physics, chemistry, and medicine; (4) their metaphysical system as a theory of necessary and possible being; (5) their doctrine that God knows particulars in so far as He is the source of their essence and existence; and (6) their insistence that the ethical life can be attained by the guidance of reason.[54] A main difference between a *mutakallim* and a *failasuf* lies in the methodological approach to the object of their study: while the practitioner of *kalām* takes the truth of Islam as his starting-point, the man of philosophy, though he may take pleasure in the rediscovery of *Qurʾānic* doctrines, does not make them his starting-point, but follows a 'method of research independent of dogma, without, however, rejecting the dogma or ignoring it in its sources'.[55]

We may credit the Arabic philosophers with the origin of the modern cosmological argument based on contingency. For though Aristotle hinted at it and the *mutakallimūn* called the world contingent because of their metaphysical atomism, it was the Arabic philosophers who spelled out the distinction between necessary and possible being on the basis of the essence/existence distinction. They therefore deserve to be credited with the origin of this important version of the cosmological argument.

With the passing of ibn Rushd (1126–1198), the exotic flower of *falsafa* in the Islamic world faded quickly, never to reappear. The Golden Age of *kalām* ended soon afterward with the death of Fakhr al-Dīn al-Rāzi (1149–1209), who was considered to be the reviver of Islam in the twelfth century just as Ghāzāli had been in the eleventh. But the *falsafa* and the *kalām* cosmological arguments did not die with them. The Arabic theologians and philosophers bequeathed their developments of the cosmological argument along with the legacy of Aristotle to the Latin West, with whom they rubbed shoulders in Muslim Spain.[56] Christians lived side by side with Muslims in Toledo, and it was inevitable that Arabic intellectual life should become of keen interest to them. The medium of this transmission was the Jews, whose own language was close to Arabic.[57] The Jewish thinkers fully participated in the intellectual life of the Muslim society, many of them writing in Arabic and translating Arabic works into Hebrew.[58] And the Christians in turn read and translated works of these Jewish thinkers. The *kalām* argument for the beginning of the universe became a subject of heated debate, being opposed by Aquinas, but adopted and supported by Bonaventure.[59] The *falsafa* argument from necessary and possible being was widely used in various forms and eventually became the key Thomist argument for God's existence. Thus it was that the cosmological argument came to the Latin-speaking theologians of the West, who receive in our Western culture a credit for originality that they do not fully deserve, since they inherited these arguments from the Arabic theologians and philosophers, whom we tend unfortunately to neglect.

In this study we shall be exclusively concerned with the *kalām* cosmological argument. So that we might acquire an accurate understanding of the proof as it was propounded historically, I have chosen to examine the arguments of three of the proof's most significant defenders, whom we shall consider in chronological order.

al-Kindi

Universally recognised as the first true philosopher of the Islamic world, Abū Yūsuf Ya'qūb b. Isḥāq al-Kindi (c. 801–c. 873) is known as 'the Philosopher of the Arabs'.[60] Taking his theological stance in the Mu'tazilite tradition, Kindi proceeds to develop a philosophy that can best be characterised as a Neoplatonised Aristotelianism. Kindi stands historically as the bridge between *kalām* and *falsafa*, and it was his conviction that revelation and philosophy attain identical truths, albeit in different ways.[61] Therefore, it is not surprising to find in him a strange blend of philosophical and theological doctrines not to be seen in the more purely philosophical thinkers who followed him. While his concept of God is thoroughly Neoplatonic,[62] he nevertheless sided with the theologians with regard to his argument for the existence of God. For unlike his philosophical successors, Kindi argued that God's existence may be demonstrated by proving that the universe was created in time. Indeed, the 'most important argument for God's existence in the philosophy of al-Kindi' is his argument for creation, and he stands apart as the only Arabian philosopher not believing in the eternity of the universe and matter.[63] Despite the influence of Aristotle and Plotinus upon his thought, he consistently upheld *creatio ex nihilo*: God creates the universe out of nothing (*al-mubdi'*), and Kindi uses the word *ibdā'* to specifically denote God's action as a creation in time out of nothing.[64] He reasons that if it may be proved that the universe began to exist a finite number of years ago, then the existence of a Creator may be legitimately inferred. Kindi's argument for creation may be found in his treatise *On First Philosophy*.[65] Here he utilises three arguments for the creation of the universe: an argument from space, time, and motion, an argument from composition, and another argument from time.

The first argument may be summarised as follows:[66] There are several self-evident principles: (1) two bodies of which one is not greater than the other are equal; (2) equal bodies are those where the dimensions between their limits are equal in actuality and potentiality; (3) that which is finite is not infinite; (4) when a body is added to one of two equal bodies, the one receiving the addition becomes greater than it was before and, hence, the greater of the two bodies; (5) when two bodies of finite magnitude are joined, the resultant body will also be of finite magnitude; (6) the smaller of two generically related things is inferior to the larger. Given these premises, it may be shown that no actual infinite can exist. For if one has an infinite body and removes from it a body of finite magnitude, then the remainder will be either a finite or infinite magnitude. If it is finite, then when the finite body that was taken from it is added back to it again, the result would have to be a finite magnitude (principle five), which is self-contradictory, since before the finite body was removed, it was infinite. On the other hand, if it remains infinite when the finite body is removed, then when the finite body is added back again, the result will be either greater than or equal to what it was before the addition. Now if it is greater than it was, then we have two infinite bodies, one of which is greater than the other. The smaller is, then, inferior to the greater (principle six) and equal to a portion of the greater. But two things are equal when the dimensions between their limits are the same (principle two). This means the smaller body and the portion to which it is equal have limits and are therefore finite. But this is self-contradictory, for the smaller body was said to be infinite. Suppose, then, on the other hand, that the result is equal to what it was before the addition. This means that the two parts together make up a whole that is equal to one of its parts; in other words, the whole is not greater than its part—which, according to Kindi, is hopelessly contradictory. All this goes to show that no actual infinite magnitude can exist. This has two consequences: (1) The universe must be spatially finite. For it is impossible for an actually infinite body to exist. (2) The universe must be temporally finite. For time is quantitative and thus cannot be infinite in actuality. Time must have had a beginning. Now time is not an independent existent, but is the duration of the body of the universe. Because time is finite, so is the being of the universe. Or to put it another way: time is the measure of motion; it is a duration counted by motion. Now motion cannot exist without a body—this is obvious, for change is always the change of some *thing*. But it is equally true that a body cannot exist without motion.[67] It is said that perhaps the body of the universe was originally at rest and then began to move. But this is impossible. For the universe is either generated from nothing or eternal. If it is generated from nothing, then its very generation is a type of motion. Thus, body would not precede motion. On the other hand, if the universe is eternal and was once at rest, motion could never arise. For motion is change, and the eternal does not change. The eternal simply is and does not change or become more perfect. It is fully actual and thus cannot move. Therefore, it is self-contradictory to say the universe is eternal and yet motion has a beginning. Motion and the universe are thus co-terminous; body cannot exist without motion. The upshot of all this is that body implies motion and motion implies time; therefore, if time had a beginning, then motion and body must have had a beginning as well. For it is impossible for body or motion to exist without time. We have shown that time must be finite. Therefore, the being of the universe must be finite as well.

Al-Kindi's second argument may be summarised as follows:[68] Composition involves change, for it is a joining and organising of things. Bodies are composed in two ways: (1) They are composed of the substance which is its genus and of its three dimensions, which are its specific difference. (2) They are composed of matter and form. Composition involves motion from a prior uncomposed state. Thus, if there were no motion, there could be no composition, and if there were no composition, there could be no bodies. Now time is the duration counted by motion. Body, motion, and time thus occur simultaneously in being. Therefore, since time is finite, motion is finite; and since motion is finite, composition is finite; and since composition is finite, bodies are finite, too.

We may summarise the third argument as follows:[69] It must be the case that before every temporal segment there is another segment of time until we reach a beginning of time, that is, a temporal segment before which there is no segmented duration. For if this were not the case, then any given moment in time would never arrive. The duration from the past infinity to the given moment is equal to the duration from the given moment regressing back into infinity. And if we know what the duration is from past infinity to the given moment, then we know what the duration from the given moment back to infinity is. But this means the infinite is finite, an impossible contradiction. Moreover, any given moment cannot be reached until a time before it has been reached, and that time cannot be reached until a time before it has been reached, and so on, *ad infinitum*. But is impossible to traverse the infinite; therefore, if time were infinite, the given moment would never have arrived. But clearly a given moment has arrived; therefore, time must be finite. Bodies, then, do not have infinite duration, and as bodies cannot exist without duration, the being of body is finite and cannot be eternal. (Nor can future time be infinite in actuality. For past time is finite, and future time consists of adding consecutive, finite times to the time already elapsed. And two things quantitatively finite added together produce a finite thing [principle five]. Thus, future time never reaches the actually infinite. If someone were to assert that a definite past added to a definite future produces an infinite whole, this can be shown to be false. For time is a continuous quantity, divided by the present into past and future. Every definite time has a first limit and a last limit; in this case, the past and the future share a common limit: the present. But if we know one limit of each of the times, the other limit is also definite and knowable. Thus, the whole continuous quantity of time—past, present, and future—must be definite and limited. Therefore, the future can never be actually infinite.)

We have already mentioned the influence of John Philoponus upon Arabic cosmological thought, and al-Kindi is no exception to the rule. According to Walzer, Kindi was familiar with either Philoponus's actual works or, more probably, a summary of his main tenets.[70] According to Davidson, there were different sets of Philoponus's arguments being circulated, and Kindi's three proofs from creation suggest that he used such a set as the springboard for his own formulation of the case for temporal creation.[71] The second proof in particular shows the influence of the Christian philosopher. He had contended that composition of matter and form and of tri-dimensionality was sufficient to prove the finitude of the universe, and Kindi, with some modifications, follows him in this.[72] The third proof also derives directly from Philoponus, who had reasoned that an infinite number of motions would have had to occur before present motions can take place, if the world were eternal.[73] The significant difference between this and Kindi's version of the proof is that Kindi substitutes time for motion, arguing that an infinite number of temporal segments would have had to elapse before any given moment could arrive. As for the first proof, which is Kindi's most important, Philoponus's influence is at best only indirect. He argued against the infinitude of the body of the universe and employed arguments showing the absurdity of infinites of different sizes, but he did not use Kindi's deductive reasoning against the possibility of the existence of the actual infinite. This would appear to be the argument in which Kindi's own contribution is most marked.

Kindi's three proofs may be outlined in this way:

1. There are six self-evident principles:
   (a) Two bodies of which one is not greater than the other are equal.
   (b) Equal bodies are those where the dimensions between their limits are equal in actuality and potentiality.
   (c) That which is finite is not infinite.
   (d) When a body is added to one of two equal bodies, the one receiving the addition becomes greater than it was before and, hence, the greater of the two bodies.
   (e) When two bodies of finite magnitude are joined, the resultant body will also be of finite magnitude.
   (f) The smaller of two generically related things is inferior to the larger.
2. No actual infinite can exist because:
   (a) If one removes a body of finite magnitude from a body of infinite magnitude, the remainder will be a body of either finite or infinite magnitude.

(b) It cannot be finite
    (*i*) because when the finite body that was removed is added back to the remainder, the resultant body would be finite
        (*a*) because of principle 1.(e).
    (*ii*) The body would then be both infinite and finite.
    (*iii*) But this is self-contradictory
        (*a*) because of principle 1.(c).
(c) It cannot be infinite
    (*i*) because when the finite body that was removed is added back to the remainder, the resultant body would be either greater than or equal to what it was before the addition.
        (*a*) It cannot be greater than it was before the addition
            (*i*) because then we would have two infinite bodies, one of which is greater than the other.
            (*ii*) The smaller would be inferior to the greater
                (*a*) because of principle 1. (f)
            (*iii*) And the smaller would be equal to a portion of the greater.
            (*iv*) Thus, the smaller body and the portion would be finite
                (*a*) because they must have limits
                    α. because of principle 1.(b).
            (*v*) The smaller body would then be both infinite and finite.
            (*vi*) But this is self-contradictory
                (*a*) because of principle 1.(c).
        (*b*) It cannot be equal to what it was before the addition
            (*i*) because the whole body composed of the greater portion and the smaller portion would be equal to the greater portion alone.
            (*ii*) Thus, a part would be equal to the whole.
            (*iii*) But this is self-contradictory.
3. Therefore, the universe is spatially and temporally finite because:

(a) The universe is spatially finite
    (*i*) because an actually infinite body cannot exist.
(b) The universe is temporally finite
    (*i*) because time is finite.
        (*a*) Time is finite
            (*i*) because time is quantitative,
            (*ii*) and an actually infinite quantity cannot exist.
        (*b*) Time is the duration of the body of the universe.
        (*c*) Therefore, the being of the body of the universe is finite.
    (*ii*) because motion is finite.
        (*a*) Motion cannot exist prior to body
            (*i*) because motion is the change of some *thing*.
        (*b*) Body cannot exist prior to motion
            (*i*) because the universe is either generated from nothing or eternal.
                (*a*) If it is generated from nothing, body would not precede motion
                    α. because its very generation is a motion.
                (*b*) If it is eternal, body would not precede motion
                    α. because motion is change,
                    β. and the eternal cannot change
                        (α) because it simply *is*, in a fully actual state.
        (*c*) Thus, body and motion can only exist in conjunction with each other.
        (*d*) Motion implies time
            (*i*) because time is a duration counted by motion.
        (*e*) Time is finite
            (*i*) because of 3.(b)(*i*)(*a*).
        (*f*) Therefore, motion is finite.
        (*g*) Therefore, the being of the body of the universe is finite.
    (*iii*) because the universe is composed.
        (*a*) Composition involves change (motion)
            (*i*) because it is a joining of things together.

  (*b*) Bodies are composed
    (*i*) because they are made up of substance and of three dimensions,
    (*ii*) because they are made up of matter and form.
  (*c*) Motion involves time
    (*i*) because time is a duration counted by motion.
  (*d*) Time is finite
    (*i*) because of 3.(b)(*i*)(*a*).
  (*e*) Therefore, motion is finite.
  (*f*) Therefore, composition is finite.
  (*g*) Therefore, the being of body is finite.
 (*iv*) because time must have a beginning.
  (*a*) Otherwise, any given moment in time would never arrive
    (*i*) because infinite time is self-contradictory.
     (*a*) The duration from past infinity to any given moment is equal to the duration from the given moment regressing back into infinity.
     (*b*) Knowledge of the former duration implies a knowledge of the latter duration.
     (*c*) But this makes the infinite to be finite.
     (*d*) This is self-contradictory
      α. because of principle 1.(c).
    (*ii*) because infinite time could not be traversed.
     (*a*) Before any given moment could be reached, an infinity of prior moments would have to have been reached.
     (*b*) But one cannot traverse the infinite.
     (*c*) So any given moment could never be reached.
     (*d*) But moments are, in fact, reached.
  (*b*) Moreover, future time cannot be actually infinite.
    (*i*) The future consists of consecutive additions of finite times.

(*ii*) Past time is finite
    (*a*) because of 3.(b)(*iv*)(*a*).
(*iii*) Therefore, future time is finite
    (*a*) because of principle 1.(e).

A brief examination of each of these steps will be worthwhile. First, *there are six self-evident principles.* Kindi actually refers to them as 'true first premisses which are thought with no mediation'.[74] In his subsequent argumentation, he only employs the second, third, fifth, and sixth principles. In fact, he could dismiss point 2.(c)(*i*)(*b*) at once as a violation of the fourth principle, but he does not. Hence, the first and fourth principles need not concern us. The remaining principles are easy enough to understand, whether one agrees with them or not. Principle 1.(c) is clearly what we would call an analytic statement. Judging by Kindi's use of principle 1.(f), the same could be said of it; 'inferior' carries here no judgement of worth. One might argue that Kindi is unfair in principle 1.(b), for one can imagine equal bodies that would not involve limits. For example, one might imagine two infinite parallel planes in space or two parallel planes that start at the same place and extend infinitely in one direction. Under principle 1.(a), they could be called equal, for one is not greater than the other. Indeed, it might be argued that principle 1.(a) contains the better definition of 'equal' and that principle 2.(a) is question-begging. Principle 1.(e) appears true enough; the real questions arise when one asks whether finites can ever add up to an infinite, or what happens when one adds a finite to an infinite. But for now, we may let that pass and agree with Kindi for argument's sake that there are six self-evident principles.

Principles in hand, Kindi next desires to demonstrate that *no actual infinite can exist.* His use of the word 'actual' is of paramount importance. Kindi's use of this term as well as the word 'body' in step 2.(a) makes it quite clear that he is arguing that no infinite quantity can exist *in reality.* He is quite willing to grant that an infinite quantity may exist *potentially.* He explains,

As it is possible through the imagination for something to be continually added to the body of the universe, if we imagine something greater than it, then continually something greater than that— there being no limit to addition as a possibility—the body of the universe is potentially infinite, since potentiality is nothing other than the possibility that the thing said to be in potentiality will occur. Everything, moreover, within that which has infinity in potentiality also potentially has infinity, including motion and time. That which has* infinity exists only in potentiality, whereas in actuality it is impossible for something to have infinity. . . .

* Reading فان الذي . . . .[75]

Kindi grants that space and time are both potentially infinite, but he denies that such a potentiality could ever be fully instantiated in reality. Though we can imagine the infinite, it is impossible for it to actually exist. The point is, of course, Aristotle's,[76] but al-Kindi turns the Greek philosopher's own principle back upon him and argues that a consistent application of the principle would prohibit Aristotle's doctrine of eternal motion and infinite time. Al-Kindi's use of the word 'body' also deserves comment. We have already remarked that this underlines the fact that he is talking about extra-mentally existing entities, and not just abstract magnitudes. He never speaks of magnitudes in a conceptual way; he is arguing about the real world and always speaks of *bodies* of finite or infinite magnitude. On the other hand, it is clear that by 'body', Kindi does not mean only an extended thing, for he applies his analysis to time as well. In speaking of time, he makes it evident that his analysis of the actual infinite applies to any extra-mentally existing quantitative entity:

It has now been explained that it is impossible for a body to have infinity, and in this manner it has been explained that any quantitative thing cannot have infinity in actuality. Now time is quantitative, and it is impossible that time have infinity in actuality, time having a finite beginning.[77]

In this way time as well as space will fall within the pale of his argument.

As for the argument itself, it is easy enough to follow. He presents a hypothetical involving a dilemma. This seems to be his favourite form of argument, for he employs it repeatedly throughout the course of his proof. His reason for denying the first disjunct seems obvious enough, but a comment on the second may be helpful. Here he posits a second hypothetical and dilemma. It is interesting that he does not regard step 2.(c)$(i)(a)(i)$, which establishes two actually existing infinities of which one is greater than the other, as an obvious absurdity. He argues that the smaller infinite body must be equal to a portion of the larger infinite body and, on his definitions, equal bodies have limits. Therefore, they must be finite. Now besides questioning the validity of his definition of 'equal', one might also wonder if having limits is synonymous with finitude. This is the problem of the infinitesimal, and one might ask if one could not have two bodies of nearly equal length each containing an infinite number of atoms. Such speculation was at the heart of Mu'tazilite atomism and could hardly have been unknown to al-Kindi. Yet he simply takes it for granted that a body with limits is finite. As for step 2.(c)$(i)(b)$, we have already noted that this disjunct could be dismissed as a violation of principle 1.(d), which holds that when a body is added to another body, the one receiving the addition becomes greater than it was before. Instead of this, Kindi refutes the point, utilising a principle that should have been added to his six: the whole is greater than a part. Having now refuted all the consequents, Kindi may now deny the ground: no actual infinite can exist.

Kindi then applies this reasoning to the universe: *therefore, the universe is spatially and temporally finite.* Step 3.(a) is really extraneous to his proof, since what Kindi is really about is to prove the universe began in time—its physical dimensions are interesting but irrelevant. As our outline reveals, Kindi's three proofs for the temporal finitude of the universe actually break down into four. This may be because the second argument appears to be a sort of after-thought on the first and serves to answer a possible objection to the first; so Kindi treats them as one. An actually infinite magnitude cannot exist, he reasons; therefore, time must be finite. The argument regards time as a magnitude, since it is capable of being measured. Since time is the duration of the body of the universe, the being of that body must be as finite as time itself. This reasoning depends upon Kindi's definition of time. This is not the Aristote-

lian definition, which links time to motion, not just to duration
in being. In this first proof, Kindi seems to anticipate the
idea of spacetime, a nexus in which space and time are inextricably bound up together.[78] He says,

> Time is the time, i.e., duration, of the body of the universe.
> If time is finite, then the being* of [this] body is finite,
> since time is not an [independent] existent.
>
> * أنية ....[79]

But someone might object that since, according to Aristotle,
time is the measure of motion, it would be possible to have
finite time, but at the same time an eternal universe. One
might imagine an absolutely still, eternal universe, which then
began to move so many years ago. Therefore, Kindi leaves
his first definition and hastens to add,

> Nor is there any body without time, as time is but the
> number of motion, i.e., it is a duration counted by motion.
> If there is motion, there is time; and if there were not
> motion, there would not be time.[80]

This serves to introduce his argument from motion, which
proceeds according to the Aristotelian concept of time. Step
3.(b)(*ii*)(*a*) is extraneous to his proof, since he wants to prove
that if motion had a beginning, the universe had a beginning.
Therefore, he must demonstrate 3.(b)(*ii*)(*b*), that body cannot
exist prior to motion. He posits a disjunction and proceeds
to show how either disjunct proves his case. The first argument
is Aristotle's: the very generation of the universe is a motion.[81]
(Kindi considers generation and corruption to be motions,
whereas Aristotle would technically refer to them as change,
not motion.) Besides this, the very point al-Kindi is out to
prove is the generation of the universe, so that it does the
opponent no good to yield it to him here. The second disjunct
is clearly the crucial one: can the universe be eternal and
begin to move at a point a finite number of years ago? Kindi
says no; the eternal cannot change. Unfortunately, his proof
is little more than assertion:

Motion is change, and the eternal does not move, for
it neither changes nor removes from deficiency to perfection.
Locomotion is a kind of motion, and the eternal does not
remove* to perfection, since it does not move.

* لا ينتقل .... .82

This appears to be circular: the eternal cannot change because
it is perfect; it is perfect because it cannot change. But he
later gives us a clue to his reasoning:

If . . . the body [of the universe] is eternal, having rested
and then moved, . . . then the body of the universe . . .
will have moved from actual rest to actual movement, whereas
that which is eternal does not move, as we have explained
previously. The body of the universe is then moving and
not moving, and this is an impossible contradiction and it
is not possible for the body of the universe to be eternal,
resting in actuality, and then to have moved into movement
in actuality.83

The terminology here immediately calls to mind the Aristotelian
distinction of actuality and potentiality. Al-Kindi appears to
reason that anything existing eternally at rest must be a being
of complete actuality, with no potential for movement. Having
no potentiality, it could never change; it simply *is*. Therefore,
it would be impossible for motion to arise in it. Body and
motion can only exist in conjunction with one another. Aristotle
would have accepted all this and agreed that it is impossible
for motion to have a beginning, though for other reasons, as
we shall see. But he would have argued that motion is therefore
eternal. Kindi now turns his attack on this stronghold of Aristotelianism. Motion implies time; time is finite; therefore, motion
is finite. Since body cannot exist without motion, the being
of the body of the universe has to be finite.

Kindi then turns to the third argument for the temporal
finitude of the universe, a proof from composition. He will
not admit the possibility of anything's being composed from
eternity; composition involves change that joined the uncomposed entities together. Bodies are composed in two ways; we
have seen al-Kindi's debt to Philoponus on this score. Hence,

all bodies must be bound up with change, the condition of
their composition. But motion or change involves time, as we
have seen, and time is finite, as we have seen; therefore, change
cannot have been going on eternally. Since composition requires
change, it also must have had a beginning. But bodies cannot
exist without composition; therefore, the being of the body
of the universe must have had a beginning. This proof only
serves to underline the earlier proofs. It is different in that
it tries to tie bodies to time without referring to the question
of whether the universe was generated or is eternal.

The final proof for an origin of the universe breaks some
new ground. Al-Kindi gives two reasons why any given moment
could never arrive if time were infinite. First, he attempts
to reduce the notion of infinite time to self-contradiction. This
really has nothing to do with the *arrival* of any given moment;
the argument ought to stand alone. His reasoning appears to
be this: in order to select any given moment in time, we
must know what time it is. But if we know what time it
is, then we know how long it has been from that moment
back to eternity. So time is not infinite at all, since we know
how much has transpired. The assumption, of course, is that
to select any given moment, we must know that moment in
relation to the past time before it instead of in relation to
the present moment in time. The second reason is more to
the point. Any moment, such as the present, could never be
reached if time were infinite. Before the present moment could
be reached, an infinite number of former times would have
to have elapsed. For example, if we were to divide time up
into, say, hours, then before this present moment could be
reached an infinite number of hours would have to have elapsed.
But the infinite cannot be traversed. That means the present
moment could never arrive, which is absurd. Kindi does not
argue here that time is finite because an actual infinite is
impossible, and in that sense, this fourth proof stands apart.
Rather the proof depends on the notion of traversing the infinite.
Kindi's discussion of future time is extraneous to his proof
for God, although it is interesting as an example of a potential
infinite. For these reasons, then, al-Kindi contends that the
universe is spatially and temporally finite.

Kindi does not immediately infer from this conclusion that
God exists, however. He has proved that the universe has a

beginning in being, but that does not prove that it did not somehow bring itself into being. Hence, he argues,

> An investigation whether it is or is not possible for a thing to be the cause of the generation of its essence, shall now follow the previous [discussion]. We say that it is not possible for a thing to be the cause of the generation of its essence.[84]

We may ask what Kindi means by 'essence'. He explains, 'I mean by "the generation of its essence" its becoming a being, either from something or from nothing. . . .'[85] He later asserts, '. . . the essence of every thing is that thing.'[86] Hence, we should not look in al-Kindi for some sort of ontological essence/existence distinction. His thought is much closer to Aristotle than to Thomas Aquinas. The essence of a thing seems to be what a thing is, but a thing and its essence are only conceptually distinct.[87] Kindi is really asking if a thing can be the cause of itself.

We may summarise his argument as follows: If a thing is the cause of itself, then either (1) the thing may be non-existent and its essence non-existent; (2) the thing may be non-existent and its essence existent; (3) the thing may be existent and its essence non-existent, or (4) the thing may be existent and its essence existent. Number one is impossible because then there would be absolutely nothing, and nothing cannot be the cause of anything. Number two is impossible because the thing is nothing and nothing cannot be the cause of anything. Number three is impossible because a thing and its essence are the same being, so that one could not be existent and the other non-existent. Number four is impossible because then the thing would be the cause and the essence the effect, and cause and effect are two different things, whereas a thing and its essence are the same. Basically Kindi is arguing that a thing cannot cause itself to come into being because (1) nothing cannot cause something to be, and (2) to cause itself, a thing would have to be different from itself.

But even at this point, Kindi does not conclude to God's existence. Instead he plunges into an elaborate Plotinian discussion of unity and multiplicity and concludes that the association of unity and multiplicity in the world cannot be due to change, but must be caused.[88] This cause he calls, in good Neoplatonic nomenclature, the True One, and by abstracting all multiplicity from it, Kindi, by use of this *via negativa*, is able to tell us,

> The True One, therefore, has neither matter, form, quantity, quality, or relation, is not described by any of the remaining intelligible things, and has neither genus, specific difference, individual, property, common accident or movement; and it is not described by any of the things which are denied to be one in truth. It is, accordingly, pure and simple unity, i.e., [having] nothing other than unity, while every other one is multiple.[89]

It is only at this juncture that Kindi now identifies the True One as the cause of the universe. We may schematise Kindi's total proof, omitting the unessential details of the argumentation, as follows:

1. There are several self-evident principles.
2. The universe had a beginning in time.
   (a) Time is finite.
       (*i*) Argument from infinite quantity.
            (*a*) No actual infinite quantity can exist.
            (*b*) Time is quantitative.
            (*c*) Therefore, infinite time cannot exist.
       (*ii*) Argument from the selection of the given moment.
            (*a*) To select a given moment in time, we must know what time it is.
            (*b*) If we know what time it is, then we know how long it has been from the given moment back to eternity.
            (*c*) Thus, we know how much time has transpired.
            (*d*) Therefore, time must be finite.
       (*iii*) Argument from the arrival of the given moment.
            (*a*) Before any given moment in time could arrive, an infinite number of prior times would have to be traversed if time were infinite.
            (*b*) But the infinite cannot be traversed.
            (*c*) Therefore, no given moment could arrive.
            (*d*) But this is absurd.

(b) The universe cannot exist without time.
    (*i*) If time is simply duration, then the universe could not exist without duration.
    (*ii*) If time is the measure of motion, the universe could not exist without time.
        (*a*) The universe cannot exist without motion.
            (*i*) If the universe were fully at rest from eternity, it could not begin to move.
            (*ii*) Therefore, there would now be no motion.
            (*iii*) But this is absurd.
(c) Therefore, the universe must have had a beginning in time.
3. The universe could not cause itself to come into existence.
    (a) Nothing cannot cause something to exist.
    (b) To cause itself, a thing would have to be something other than itself.
4. Multiplicity in the universe must be caused.
5. The cause of multiplicity in the universe is the cause of the universe itself, and it is the True One.

The True One is the source of all unity and coming to be.[90] Kindi declares,

> As the True One, the First, is the cause of the beginning of the motion of coming to be, . . . it is the creator of all that comes to be. As there is no being except through the unity in things, and their unification is their coming to be, the maintenance of all being due to its unity, if [things which come to be] departed from the unity, they would revert and perish. . . . The True One is therefore the First, the Creator who holds everything He has created, and whatever is freed from His hold and power reverts and perishes.[91]

In concluding to the existence of God, al-Kindi has made a Plotinian move to supplement his argument from creation. The source of the being of the universe is also the ultimate source of its multiplicity.

God is thus declared to be the ultimate cause. Kindi takes this notion quite seriously, and it involves him in a rigorous determinism. As Fakhry explains, for Kindi causal action is primarily a process of bringing things forth out of nothing

into being, and this action belongs to God alone.[92] Even so-called
secondary causes are merely recipients of God's sovereign action
who in turn pass it on successively.[93] God is therefore the
only real agent or cause in the world.

This serves to point up an important final issue. Kindi's
argument from the temporal finitude of the world has at its
heart the presupposition of the principle of efficient causality.
But it is important to see exactly how this is so. Al-Kindi
does not argue that every event has to have a cause and that
the series of causes cannot be infinite. The use of the causal
principle is not to be found here, for Kindi's arguments are
based simply on the notion of the succession of temporal segments. One could hold (as al-Ghāzāli did) that causal connection
is only a psychological disposition habitually formed from observation of constant conjunction and yet argue that there cannot
be an infinite temporal regress of such successive states because
of reasons revolving around the impossibility of an actually
existing infinite. The use of the causal principle arises after
al-Kindi has proved that the universe began to exist a finite
number of years ago. Having proved that the universe came
into being from nothing and that it could not cause itself
to come into existence, he then infers that it and the multiplicity
in it must have a Creator cause. Now this may be a natural
and entirely justified inference, but it is important to point
out that it does presuppose the validity of the causal principle;
that is to say, it assumes that the universe could not come
into existence wholly uncaused, as David Hume was to later
assert that it might have. Al-Kindi assumes that having proven
that the universe began and that it could not cause itself to
begin, then it must have an efficient cause to make it begin.
In the words of El-Ehwany, 'The Kindian arguments for the
existence of God depend on the belief in causality. . . . Given
that the world is created by the action of *ibda'* in no time,
it must be in need of a creator, i.e., God.'[94]

Saadia

Standing in the gap between the Arabic thinkers and the Christian theologians of the West, the Jewish philosophers were instrumental in the transmission of Aristotelian and Arabic philosophy to medieval Europe. These Jewish thinkers were themselves to exercise considerable influence upon Christian scholasticism, so their formulations of the cosmological argument deserve our attention.[95] Spawned within Islamic culture, Jewish philosophy was to a considerable extent dependent upon Arabic philosophical thought.[96] Often writing in Arabic rather than their native tongue, Jewish philosophers tended to adopt the Arabic treatment of philosophical issues. The peculiar feature of medieval Jewish philosophy is that it preoccupied itself with specifically religious issues; accordingly, it might be more properly described as philosophy of religion, as Julius Guttmann observes:

> Even more than Islamic philosophy, it was definitely a philosophy of religion. Whereas the Islamic Neoplatonists and Aristotelians dealt with the full range of philosophy, Jewish thinkers relied for the most part on the work of their Islamic predecessors in regard to general philosophical questions, and concentrated on more specifically religio-philosophic problems . . . the great majority of Jewish thinkers made the philosophic justification of Judaism their main subject, dealing with problems of metaphysics in a religio-philosophic context.[97]

Jewish philosophy was thus a more specialised discipline than
Arabic philosophy, but for all that, it was still .cast in the
same mould as its Islamic predecessor. Jewish philosophy of
religion was the offspring of the Muslim *kalām* and, as Guttmann
remarks, the same needs that brought about the development
of Islamic philosophy of religion on the part of the Mu'tazilites
produced its Jewish counterpart, with the result that the 'Islamic
background determined the character of medieval Jewish philosophy from beginning to end'.[98] In fact, with specific regard
to the arguments for the existence of God, we find within
Jewish thought the same bifurcation between *kalām* and *falsafa*
that we encountered in Muslim speculation about God. Thus,
some Jewish philosophers employ with alacrity the *kalām* arguments from creation for the existence of God, while others
disdain them, preferring to utilise arguments from motion and
from necessary and possible being. But it is interesting to note
that, whether their arguments were derived from the *mutakallimūn* or from the philosophers, the only argument for the existence
of God employed by the Jewish thinkers was, according to
H. A. Wolfson, the cosmological argument.[99] Therefore, Wolfson
calls the cosmological argument based on the principle of causality 'the standard proof of the existence of God in Jewish
philosophy'.[100]

The chief exponent of the *kalām* argument from creation
for the existence of God was Saadia ben Joseph (882–942),
the 'first important Jewish philosopher'.[101] Although Saadia
repudiated the metaphysical atomism of the Mu'tazilites, he
remained dependent upon them for his proofs for God's existence.[102] Saadia presents four *kalām* arguments for creation:
a proof from the finitude of the world, a proof from composition,
a proof from the temporality of accidents, and a proof from
the finitude of time.[103] Only the fourth argument is of real
interest, however. There Saadia attempts to reduce the hypothesis of infinite time to absurdity:

> The fourth proof is [based] on [the conception of] time.
> That is to say, I know that there are three [distinct] periods
> of time: past, present, and future. Now even though the
> present is shorter than any moment of time, I assumed . . .
> that this present moment is a point and said. . . : 'Let it
> be supposed that a person should desire mentally to advance

in time above this point. He would be unable to do it for the reason that time is infinite, and what is infinite cannot be completely traversed mentally in a fashion ascending [backward to the beginning].'

Now this same reason makes it impossible for existence to have traversed infinity in descending fashion so as to reach us. But if existence had not reached us, we would not have come into being. . . . Since, however, I find that I do exist, I know that existence has traversed the whole length of time until it reached me and that, if it were not for the fact that time is finite, existence could not have traversed it.[104]

Davidson demonstrates at some length Saadia's dependence on Philoponus for this proof.[105] But there are differences: for example, Saadia transforms Philoponus's argument against an infinite temporal regress of causes into an argument against an infinite regress of moments of time. According to Davidson, these changes reflect Arabic influence, indicating that Saadia received the proofs only after they had been reformulated by *kalām*.[106] We may outline Saadia's argument as follows:

1. It is impossible to regress mentally through time to reach the beginning of time because:
   (a) the infinite cannot be traversed,
   (b) and time is, *ex hypothesi*, infinite.
2. It is impossible for existence to progress through time to reach the present moment because:
   (a) existence must traverse exactly the same series that our thoughts traversed,
   (b) but the traversal of such a series has been shown to be impossible.
3. Therefore, we do not now exist, which is absurd.
4. Therefore, time must be finite because:
   (a) otherwise existence could never have traversed it and reached the present moment.

Saadia's first point is that *it is impossible to regress mentally through time to reach the beginning of time*. He actually speaks of ascending through time. In medieval terminology an ascending series was one that regressed from effect to cause, while a descending series was one that progressed from cause to effect.[107] Thus, Saadia contends that we cannot mentally ascend through the entire series of past moments of time since time is *ex hypothesi* infinite. No matter how far back in time our thoughts regress, an infinity of prior time always remains.

For the same reason, Saadia continues, *it is impossible for existence to progress through time to reach the present moment.* As Diesendruck points out, Saadia is arguing that the series which our thoughts traverse and the series which existence traverses are one and the same series.[108] Existence must reach the present by traversing in the opposite direction the same infinite series of temporal moments that our thoughts proved incapable of traversing. If the series of moments cannot be traversed one way, Saadia asks, why should we think that it can be traversed the other way? Saadia speaks as though time were spatialised and existence were a thing moving from one point to another along the time line. The problem with such a conception is that there is no occult entity 'existence' that moves through time as a body moves through space. But although the imagery may be defective, the point of the argument remains clear: things existing at the present moment cannot come to exist until an infinite number of prior moments and existents have elapsed. But such a series cannot elapse (be traversed). There-fore, the present moment with its existents could never arrive. Stated in this way, the argument foreshadows the thesis of Kant's first antinomy of pure reason.

It is most interesting that Saadia immediately discerns the relevance of the Zeno paradoxes to the problem of traversing past infinity, a point that modern writers on the paradoxes have failed to notice. For subsequent to the statement of the proof itself, Saadia goes on to urge that the traversal of a finite spatial distance does not actually involve traversing an infinite because in this case no actual infinite exists, only an infinitely divisible finite distance.[109] In this case infinity exists only potentially, not actually. But in contrast to this, an infinity of past time would be an actual infinity, and no actual infinity can be traversed. It might be thought that this involves Saadia in an atomistic view of time as composed of discrete moments, but this is not necessarily so. For he could admit that any finite time segment is infinitely divisible and yet traversible just as a finite distance is, but maintain that an actually infinite duration of time could no more elapse than could an actually infinite distance be traversed. In this case the present moment and its existents could never come to be.

Therefore, we do not now exist, which is absurd, Saadia concludes. The present moment has obviously arrived and existence has obviously traversed the time series. *Therefore, time must be finite*; for only if time is finite could existence reach the present moment. In this way Saadia proves that the world and time must have had a beginning. He then proceeds to argue that since nothing can cause itself to come into existence, the world must have a Creator.[110]

These further arguments need not concern us, and a schematisation of Saadia's proof would virtually reproduce our outline, so I omit it here. The most interesting portion of his proof is his case against infinite time, which, like all problems concerning the infinite, is extremely fascinating and possesses such allure that even Kant adopted a nearly identical argument, which he regarded as cogent in itself, for proving the thesis of his first antimony.

al-Ghāzāli

Jurist, theologian, philosopher, and mystic, Abu Ḥāmid Muḥammad ibn Ṭā'ūs Aḥmad al-Ṭūsi al-Shāfi'i, generally known simply as al-Ghāzāli (1058–1111; known in the West as Algazel), has been acclaimed the Proof of Islam, the Ornament of Faith, and the Renewer of Religion.[111] For in him we find the 'final triumph of Ash'arite theology' and the victory of *kālam* over *falsafa*.[112] Ghāzāli was 'the greatest figure in the history of the Islamic reaction to Neo-Platonism',[113] and, despite ibn Rushd's attempted refutation of Ghāzāli's objections, he dealt a blow to Islamic philosophy from which it would never recover. Ghāzāli struck his blow with the publication in 1095 of his *Incoherence of the Philosophers*, a withering attack on Arabic philosophy, particularly as exemplified in Aristotle, Fārābi, and especially ibn Sīnā. It was only after he had thoroughly immersed himself in the teachings of the *falasifa* and even published an exposition of their tenets in the *Intentions of the Philosophers* that he felt equipped to defeat the philosophers on their own grounds.

Nearly a quarter of the *Incoherence* is devoted to the issue of whether the universe had a beginning in time, and on this question Ghāzāli ardently upholds the traditional *kalām* argument. It is with this argument that we shall be occupied, but it ought to be noted that this is not the only argument for God's existence employed by Ghāzāli; in his excellent treatment of Ghāzāli's argument from creation, Goodman lists citations for the teleological argument, the argument from self-authenticating authority, and the *kalām* argument from the temporal character of the universe.[114] Ghāzāli also hints at the Prime Mover argument from motion.[115] Interestingly, he at one time even propounded the contingency argument used by the Neoplatonists.[116] But he came to discard the proof because he believed it to be ultimately counterproductive, as Goodman explains,

> If it is possible to reason from a contingent world to a necessary God, it may equally be thought possible to reason from a necessary God to the contingent world. If the world's contingent existence is attributable to a necessary Being whose nature is to impart being to all that exists besides Him, then it might well be claimed that the world's existence itself is no longer contingent, but necessary in relation to its Cause. . . . God is the ground of being, but nothing more; the world remains 'dependent' on God, but hangs only by the most tenuous metaphysical thread, vaguely characterized as 'ontological dependence.'
>
> Ghazâlî's suspicion is that 'ontological dependence' may prove a vacuous relation. By Aristotelian standards, what always exists must exist: if the world is eternal then, it is its own necessary being. . . . *Ex hypothesi* there must be some self-sufficient being; but, as Ghazâlî puts it, if the world is eternal, that being has already been reached. There is no need that it be God. The contingency argument, then, is self-undermining. . . . If the world is eternal, it is Ghazâlî's firm belief, neither the contingency argument nor any other argument can establish the need for the existence of God.[117]

This explains the urgency with which Ghāzāli pursued the proof that the universe has a beginning in time, for to his mind the thesis of an eternal universe was quite simply equivalent to atheism.[118]

In the *Incoherence*, Ghāzāli's position is one of attack, not construction.[119] His faith had gone through a crisis period of scepticism, and in the *Incoherence*, according to W. Montgomery Watt, Ghāzāli 'is trying to show that reason is not self-sufficient in the field of metaphysics and is unable out of itself to produce a complete world-view'.[120] Therefore, we should not expect to find him setting forth a reasoned case for theism. But he does argue for the temporal beginning of the universe, and, placed within the context of his total thought as expressed elsewhere, this does constitute an argument for God's existence. The logical context for the arguments in the *Incoherence* may be found in the *Iqtiṣād* and 'The Jerusalem Letter' of Ghāzāli. In the first of these two works, Ghāzāli presents this syllogism: 'Every being which begins has a cause for its beginning; now the world is a being which begins; therefore, it possesses a cause for its beginning.'[121] Defining his terms, Ghāzāli states, 'We mean by "world" every being except God; and by "every being which begins" we mean all bodies and their accidents.'[122] Ghāzāli regards the first premiss as indubitable, calling it 'an axiom of reason' in his 'Jerusalem Letter'.[123] But he does supply a supporting argument: anything that comes to be does so in a moment of time; but since all moments are alike prior to the existence of the thing, there must be 'some determinant to select the time' for its appearance.[124] Thus, the cause demanded in the first premiss is really the determinant, as Beaurecueil explains,

> The first premiss of his syllogism furnishes a starting point which, in his eyes, presents no difficulty at all ... we must understand by *a being which begins* that which did not exist at one time, which was nothing, and which finally came to existence; as for the *cause* which he requires, it is precisely that which gives preference to the existence of one being over its non-existence. The coming to existence, established by the senses in the world of bodies, demands the intervention of a determinant principle among the possibles. . . .[125]

Ghāzāli now essays to prove in the second premiss that the world has come to be. This is the logical juncture at which the arguments in the *Incoherence* fit in, for it is evident that his argument from temporal regress is designed to prove that the world must have had a beginning.[126] We noted earlier that Ghāzāli mounts two lines of attack on the thesis of the world's eternity: (1) that the philosophers fail to demonstrate the impossibility of the creation of a temporal entity from an eternal being and (2) that the beginning of the universe is demonstrable. It is to the second point that we shall now turn our attention. Ghāzāli summarises his proof as follows:

> You reject as impossible the procession of a temporal from
> an eternal being. But you will have to admit its possibility.
> For there are temporal phenomena in the world. And some
> other phenomena are the causes of those phenomena. Now
> it is impossible that one set of temporal phenomena should
> be caused by another, and that the series should go on
> *ad infinitum*. No intelligent person can believe such a thing.
> If it had been possible, you would not have considered it
> obligatory on your part to introduce the Creator [into your
> theories], or affirm the Necessary Being in whom all the
> possible things have their Ground.
> So if there is a limit at which the series of temporal pheno-
> mena stops, let this limit be called the Eternal.
> And this proves how the possibility of the procession of
> a temporal from an eternal being can be deduced from their
> fundamental principles.[127]

We have already commented on the origin of this popular
kalām argument for God's existence. Ghāzāli's terse summary
may be outlined as follows:

1. There are temporal phenomena in the world.
2. These are caused by other temporal phenomena.
3. The series of temporal phenomena cannot regress infinitely.
4. Therefore, the series must stop at the eternal.

We shall now fill out the structure of this outline by a step
by step analysis. The first point, that *there are temporal phenomena
in the world*, is straightforward. We experience in the world
of the senses the coming to be and the passing away of things
around us. Ghāzāli takes the point as obvious.

Secondly, *these are caused by other temporal phenomena*. This step
assumes the principle of secondary causation, which, we have
seen, Ghāzāli thoroughly repudiates. It is therefore odd for
him to be propounding the principle here himself. Probably
the best explanation is that it is a concession to his opponents.
The argument is addressed to the philosophers, who believed
in the existence of real causes in the world.[128] Rather than
raise here an extraneous issue that could only sidetrack the
discussion, he gives the philosophers their four Aristotelian causes
operating in the world. Ghāzāli himself did not believe in the

efficacy of secondary causes, and his argument for a beginning of the universe does not depend on their presence. For he could just as easily have argued that there are temporal phenomena in the world, these temporal phenomena are preceded by other temporal phenomena, and so forth. The proof is not dependent at this point upon the causal principle, and it seems likely that Ghāzāli admits it simply for the sake of his opponents, who would not think to dispute it.[129] Thus, he willingly acknowledges of temporal phenomena that these are caused by other temporal phenomena.

The third premiss, *the series of temporal phenomena cannot regress infinitely*, is the crux of the argument. Ghāzāli supports the premiss by showing the absurdities involved in the supposition of the eternity of the world, that is, in an infinite regress of temporal phenomena. For example, it leads to the absurdity of infinites of different sizes.[130] For Jupiter revolves once every twelve years, Saturn every thirty years, and the sphere of the fixed stars every thirty-six thousand years. If the world were eternal, then these bodies will each have completed an infinite number of revolutions, and yet one will have completed twice as many or thousands of times as many revolutions as another, which is absurd. Or again, there is the problem of having an infinite composed of finite particulars.[131] For the number of these revolutions just mentioned is either odd or even. But if it is odd, the addition of one more will make it even, and *vice versa*. And it is absurd to suppose that the infinite could lack one thing, the addition of which would make the number of the total odd or even. If it is said that only the finite can be described as odd or even and that the infinite cannot be so characterised, then Ghāzāli will answer that if there is a totality made up of units and this can be divided into one-half or one-tenth, as we saw with regard to the different ratios of revolutions per year on the part of the planets, then it is an absurdity to state that it is neither odd nor even.[132] If it is objected to this that the revolutions do not make up a totality composed of units, since the revolutions of the past are non-existent and those of the future not yet existent, Ghāzāli will reply that a number must be odd or even, whether it numbers things that now exist or not.[133] Hence, the number of the revolutions must be odd or even. Or again, there is the problem of souls.[134] If the world is eternal then there will be an infinite number of actually existing souls of deceased men. But an infinite magnitude cannot exist. Ghāzālī implicitly assumes here the truth of Aristotle's analysis of the infinite, knowing that his opponents also accept it. Ghāzālī's arguments may appear rather quaint, presupposing as they do the constancy of the solar system and the life of man upon earth. But the problems raised by the illustrations are real ones, for they raise the question of whether an infinite number or numbers of things can actually exist in reality. Ghāzālī argues that this results in all sorts of absurdities; therefore, the series of temporal phenomena cannot regress infinitely.

The conclusion must therefore be: *the series must stop at the eternal.* The series of temporal phenomena must have a beginning. Therefore, according to the principle of determination (premiss one in the *Iqtiṣād*), an agent must exist who creates the world. Ghāzālī states,

> . . . the people of the truth . . . hold that the world began in time; and they know by rational necessity that nothing which originates in time originates by itself, and that, therefore, it needs a creator. Therefore, their belief in the Creator is understandable.[135]

This also means for Ghāzālī that time itself had a beginning and was created.[136] As Michael E. Marmura points out, Ghāzālī does not challenge the Aristotelian definition of time as the measure of motion, nor does he question the legitimacy of the inference of the eternity of motion from the eternity of time.[137] For him if temporal phenomena, or things changing in time, have an origin, then time, as the measure of such change, must have an origin as well. Prior to the beginning of the world was simply God and no other being. Time came into existence with the universe. It is only through the weakness of our imagination that we think there must be a 'time' before time:

> . . . all this results from the inability of the Imagination to apprehend the commencement of a being without supposing something before it. This 'before,' which occurs to the Imagination so inevitably, is assumed to be a veritable existent—

viz., time. And the inability of the Imagination in this case is like its inability to suppose a finite body, say, at the upper level, without something above its surface. Hence its assumption that beyond the world there is space—i.e., either a plenum or a void. When therefore it is said that there is nothing above the surface of the world or beyond its extent, the Imagination cannot accept such a thing—just as it is unable to accept the idea that there is nothing in the nature of a verifiable being before the existence of the world.[138]

So just as we realise the universe is finite and nothing is beyond it, though we cannot imagine such a thing, we know that time, too, is finite and nothing is before it. Similarly, to suppose that God could have created the world earlier is simply 'the work of the Imagination'.[139] Ghāzāli is fond of emphasising that it is the imagination that leads one astray with regard to questions of time and space; we must accept the conclusions of reason despite the problems the imagination might confront. So with regard to the problem of God's creating the world earlier, this is obviously nonsensical since no time existed before the universe. Thus, it could not have been created sooner in time, and to think it might have is only to be deceived by the imagination.

Now placing this argument within the logical context of Ghāzāli's thought, we can see why Ghāzāli concludes that the world must have a cause: the universe had a beginning; while it was non-existent, it could either be or not be; since it came to be, there must be some determinant which causes it to exist. And this is God. Thus, Ghāzāli says, 'So either the series will go on to infinity, or it will stop at an eternal being from which the first temporal being should have originated'.[140] Ghāzāli assumes that the universe could not simply spring into existence without a determinant, or cause. We may schematise his argument as follows:

1. Everything that begins to exist requires a cause for its origin.
2. The world began to exist.
   (a) There are temporal phenomena in the world.
   (b) These are preceded by other temporal phenomena.
   (c) The series of temporal phenomena cannot regress infinitely.

(*i*) An actually existing infinite series involves various absurdities.

(d) Therefore, the series of temporal phenomena must have had a beginning.

3. Therefore, the world has a cause for its origin: its Creator.

In conclusion, it is significant to note that Ghāzāli does not, like al-Kindi, base his argument on the finitude of time. Rather he argues from temporal *phenomena*, not time itself. These phenomena cannot regress infinitely, for this is absurd. We might also note that Ghāzāli, like Kindi, argues against the *real* existence of an infinite quantity. This is especially clear when in the *Iqtiṣād* Ghāzāli states that God's knowledge of infinite possibles does not refute his case against the infinite magnitude, for these 'knowables' are not real, existent things, to which his argument is confined.[141] Finally, we should reiterate that the role of the causal principle is not in the relation between phenomena, but in the demand for a determinant which causes the phenomena to be. This fact alone serves to clearly demarcate Ghāzāli's proof from arguments relying upon the reality of secondary causes, for example, the first three ways of Aquinas. Since God is the only cause, a causal series of any sort cannot exist. In sum, Ghāzāli's cosmological argument is squarely based on two principles, as pointed out by Beaurecueil:

'There remain ... to the scepticism of Ghāzāli two great limits, which appear now with a majestic clarity: one, the impossibility of the infinite number, and the other, the necessity of a principle of determination amongst the possibles.'*

These are the two pillars of all Ghāzāli's reasoning in his proof for the existence of God: the impossibility of the infinite number permits him to establish that the world has a beginning; on the other hand, if it has begun, it is necessary that one being should give preference to its existence over its non-existence: this being is God, its creator.

*Carra de Vaux, *Gazali*, pp. 80–81.[142]

Having now completed a historical exposition of the arguments of three of *kalām*'s greatest proponents, let us turn to a critical discussion of these arguments in the light of contemporary thought.

Notes

1. For example, Burrill makes no mention of the Arabic contribution. (Donald Burrill, *The Cosmological Argument* [New York: Doubleday & Co., 1967].) On the other hand, Sturch devotes three chapters exclusively to Arabic developments of the cosmological argument. (R. L. Sturch, 'The Cosmological Argument' [Ph.D. thesis, Oxford University, 1970], pp. 59-120a.)

2. Frederick Copleston, *A History of Philosophy*, vol. 2, *Mediaeval Philosophy: Augustine to Scotus* (London: Burnes, Oates & Washbourne, 1950), pp. 186–200. See also his chapter in Frederick Copleston, *A History of Medieval Philosophy* (London: Methuen & Co., 1972), pp. 104-24.

3. F. E. Peters, *Aristotle and the Arabs: The Aristotelian Tradition in Islam* (New York University Press, 1968; London: University of London Press, 1968), pp. 135-6. See also De Lacy O'Leary, *Arabic Thought and Its Place in History*, rev. ed. (London: Kegan Paul, Trench, Trubner, & Co., 1939; New York: E. P. Dutton & Co., 1939), p. 135.

4. *Encyclopaedia of Islām*, 1st ed., s.v. 'Kalām', by D. B. Macdonald.

5. According to T. J. De Boer,

> An assertion, expressed in logical or dialectical fashion, whether verbal or written, was called by the Arabs—generally but more particularly in religious teaching—a *Kalam* (λόγος). . . . The name was transferred from the individual assertion to the entire system, and it covered also the introductory, elementary observations on Method,—and so on. (T. J. De Boer, *The History of Philosophy in Islam*, trans. Edward R. Jones [London: Luzac & Co., 1933], pp. 42-3.)

For a history of the origin and development of this movement, see Peters, *Arabs*, pp. 135-55; Majid Fakhry, *A History of Islamic Philosophy* (New York & London: Columbia University Press, 1970), pp. 56–81.

6. Richard Walzer, 'Early Islamic Philosophy', in *The Cambridge History of Later Greek and Early Mediaeval Philosophy*, ed. A. H. Armstrong (Cambridge: Cambridge University Press, 1970), p. 648.

7. Peters, *Arabs*, p. 140.

8. For a fine synopsis of the origin and development of Islamic atomism, see Husâm Muhî Eldîn al-Alousî, *The Problem of Creation in Islamic Thought: Qur'an, Hadith, Commentaries, and Kalam* (Baghdad: National Printing and Publishing Co., 1965), pp. 269–97.

9. See D. B. Macdonald, 'Continuous re-creation and atomic time in Muslim scholastic theology', *Isis* 9 (1927): 326–44.

10. Fakhry, *History*, p. 70.

11. W. D. Ross, *Aristotle*, 5th ed. (London: Methuen & Co., 1964; New York: Barnes & Noble, 1964), p. 177.

12. They thus arrived at a metaphysical system not dissimilar from G. W. F. Leibniz's monadology. But Leibniz's monads were 'windowless' because of his doctrine that every predicate is contained in the analysis of its subject, whereas the atoms of the *mutakallimūn* could not affect each other because each one ceased to exist the instant it was created. Moreover, Leibniz's conclusion was that everything operates according to a pre-established harmony infused in each monad, while the *mutakallimūn* concluded that God is the only and ever-present cause of all that happens. Whether Leibniz's system is in the end any less deterministic than that of the Islamic theologians is a matter of some controversy.

13. Majid Fakhry, *Islamic Occasionalism and Its Critique by Averroës and Aquinas* (London: George Allen & Unwin, 1958), p. 30.

14. Al-Ghazali, *Tahafut al-Falasifah* [*Incoherence of the Philosophers*], trans. Sabih Ahmad Kamali (Lahore: Pakistan Philosophical Congress, 1958), pp. 185–96.

15. David Hume, *Enquiries Concerning Human Understanding and Concerning the Principles of Morals*, 2d ed., ed. L. A. Selby-Bigge (Oxford: Clarendon Press, 1902), pp. 17–24, 42–7, 79; David Hume, *A Treatise of Human Nature*, 2 vols., with an Introduction by A. D. Lindsay (London: Dent, 1968; New York: Dutton, 1968), pp. 11, 81–5. Ghāzāli is compared to Hume by, for example, A. F. M. Hafeezullah Bhuyan, 'The Concept of Causality in Al-Ghazzali', *Islamic Culture*, April 1963, pp. 88–9.

16. In the *Tahafut*, he responds to an objector who urges that fire alone is the cause of burning in cotton and that the fire cannot but burn the cotton, since it is its nature to burn a flammable object brought into contact with it:

> This is what we deny. We say that it is God who ... is the agent of the creation of blackness in cotton, of the disintegration of its parts, and of their transformation into a smouldering heap of ashes. Fire, which is an inanimate thing, has no action. How can one prove that it is an agent? The only argument is from the observation of the fact of burning at the time of contact with fire. But observation only shows that one is *with* the other, not that it is *by* it and has no other cause than it. (Al-Ghazali, *Tahafut*, p. 186.)

In his greatest religious work, Ghāzāli asserts, '. . . everything is from God. That is, God is the primal, first Cause of all (*musabibülasbāb*),' and he expounds a rigorous determinism in which everything, even man's 'free' acts, are from God. (Al-Ghazāli, *The Revival of Religious Sciences*, trans. Bankey Behari [Farnham, England: Sufi Publishing Co., 1972], p. 129.)

17. Hume fled from what he called Pyrrhonic scepticism to a more workable mitigated scepticism. He realised that a consistent application of his sceptical principles would be completely unliveable; he therefore appealed to Nature as the guarantor of the reasonableness of our causal inferences based on experience. Thus, beneficent Nature establishes our *belief* in causation, which we cannot prove by reason. The contrast of Hume's faith in the causal principle with Ghāzāli's denial of secondary causality is clearly seen in Hume's attack on just the sort of occasionalism espoused by Ghāzāli. (Hume, *Enquiries*, pp. 158–65, 70–73; Hume, *Treatise*, pp. 178–9, 254.)

18. Nicolas Malebranche, *Dialogues on Metaphysics and on Religion*, trans. Morris Ginsberg (London: George Allen & Unwin, 1923), pp. 177–201. For Malebranche God is the true and only cause of every event, so-called secondary causes being the mere occasions on which God acts. (Ibid., pp. 185-6, 189–90.) See also Fakhry, *Occasionalism*, pp. 9–14.

19. Fakhry, *Occasionalism*, pp. 14, 56–7; Macdonald, 'Recreation,' pp. 328, 333.

20. See Peters, *Arabs*, pp. 144–5; Fakhry, *History*, pp. 69–70.

21. On the issue of divine attributes, the Ash'arites believed that God did possess the attributes ascribed to him in the *Qur'ān*, but that these ascriptions are entirely equivocal so that they do not mean the same thing when predicated of man. As for determinism, the Ash'arites adhered to strict determinism by God, but also believed that God creates in man an accident whereby an act can be imputed to the alleged agent. For a discussion of these and other issues, see al-Ash'ari's *Kitāb al-Luma'* and *Risālat Istiḥsān al-Khawḍ fi 'Ilm al-Kalām*, which are translated in Richard J. McCarthy, *The Theology of al-Ash'ari* (Beirut: Imprimerie Catholique, 1953).

22. Peters, *Arabs*, p. 187.

23. Writing in the twelfth century, ibn Rushd distinguishes three schools of thought within Islam concerning the problem of God's existence: (1) The literalists who disdain rational argument altogether and claim that God's existence is known on the basis of authority alone; (2) the Ash'arites (and implicitly, the Mu'tazilites) who contend that the existence of God may be rationally demonstrated from temporality (*ḥuduth*) or contingency (*jawāz*), and (3) the Sufis who believe in a direct apprehension of God apart from speculative argument. (Ibn Rushd, *Al-Kashf 'an Manāhij al-Adillah*, cited in Majid Fakhry, 'The Classical Islamic Arguments for the Existence of God', *Muslim World* 47 [1957]: 133–34.) We are considering the argumentation employed by the second group. For a good overview, see in addition to Fakhry's article A. J. Wensinck, 'Les preuves de l'existence de Dieu dans la théologie musulmane', *Mededeelingen der Koninklijke Academie van Wetenschappen* 81 (1936): 41–67. According to Fakhry, prior to the rise of the Mu'tazilites, the question of the demonstrability of God's existence did not arise; belief in God was based on revelation or authority. (Fakhry, 'Arguments', p. 135.)

24. Ibid.

25. Al-Alousî, *Creation*, pp. 298–320.

26. Simplicius *In Aristotelis de caelo commentaria*; Simplicius *In Aristotelis physicorum libros quattuor posteriores commentaria*.

27. Joannes Philoponus *De aeternitate mundi contra Proclum*.

28. Ibn al-Khammār, ibn Rushd, and al-Suhrawardi all mention that Yahyā al-Nahwī argued for the temporality of the world on the basis of its finitude. (Al-Alousî, *Creation*, p. 311.) Al-Fārābī also knew Philoponus, perhaps in a direct Arabic translation, as his quotations differ from those of Simplicius. (Herbert A. Davidson, 'John Philoponus as a Source of Medieval Islamic and Jewish Proofs of Creation', *Journal of the American Oriental Society* 89 [1969]: 359–60.) According to Davidson, references to Philoponus also occur in Sijistānī, ibn al-Haytham, and ibn Sīnā. (Ibid., pp. 360–1.)

29. Ibid., p. 361.

30. Ibid., pp. 362–3. See also Schmuel Sambursky, 'Note on John Philoponus' Rejection of the Infinite', in *Islamic Philosophy and the Classical Tradition*, ed. S. M. Stern, Albert Hourani, and Vivian Brown (Columbia, S.C.: University of South Carolina Press, 1972), pp. 351–3. For a general overview of the Islamic–Jewish treatment of the problem of infinity, see Louis-Émile Blanchet, L'infini dans les pensées Juive et Arabe', *Laval théologique et philosophique* 32 (1976): pp. 11–21.

31. See Al-Alousî, *Creation*, pp. 304, 310–11; Davidson, 'Philoponus', pp. 376–7.

32. Fakhry, 'Arguments', p. 139.

33. Simon Van Den Bergh, Notes to *Tahafut al-Tahafut* [*The Incoherence of the Incoherence*], 2 vols., by Averroes, trans. by Simon Van Den Bergh (London: Luzak & Co., 1954) 2: 2, 17–18.

34. See Al-Alousî, *Creation*, pp. 224–68.

35. Al-Suyūti, cited in *The Encyclopaedia of Islam*, 1971 ed., s.v. "*illa*', by H. Fleisch and L. Gardet. This distinction was apparently not shared by the philosophers, for both al-Fārābī and ibn Sīnā use *sabab* as a synonym of *'illa*. (Ibid.; A.-M. Goichon, *Lexique de la langue philosophique d' Ibn Sīnā* [Paris: Desclée de Brouwer, 1938], pp. 149, 237–8.) As a result they argued for the eternity of the universe. A cause in actuality cannot exist without its effect; therefore, as eternal First Cause God cannot but produce the world from eternity.

36. Al-Alousî, *Creation*, pp. 238–9. Note that al-Alousī is using 'determinant' exclusively in the third sense listed by Van Den Bergh above. The argument is that if the world is not eternal, then there must be a sufficient reason why God chose one moment to create rather than another, which is impossible because all moments are alike.

37. Al-Alousî, *Creation*, pp. 247–8.

38. Al-Ghazali, *Tahafut*, pp. 14–15, 23–4. One passage reads:

'The procession of a temporal [being] from an eternal [being] is absolutely impossible. For, if we suppose the eternal at a stage when the world had not yet originated from Him, then the reason why it had not originated must have been that there was no determinant for its existence, and that the existence of the world was a possibility only. So, when later the world comes into existence, we must choose one of the two alternatives [to explain it]—namely, either that the determinant has, or that it has not, emerged. If the determinant did not emerge, the world should still remain in the state of bare possibility, in which it was before. But if it has emerged, who is the originator of the determinant itself? And why does it come into being now, and did not so before? . . . In fine since all the states of the Eternal are alike, either nothing shall originate from Him, or whatever originates shall continue to originate forever.' (Ibid., p. 14.)

39. Ibid., pp. 16, 32.
40. This fact seems to elude Fakhry, who struggles to explain away the 'flagrant contradiction' of how Ghāzāli could deny the concept of causality and yet maintain that since the universe had a beginning, before its existence there must have been a determinant which caused it to exist. (Fakhry, 'Arguments', p. 141.) Fakhry attempts to resolve the contradiction by stating that what the world needs is not a cause, but a determinant. But this, of course, explains precisely nothing, for Ghāzāli repudiates the need for a determinant in the sense of a reason, but affirms the need for a cause. This involves no contradiction, for Ghāzāli does not deny the causal principle; he denies *secondary* causality. (Peters, *Arabs*, p. 190; Fakhry, *History*, p. 257.) God is the only cause of all there is. (De Boer, *History*, pp. 160–62; Bhuyan, 'Causality', pp. 89–91.) Hence, Ghāzāli is perfectly consistent in demanding a cause for the world's existence.
41. Al-Ghazali, *Tahafut*, p. 25.
42. Ibid., p. 27. This is the Arabic version of the more famous Buridan's ass, the helpless animal which starved to death as it wavered indecisively between two equally appetising bundles of straw. The original problem is from Aristotle *De caelo* B 13. 295b32, where a man equally hungry and thirsty is caught between food and drink at an equal distance. According to Leibniz's principle of sufficient reason, *everything*, even God's choices, must have a reason; therefore, Buridan's ass would have certainly starved (G. W. Leibniz, *Theodicy: Essays on the Goodness of God, the Freedom of Man, and the Origin of Evil*, trans. E. M. Huggard [London: Routledge & Kegan Paul, 1951], pp. 149–50; cf. Gottfried Martin, *Leibniz: Logic and Metaphysics*, trans. K. J. Northcott and Lucas [Manchester: Manchester University Press, 1960], pp. 9–10), though such a situation could never occur in reality, Leibniz cautions, for two alternatives are never absolutely identical.
43. Cf. Leibniz's principle of the best, which serves to solve the same problem in a different way. (G. W. Leibniz, 'Mr. Leibniz's Fifth Paper: Being an answer to Dr. Clarke's Fourth Reply', in G. W. Leibniz, *The Philosophical Works of Leibnitz*, trans. George Martin Duncan [New Haven, Conn.: Tuttle, Morehouse & Taylor, 1890], pp. 255–6.) Leibniz argued that God must always choose the best and that this is therefore the best of all possible worlds. Although some *mutakallimūn* would have agreed, most would have said that God's will chooses without necessarily choosing the best and why He chooses one alternative rather than another is that it is simply His choice.
44. Al-Alousî, *Creation*, p. 252. See also Herbert A. Davidson, 'Arguments from the Concept of Particularization in Arabic Philosophy', *Philosophy East*

and West 18 (1968): 299–314.
    45. Al-Ghazali, *Tahafut*, pp. 83–4.
    46. Davidson, 'Particularization', p. 314.
    47. Al-Ghāzāli, 'The Jerusalem Tract', trans. and ed. A. L. Tibawi, *The Islamic Quarterly* 9 (1965): 98. Ghāzāli's statement of the proof is simply the culmination of the thinking of the Ash'arite school, which argued in a similar fashion: 'The world is contingent. Every contingent thing must have a cause, therefore, the world must have a cause, and as no contingent thing can be the cause, that cause must be God.' (M. Abdul Hye, 'Ash'arism', in *A History of Muslim Philosophy*, ed. M. M. Sharif [Wiesbaden: Otto Harrassowitz, 1963], p. 238.)
    48. Lenn E. Goodman, 'Ghazâlî's Argument from Creation', *International Journal for Middle East Studies* 2 (1971): 76, 83. Cf. Fakhry, *History*, pp. 258–9.
    49. Walzer, 'Philosophy', p. 648.
    50. *Encyclopaedia of Islām*, 1st ed., s.v. 'Falsafa', by R. Arnaldez.
    51. Peters, *Arabs*, p. 157.
    52. See Etienne Gilson, *History of Christian Philosophy in the Middle Ages* (London: Sheed & Ward, 1955), pp. 181–3; Fakhry, *Occasionalism*, pp. 22–4.
    53. *Encyclopaedia of Islām*, 1st ed., s.v. 'Falsafa'.
    54. *Encyclopaedia of Islām*, 1st ed., s.v. 'Falāsifa', by R. Arnaldez.
    55. *Encyclopaedia of Islām*, 1st ed., s.v. 'Falsafa'.
    56. See O'Leary, *Thought*, pp. 275–94.
    57. Ibid., p. 269.
    58. De Boer, *History*, pp. 208–13.
    59. Bonaventure argued that the existence of God is incompatible with the eternity of the universe and marshalled several arguments to demonstrate that the universe had a beginning (Bonaventure 2 *Sententiarium* 1.1.1.2.1–6): (1) because it is impossible to add to the infinite, the number of days elapsed till the present cannot be infinite; (2) because it is impossible to order an infinity of terms according to beginning, middle, and end, the series of temporal events in the world could not exist from eternity; (3) because an infinite cannot be traversed, the present day could never have arrived if celestial revolutions have been going on eternally; (4) because since the Intelligences know the revolutions of their respective spheres, an infinite number of revolutions would mean that the finite could comprehend the infinite, which is impossible; and (5) infinite time would necessitate an infinite number of souls of the deceased, which is impossible because an actual infinite cannot exist. See Etienne Gilson, *The Philosophy of St. Bonaventure*, trans. Dom Illtyd Trethowan and F. J. Sheed [London: Sheed & Ward, 1938], pp. 190–4. See also Francis J. Kovach, 'The Question of the Eternity of the World in St. Bonaventure and St. Thomas—A Critical Analysis', *Southwestern Journal of Philosophy* 5 (1974): 141–72: Bernardino Bonansea, 'The Impossibility of Creation from Eternity according to St. Bonaventure', *Proceedings of the American Catholic Philosophical Association* 48 (1974): 121–35; Bernardino Bonansea, 'The Question of an Eternal World in the Teaching of St. Bonaventure', *Franciscan Studies* 34 (1974): 7–33.
    60. D. M. Dunlop, *Arab Civilization to A.D. 1500* (London: Longman, 1971), p. 175.

61. Ahmed Fouad El-Ehwany, 'Al-Kindi', in *History*, ed. Sharif, pp. 425–7.

62. Ya'qūb ibn Isḥāq al-Kindi, *Al-Kindi's Metaphysics: A Translation of Ya'qūb ibn Isḥāq al-Kindi's Treatise 'On First Philosophy'*, with an Introduction and Commentary by Alfred L. Ivry (Albany, N.Y.: State University of New York Press, 1974), pp. 12–16; Alfred L. Ivry, 'Al-Kindi as Philosopher: The Aristotelian and Neoplatonic Dimensions', in *Philosophy*, ed. Stern, Hourani, and Brown, pp. 117–24.

63. George N. Atiyeh, *Al-Kindi: The Philosopher of the Arabs* (Rawalpindi: Islamic Research Institute, 1966), p. 49. Kindi accepted the Mu'tazilite creed. (Richard Walzer, 'Islamic Philosophy', in *History of Philosophy, Eastern and Western*, 2 vols., ed. S. Radhakrishnan [London: Allen & Unwin, 1953], 2: 131.) However, even some of the Mu'tazilites before him, such as Abū Hudhayl, had tried to reconcile Aristotle's statements concerning the eternity of the world with the doctrine of creation found in the *Qur'ān* by maintaining that

> ... the universe ... existed eternally, but in perfect quiescence and stillness, as it were latent and potential, rather than actual.... Creation meant that God brought in movement so that things began to exist in time and space.... (O'Leary, *Arabic Thought*, p. 125.)

But al-Kindi clearly rejects any such compromise and argues strongly for a genuine creation of the universe from nothing. In fact, Fakhry credits al-Kindi with the earliest statement of the argument from creation for the existence of God. (Fakhry, 'Arguments', p. 140.) For a helpful discussion of Kindi's relationship to the Mu'tazilites, see Ivry's introduction in al-Kindi, *On First Philosophy*, pp. 22–34.

64. Atiyeh, *Al-Kindi*, p. 52. On the significance of Kindi's use of the term *ibda'*, see Richard Walzer, 'New Studies on Al-Kindi', in Richard Walzer, *Greek into Arabic: Essays on Islamic Philosophy*, Oriental Studies (Oxford: Bruno Cassier, 1962), pp. 187–90. Walzer cites references to Kindi's definitions of the term: 'to make a thing appear out of nothing'; 'to produce real things from nothing.' (Ibid., p. 187.) Contrast this with ibn Sīnā's use of *ibda'* to mean creative emanation of being as opposed to temporal creation. (*Encyclopaedia of Islām*, 1971 ed., s.v. '*ibda'*', by L. Gardet.)

65. Al-Kindi, *On First Philosophy*, pp. 67–75. See two other treatises by al-Kindi which are translated in N. Rescher and H. Khatchadourian, 'Al-Kindi's Epistle on the Finitude of the Universe', *Isis* 57 (1966): 426–33; F. A. Shamsi, 'Al-Kindi's Epistle on What Cannot Be Infinite and of What Infinity May Be Attributed', *Islamic Studies* 14 (1975): 123–44.

66. Al-Kindi, *On First Philosophy*, pp. 67–73.

67. We here omit Kindi's attempt to prove motion must exist, as it is not really to the point and is poorly reasoned.

68. Al-Kindi, *On First Philosophy*, pp. 73–4.

69. Ibid., pp. 74–5.

70. Walzer, 'Studies', p. 191.

71. Davidson, 'Philoponus', pp. 370–1.

72. Ibid., pp. 371–2.

73. Ibid., pp. 372–3.

74. Al-Kindi, *On First Philosophy*, p. 68. In his treatise 'On the Unity of God and the Finiteness of the Body of the World', Kindi calls them the evident first premises. Ivry comments, '"which are thought with no mediation": ... i.e. as intellectual intuitions, free of prior logical, as well as physical, mediation. ...' (Alfred L. Ivry, Commentary to *On First Philosophy*, by al-Kindi, p. 147.)

75. Al-Kindi, *On First Philosophy*, p. 70.

76. For Aristotle on the impossibility of an actually existing infinite, see Aristotle *Physica* 3. 4–8. 202b30–208a20. It is his view that the infinite can exist only potentially, as, for example, in infinite divisibility.

77. Al-Kindi, *On First Philosophy*, p. 69.

78. Cf. H. Minkowski, 'Space and Time', in *Problems of Space and Time*, ed. with an Introduction by J. J. C. Smart, Problems of Philosophy Series (New York: Macmillan, 1964; London: Collier-Macmillan, 1964), pp. 297–312.

79. Al-Kindi, *On First Philosophy*, p. 70.

80. Ibid.

81. I think Ivry misunderstands Kindi's argument here. Ivry says that Kindi tries to show that both *creatio ex nihilo* and infinite temporal regression are impossible, and therefore the problem of the origin of the universe is an irresolvable antinomy. (Ivry, 'Al-Kindi', p. 120.) But this runs contrary to the whole thrust of the treatise. What Kindi is arguing here is that body cannot exist apart from motion, whether body came into being from nothing or is eternal. In the first case, its coming to be would be a motion; therefore, body does not exist without motion. Kindi does not object (as does Aristotle) to designating this as the first motion.

82. Al-Kindi, *On First Philosophy*, p. 68.

83. Ibid., p. 72.

84. Ibid., p. 76.

85. Ibid.

86. Ibid., p. 77.

87. Ibid.

88. Ibid., p. 94.

89. Ibid., p. 112.

90. Ibid., p. 113.

91. Ibid., p. 114.

92. Fakhry, *History*, p. 95.

93. El-Ehwany, 'Al-Kindi', p. 429.

94. Ibid., pp. 429–30.

95. Though not as widely ignored as the Arabic philosophers, these Jewish thinkers are nevertheless largely neglected in favour of Christian writers; I have never seen a selection from even Maimonides included in a philosophy of religion reader, and his proofs for the existence of God are sometimes grossly misrepresented (as in Jacob B. Agus, *The Evolution of Jewish Thought from Biblical Times to the Opening of the Modern Era* [London and New York: Abelard–Schuman, 1959], p. 185.).

96. Copleston, *Medieval Philosophy*, p. 105.

97. Julius Guttmann, *Philosophies of Judaism: The History of Jewish Philosophy from Biblical Times to Franz Rosenzweig*, with an Introduction by R. J. Z.

Werblowsky, trans. David W. Silverman (London: Routledge & Kegan Paul, 1964), p. 55.

98. Ibid. Blanchet observes that in Arabic and Jewish philosophy, '. . . the same preoccupations appeared: God and his existence, the creation and origin of the world, its temporal or eternal duration, its finite or infinite dimensions.' (Blanchet, 'L'infini', p. 11.)

99. Harry Austryn Wolfson, 'Notes on Proofs of the Existence of God in Jewish Philosophy', in *Hebrew Union College Annual* 1 (1924): 575.

100. Ibid., p. 584.

101. Isaac Husik, *A History of Medieval Jewish Philosophy* (Philadelphia: The Jewish Publication Society of America, 1940), p. 23. Saadia was the first to 'set up a comprehensive system of religious philosophy' demonstrating 'the superiority of Judaism' over other religious systems and over the doctrines of the philosophers [Henry Malter, *Saadia Gaon: His Life and Works*, the Morris Loeb Series (Philadelphia: The Jewish Publication Society of America, 1921), p. 175.]; accordingly, he 'deserves to be considered the father of medieval Jewish philosophy of religion'. (Guttmann, *Philosophies*, p. 61.) On other Jewish proponents of the *kalām* argument particularly Abraham ibn Daud (1110–1180), see Blanchet, 'L'infini', pp. 12–15.

102. See Martin Schreiner, 'Sa'adja b. Josef al-Fajjûmî', in *Dreizehnter Bericht über die Lehranstalt für die Wissenschaft des Judenthums in Berlin* (Berlin: 1895), p. 59; Guttmann, *Philosophies*, p. 62; Husik, *History*, pp. 25–6.

103. Saadia Gaon, *The Book of Beliefs and Opinions*, trans. Samuel Rosenblatt (New Haven, Conn.: Yale University Press, 1948), pp. 41–4. For a discussion of Saadia's first three proofs, see Harry Austryn Wolfson, 'The Kalam Arguments for Creation in Saadia, Averroes, Maimonides and St. Thomas', in *Saadia Anniversary Volume*, Texts and Studies, vol. 2 (New York: American Academy for Jewish Research, 1943), pp. 197–207; Davidson, 'Philoponus', pp. 362–70.

104. Saadia, *Book*, pp. 44.

105. Davidson, 'Philoponus', pp. 362–70.

106. Ibid., p. 370.

107. Cf. Aristotle *Analytica Posteriora* 1. 22. 83b6–7.

108. Z. Diesendruck, 'Saadya's Formulation of the Time-argument for Creation', in *Jewish Studies in Memory of George Alexander Kohut, 1874–1933*, ed. S. W. Baron and A. Marx (New York: Bloch, 1935), p. 154.

109. Saadia, *Book*, p. 45.

110. Ibid., pp. 46–7.

111. M. Saeed Sheikh, 'Al-Ghazāli: Metaphysics', in *History*, ed. Sharif, p. 581.

112. O'Leary, *Thought*, p. 219.

113. Fakhry, *History*, p. 244.

114. Goodman, 'Creation', pp. 68–75.

115. Al-Ghazāli, *Revival*, p. 237.

116. Goodman, 'Creation', p. 75. Ghāzāli does not, however, employ the essence/existence distinction in his version.

117. Ibid., p. 77.

118. Al-Ghazali, *Tahafut*, pp. 89, 140. Cf. Goodman, 'Creation', pp. 80–1.

119. Al-Ghazali, *Tahafut*, p. 8.

---

120. W. Montgomery Watt, *Muslim Intellectual: A Study of Al-Ghazali* (Edinburgh: Edinburgh University Press, 1963), p. 58.

121. Al-Ghāzālī, *Kitāb al-Iqtiṣād fī'l-I'tiqād*, with a Foreword by Íbrahim Agâh Çubukçu and Hüseyin Atay (Ankara: University of Ankara Press, 1962), pp. 15–16; cf. p. 20. For a detailed analysis of the *Iqtiṣād* proof, see S. de Beaurecueil, 'Ġazzālī et S. Thomas d'Aquin: Essai sur la preuve de l'existence de Dieu proposée dans l'*Iqtiṣād* et sa comparison avec les "voies" Thomistes', *Bulletin de l'Institut Francais d'Archaéologie Orientale* 46 (1947): 203–12. Fakhry comments on the terminology of this proof:

> The syllogism runs as follows: Everything temporal (ḥadīth) must have a cause. By *ḥadith*, Al-Ghazālī tells us, he means 'what did not previously exist and then began to exist'. Prior to its existence, this 'temporal world' was 'possible' (mumkin) i.e. 'Could equally exist or not exist.' To tilt the balance in favour of existence a 'determinant' (murajjih) was necessary)—since otherwise this possible universe would have always remained in a state of non-being.*

*[*Kitāb al-Iqtisād fī l-'Itiqād*], Cairo, N.D., p. 14. (Fakhry, 'Arguments', p. 141.)

122. Al-Ghāzālī, *Iqtiṣād*, p. 24.
123. Al-Ghāzālī, 'Jerusalem Tract', p. 98.
124. Ibid.
125. Beaurecueil, 'Ġazzālī et S. Thomas', pp. 212–13.
126. In the *Iqtiṣād* and 'The Jerusalem Letter' Ghāzālī employs a somewhat different line of reasoning. Taking as his point of departure the existence of motion and rest, he argues: (1) bodies cannot exist without motion or rest; (2) motion and rest both have a beginning; (3) therefore, bodies (of which the world is a collection) must have had a beginning. In 'The Jerusalem Letter' he employs the typical *kalām* argument that since motion and rest are accidents, and accidents are temporal, the substance in which they inhere must be temporal. The *Iqtiṣād* also includes an involved discussion of the nature of bodies and accidents, but contains as well arguments against the possibility of an infinite temporal regress. Such a regress would be absurd because: (1) the arrival of the present moment would mean that the infinite has an end; (2) the heavenly spheres would have completed an infinite number of revolutions which must be either odd or even; and (3) infinites of different sizes would exist, all of which are absurd. The second and third arguments are found in the *Incoherence*. For analyses of these, see Goodman, 'Creation', pp. 72–5; Beaurecueil, 'Ġazzālī et S. Thomas', pp. 203–12; Wensinck, 'Preuves', pp. 48–54.

127. Al-Ghazali, *Tahafut*, p. 32.
128. Seyyed Hossein Nasr, *An Introduction to Islamic Cosmological Doctrines* (Cambridge, Mass.; Belknap Press of Harvard University Press, 1964), p. 230.
129. In the same way, Ghāzālī assumes for the sake of argument Aristotelian, not atomistic, metaphysics in the *Incoherence*. (Davidson, 'Particularization', p. 309.)

130. Al-Ghazali, *Tahafut*, p. 20.

131. Ibid., pp. 20-21.

132. Ibid., p. 21.

133. Ibid., pp. 21-2.

134. Ibid., p. 22.

135. Ibid., p. 89.

136. Ibid., p. 36.

137. Michael E. Marmura, 'The Logical Role of the Argument from Time in the Tahāfut's Second Proof for the World's Pre-Eternity', *Muslim World* 49 (1959): 306.

138. Al-Ghazali, *Tahafut*, p. 38.

139. Ibid., p. 43.

140. Ibid., p. 33.

141. Beaurecueil, 'Gazzālī et S. Thomas', p. 211.

142. Ibid., p. 222.

PART II

A Modern Defence of the *Kalām* Cosmological Argument

Proposed Formulation of the Argument

In my opinion the cosmological argument which is most likely to be a sound and persuasive proof for the existence of God is the *kalām* cosmological argument based on the impossibility of an infinite temporal regress of events. We have seen that the argument rests essentially on two contentions: (1) some form of the principle of efficient causality and (2) the impossibility of an infinite regress of events. In this chapter I shall attempt to formulate and defend such a cosmological argument, taking into account the modern developments in both philosophy and science that have a bearing on the proof's cogency.

We may present the basic argument in a variety of ways. Syllogistically, it can be displayed in this manner:

1. Everything that begins to exist has a cause of its existence.
2. The universe began to exist.
3. Therefore the universe has a cause of its existence.

Or, alternatively, we may present the argument as a series of disjunctions about the universe, the existence of which is taken as given:

The point of the argument is to demonstrate the existence of a first cause which transcends and creates the entire realm of finite reality. Having reached that conclusion, one may then inquire into the nature of this first cause and assess its significance for theism.

Second Premiss: The Universe Began to Exist

The key premiss in our syllogism is certainly the second; therefore, let us temporarily pass by the first premiss and attempt to support the second, that the universe began to exist. This premiss may be supported by two lines of reasoning, philosophical and empirical.

PHILOSOPHICAL ARGUMENT

Turning first to the philosophical reasoning, I shall present two arguments in support of the premiss: (1) the argument from the impossibility of the existence of an actual infinite and (2) the argument from the impossibility of the formation of an actual infinite by successive addition.

Before we examine each of these arguments in detail, it is imperative to have a proper understanding of the concept of the actual infinite. Prior to the revolutionary work of the mathematicians Bernard Bolzano (1781–1848), Richard Dedekind (1831–1916), and especially Georg Cantor (1845–1918), the only infinite considered possible by philosopher and mathematician alike was the potential infinite. Aristotle had argued at length that no actually infinite magnitude can exist.[1] The only legitimate sense in which one can speak of the infinite is in terms of potentiality: something may be infinitely divisible or susceptible to infinite addition, but this type of infinity is potential only and can never be fully actualised. For example, space is never actually infinite, but it is infinitely divisible in that one can continue indefinitely to divide spaces. Again, number is never actually infinite, but it may be increased without limit. And time is susceptible to both infinite division and infinite increase. But while the processes of division and addition may proceed indefinitely, they never arrive at infinity: space and time are never actually infinitely divided, and number and time are never completed wholes. Since Aristotle defines the potential as that which can become actual, some have charged him with contradiction in his doctrine of the potential infinite, since a potential infinite can never be actualised.[2] But Aristotle makes it quite plain that he is here using 'potential' in another sense:

> . . . the infinite has a potential existence.
> But the phrase 'potential existence' is ambiguous. When we speak of the potential existence of a statue we mean that there will be an actual statue. It is not so with the infinite. There will not be an actual infinite.[3]

When Aristotle speaks of the potential infinite, what he refers to is a magnitude that has the potency of being indefinitely divided or extended. Technically speaking, then, the potential infinite at any particular point is always finite.

This conception of the infinite prevailed all the way up to the nineteenth century. The medieval scholastics adhered to Aristotle's analysis of the impossibility of an actual infinite, and the post-renaissance thinkers, even Newton and Leibniz with their infinitesimal calculus, believed that only a potential infinite could exist.[4] One of the foremost mathematicians of the nineteenth century, Georg Friedrich Gauss, in an oft-printed statement, decried any use of the actual infinite in mathematics:

> I protest . . . against the use of infinite magnitude as if it were something finished; this use is not admissible in mathematics. The infinite is only a *façon de parler*: one has in mind limits approached by certain ratios as closely as desirable while other ratios may increase indefinitely.[5]

This expressed the accepted view of the infinite as the limit of a convergent or divergent process: $\lim_{x \to \infty}$ . . . . But although the majority of philosophers and mathematicians adhered to this conception of the infinite, dissenting voices could also be heard. A man ahead of his time, Bolzano argued vigorously against the then current definitions of the potential infinite.[6]

He contended that infinite multitudes can be of different sizes and observed the resultant paradox that although one infinite might be larger than another, the individual elements of the two infinites could nonetheless be matched against each other in a one-to-one correspondence.[7] It was precisely this paradoxical notion that Dedekind seized upon in his definition of the infinite: a system is said to be infinite if a part of that system can be put into a one-to-one correspondence with the whole.[8] In other words, the Euclidean maxim that the whole is greater than a part was now going by the board. According to Dedekind, this assumption could hold only for finite systems.

But it was undoubtedly Cantor who won for the actual infinite the status of legitimacy that it holds today.[9] Cantor called the potential infinite a 'variable finite' and attached the sign ∞ to it; this signified that it was an 'improper infinite'.[10] The actual infinite he pronounced the 'true infinite' and assigned the symbol $\aleph_0$ (aleph zero) to it. This represented the number of all the numbers in the series $1, 2, 3, \ldots$ and was the first infinite or transfinite number, coming after all the finite numbers. According to Cantor, a collection or set is infinite when a part of it is equivalent to the whole.[11] Utilising this notion of the actual infinite, Cantor was able to develop a whole system of transfinite arithmetic which he bequeathed to modern set theory. '. . . Cantor's . . . theory of *transfinite* numbers . . . is, I think, the finest product of mathematical genius and one of the supreme achievements of purely intellectual human activity,' exclaimed the great German mathematician David Hilbert; 'No one shall drive us out of the paradise which Cantor has created for us.'[12]

Modern set theory, as a legacy of Cantor, is thus exclusively concerned with the actual as opposed to the potential infinite. At this point we may clarify the distinction between a potential and actual infinite. According to Hilbert, the chief difference lies in the fact that the actual infinite is a determinate totality, whereas the potential infinite is not:

> Someone who wished to characterize briefly the new conception of the infinite which Cantor introduced might say that in analysis we deal with the infinitely large and the infinitely small only as limiting concepts, as something becoming, happening, i.e., with the *potential infinite*. But this

is not the true infinite. We meet the true infinite when
we regard the totality of numbers 1, 2, 3, 4, . . . itself as
a completed unity, or when we regard the points of an
interval as a totality of things which exists all at once. This
kind of infinity is known as *actual infinity*.[13]

In set theory this notion of infinity finds its place in the theory
of infinite sets. According to Cantor, a set is a collection into
a whole of definite, distinct objects of our intuition or of our
thought; these objects are called elements or members of the
set. Fraenkel draws attention to the characteristics definite and
distinct as particularly significant.[14] That the members of a
set are distinct means that each is different from the other.
To say that they are definite means that given a set S, it
should be intrinsically settled for any possible object x whether
x is a member of S or not. This does not imply actual decidability
with the present or even future resources of experience; rather
a definition could settle the matter sufficiently, such as the
definition for 'transcendental' in the set of all transcendental
numbers. Unfortunately, Cantor's notion of a set as any logical
collection was soon found to spawn various contradictions or
antinomies within naive set theory that threatened to bring
down the whole structure. As a result, most mathematicians
have renounced a definition of the general concept of set and
chosen instead an axiomatic approach to set theory by which
the system is erected upon several given, undefined concepts
formulated into axioms. But presumably the characteristics of
definiteness and distinctness are still considered to hold of the
members of any set. An infinite set in Zermelo-Fraenkel axiomatic set theory is defined as any set R that has a proper
subset that is equivalent to R.[15] A proper subset is a subset
that does not exhaust all the members of the original set,
that is to say, at least one member of the original set is not
also a member of the subset. Two sets are said to be equivalent
if the members of one set can be related to the members
of the other set in a one-to-one correspondence, that is, so
that a single member of the one set corresponds to a member
of the other set and *vice versa*. Thus, an infinite set is one
in which the whole set is not greater than a part. In contrast
to this, a finite set is a set such that if n is a positive integer,
the set has n members.[16] Because set theory does not utilise

the notion of potential infinity, a set containing a potentially infinite number of members is impossible. Such a collection would be one in which the members are not definite in number, but may be increased without limit. Such a collection would best be described as indefinite. The crucial difference between an infinite set and an indefinite collection would be that the former is conceived as a determinate whole actually possessing an infinite number of members, while the latter never actually attains infinity, though it increases limitlessly. Therefore, we must in our subsequent discussion always keep conceptually distinct these three types of collection: finite, infinite, and indefinite.

First Philosophical Argument

Our first argument in support of the premiss that the universe began to exist is based upon the impossibility of the existence of an actual infinite. We may present the argument in this way.

1. An actual infinite cannot exist.
2. An infinite temporal regress of events is an actual infinite.
3. Therefore an infinite temporal regress of events cannot exist.

With regard to the first premiss, it is important to understand that by 'exist' we mean 'exist in reality', 'have extra-mental existence', 'be instantiated in the real world'. We are contending, then, that an actual infinite cannot exist in the real world. It is usually alleged that this sort of argument has been invalidated by Cantor's work on the actual infinite and by subsequent developments in set theory.[17] But this allegation seriously misconstrues the nature of both Cantor's system and modern set theory, for our argument does not contradict a single tenet of either. The reason is this: Cantor's system and set theory are concerned exclusively with the mathematical world, whereas our argument concerns the real world. What I shall argue is that while the actual infinite may be a fruitful and consistent concept in the mathematical realm, it cannot be translated from the mathematical world into the real world, for this would involve counter-intuitive absurdities. It is only the real existence of the actual

infinite which I deny. Far from being remarkable, this view
of the actual infinite as a mathematical entity which has no
relation to the real world is prevalent among the mathematicians
themselves who deal with infinite sets and transfinite arithmetic.
Bolzano's primary examples of infinite sets were admittedly
in the *'realm of things which do not claim actuality, and do not
even claim possibility'*.[18] When it came to an instance of an actual
infinite in the real world, Bolzano was reduced to pointing
to God as an infinite being.[19] But of course the infinity of
God's being has nothing to do with an actually infinite collection
of definite and distinct finite members. Cantor's definition of
a set made it clear that he was theorising about the abstract
realm and not the real world for, it will be remembered, he
held that the members of a set were objects of our intuition
or of our thought. According to Robinson, '. . . Cantor's infinites
are abstract and divorced from the physical world'.[20] This
judgement is echoed by Fraenkel, who concludes that among
the various branches of mathematics, set theory is 'the branch
which least of all is connected with external experience and
most genuinely originates from free intellectual creation'.[21] As
a creation of the human mind, state Rotman and Kneebone,

> . . . the Zermelo-Fraenkel universe of sets exists only in a
> realm of abstract thought . . . the 'universe' of sets to which
> the . . . theory refers is in no way intended as an abstract
> model of an existing Universe, but serves merely as the postu-
> lated universe of discourse for a certain kind of abstract
> inquiry.[22]

Such a picture of set theory ought not to surprise us, for virtually
every philosopher and mathematician understands the same
thing of, for example, Euclidean and non-Euclidean geometries,
namely, that these represent consistent conceptual systems that
may or may not hold in reality.

This being so, the novice is apt to be confused by the frequent
existential statements found in books on set theory, statements
such as the Axiom of Infinity that there exists an infinite set.
But such statements do not imply existence in the extra-mental
world, but only in the mathematical realm. Alexander Abian
explains,

... whenever in the Theory of Sets we are confronted with a statement such as *there exists a set* x *whose elements are sets* b *and* c, *and there exists a set* u *whose elements are the sets* x, b *and* m, then we may take this statement as implying that a table such as the following appears as part of the illusory table which describes the Theory of Sets. . . :

	a				e	
b	$\in$	a		a	$\in$	e
c	$\in$	a		b	$\in$	e
				m	$\in$	e

. . . The above considerations show how we may interpret more concretely the notion of *existence* in the Theory of Sets. In short if an axiom or a theorem of the Theory of Sets asserts that *if certain sets . . . exist, then a certain set . . . also exists,* we shall interpret this as: *if certain sets . . . are listed in the above illusory table, then a certain set . . . must also be listed in the same illusory table.*[23]

Thus, the existential statements in set theory have no bearing on the extra-mental existence of the entities described. When, therefore, the existence of an infinite set is postulated, no true existential import is carried by the statement, and no verdict is pronounced on whether such a collection could really exist at all. This analysis of the actual infinite says nothing about whether an actual infinite can exist in reality.

What Cantor accomplished was the establishing of the possibility of conceiving of the infinite as a completed, determinate whole, thus enabling us to speak abstractly of infinite sets. Rather than attempt to mentally synthesise the infinite by counting, Cantor stood outside the infinite series of natural numbers and grasped them conceptually as a totality, and from thence developed his system of transfinite arithmetic. But the ability to conceive of an actual infinite does not imply the possibility of its real existence, as Pamela Huby explains:

It is often said that Cantor legitimized the notion of the actual infinite, and it is well to get clear what this means. What it seems to mean is that we can make statements, within a certain conventional system, about *all* the members of an infinite class, and that we can clearly identify certain classes which have an infinite number of members, and even say, using new conventions, what the cardinal number of their members is. But beyond that Cantor tells us nothing about actual infinity.[24]

The use of the notion of the actual infinite in modern mathematics does not, therefore, insure the possibility of its real existence. Far from it, in fact; a basic exposition of the Cantorian system itself ought to make it intuitively obvious that it is impossible for an actual infinite to exist in reality. To begin with, we must distinguish between cardinal numbers and ordinal numbers. In ordinary language we distinguish them by naming cardinal numbers one, two, three, and so forth, and ordinal numbers first, second, third, . . . The cardinal number of a set expresses how many members there are in that set, or the *power* of that set. Thus, the cardinal number of $\{1, 2, 3, 4, 5\}$ is 5. The ordinal number of a set is an expression of the order of the elements of the set. Thus, because the set $\{1, 2, 3, 4, 5\}$ has a fifth element, its ordinal number is 5. From this it is seen that the natural numbers may express either cardinal or ordinal numbers. Indeed, for all finite collections, the cardinal and ordinal number will be identical. But when we come to infinite sets, important differences will arise.

Now suppose we wish to discover if the cardinal number of two sets is the same. We could count each element in each set and compare the totals, but another way of achieving the same result without counting is by establishing a one-to-one correspondence between the elements of the two sets. If the elements match perfectly, then one can be sure the cardinal number is identical; but if one set has members left over, then it is clear the cardinal numbers are different. For example, if a child who could not count wished to determine whether he had more multi-coloured than solid-coloured marbles in his collection, he could arrange them in pairs, matching one solid-coloured with one multi-coloured marble. If there were no marbles left over, he would know he had the same number of each type; but if he had some extras of one kind, then he could be sure he possessed more of that kind than of the other. When this method is applied to finite collections, the results are non-paradoxical; but when one comes to infinite sets, unexpected results arise. For example, if the natural number series is considered to be an actual and not merely a potential infinite, we are confronted with some very paradoxical conclusions. We may ask which is larger, the set of even numbers or the set of odd numbers. Placing them in a one-to-one correspondence, we find them to be the same, which is what we would expect:

$$1, 3, 5, \cdots$$
$$\uparrow \ \uparrow \ \uparrow$$
$$\downarrow \ \downarrow \ \downarrow$$
$$2, 4, 6, \cdots$$

But now we might ask which is greater, all the natural numbers or just the even natural numbers, and here we may be surprised. For while we would expect that the series of natural numbers is larger, we find, in fact, that the two series are equivalent:

$$1, 2, 3, \cdots$$
$$\uparrow \ \uparrow \ \uparrow$$
$$\downarrow \ \downarrow \ \downarrow$$
$$2, 4, 6, \cdots$$

The interesting feature of the correspondence here is that the number in the second series is always the double of the corresponding number in the first series. Thus, we reach the curious conclusion that even though the natural numbers contain all the even numbers and more (infinitely more!), nevertheless the number of even numbers is the same as the number of all natural numbers. This has become, as we have seen, the very defining characteristic of infinite sets, namely, that a set is infinite if it has a proper subset equivalent to itself.

But let us proceed. Having seen that part of an infinite is equivalent to the whole, we may ask which is larger, the set of all positive integers or the set of all positive and negative integers plus zero:

$$1, 2, 3, \cdots$$
$$\cdots, -3, -2, -1, 0, 1, 2, 3, \cdots$$

It would appear that the second series is larger, but this is incorrect, for the two sets may be placed in a one-to-one correspondence:

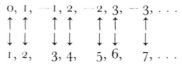

In this correspondence, the correlate of every positive number *n* in the first set is 2*n* in the second set, and the correlate of every negative number *n* is −2*n* + 1. What makes the conclusion unexpected is that both the negative and positive integers run through the entire natural number series separately, so that it seems odd to say that taken together they can still be enumerated by the same series. But the method of determining equivalence by correspondence insures that they can.

Similarly, it can be shown that the set of all rational numbers (numbers that can be expressed as a fraction with an integer as a numerator and an integer as a denominator, for example, ½, ²⁰⁄₅, ⁶⁰⁄₄₇) is equivalent to the set of the natural numbers. This may seem quite remarkable when one reflects that between any two integers, an infinity of possible fractions exist. For between any two fractions a/b and c/d, there will be the fraction a + b/c + d. So if one had an infinite number of integers, one would have between them rational numbers representing an infinity of infinities! Yet the set of rational numbers and the set of natural numbers can be shown to be equivalent by use of the following matrix; the square will record every rational number, and to number them, simply follow the arrows:

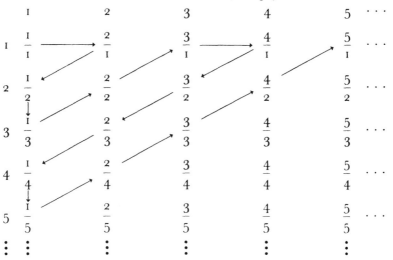

Dropping out the duplications and beginning with zero, one may enumerate the rational numbers:

$$0, \frac{1}{1}, \frac{2}{1}, \frac{1}{2}, \frac{1}{3}, \frac{3}{1}, \ldots$$

$$\uparrow \uparrow \uparrow \uparrow \uparrow \uparrow$$
$$\downarrow \downarrow \downarrow \downarrow \downarrow \downarrow$$

$$1, 2, 3, 4, 5, 6, \ldots$$

To include the negative rationals as well, simply place after every positive rational in the above sequence its negative counterpart and then enumerate:

$$0, \frac{1}{1}, \frac{-1}{1}, \frac{2}{1}, \frac{-2}{1}, \ldots$$

$$\uparrow \uparrow \uparrow \uparrow \uparrow$$
$$\downarrow \downarrow \downarrow \downarrow \downarrow$$

$$1, 2, 3, 4, 5, \ldots$$

Thus, it is clear that the set of all negative and positive rational numbers is no larger than the set of the natural numbers.

Such infinite sets as these are called *denumerably infinite* because they can be placed in a one-to-one correspondence with the natural numbers. Since these sets are actual infinites, determinate totalities, they can be assigned a cardinal and an ordinal number. But no natural number would do, since one would require an 'infinitieth' number, which is impossible. So mathematicians have adopted the symbol $\aleph_0$ as the cardinal number of a denumerably infinite set and ω as its ordinal number.

The purely theoretical nature of the actual infinite becomes clear when one begins to perform arithmetic calculations with infinite numbers. For example, ω is the ordinal number of the natural number series $\{1, 2, 3, \ldots\}$. But suppose we add one to this series: $\{1, 2, 3, \ldots, 1\}$. Now the ordinal number of such a set is $\omega + 1$. And we can begin counting all over again $\omega + 1$, $\omega + 2$, $\omega + 3$, $\ldots$ up to $\omega + \omega$ or $\omega \cdot 2$. This would be the ordinal of the set $\{1, 2, 3, \ldots, 1, 2, 3, \ldots\}$. But again, suppose we add one. Then we have $(\omega \cdot 2) + 1$ and this can continue up to $(\omega \cdot 2) + \omega$ or $\omega \cdot 3$, and this can go on until we reach $\omega \cdot \omega$ or ω^2. This could be the ordinal of an infinite series of infinites. But although the mind boggles at such a concept, we may yet proceed and add one more: $\omega^2 + 1$. Finally, we will reach $\omega^2 + \omega$. But suppose we continue to add one more: $\omega^2 + (\omega + 1)$, $\omega^2 + (\omega + 2)$, $\omega^2 + (\omega + 3), \ldots \omega^2 + (\omega + \omega) = \omega^2 + \omega \cdot 2$. On and on this may go until the following table is established:

$$1, 2, 3, \ldots$$
$$\omega, \omega + 1, \omega + 2, \ldots$$
$$\omega \cdot 2, (\omega \cdot 2) + 1, (\omega \cdot 2) + 2, \ldots$$
$$\omega \cdot 3, (\omega \cdot 3) + 1, (\omega \cdot 3) + 2, \ldots$$
$$\vdots$$
$$\omega^2, \omega^2 + 1, \omega^2 + 2, \ldots$$
$$\omega^2 + \omega, \omega^2 + \omega \cdot 2, \omega^2 + \omega \cdot 3, \ldots$$
$$\omega^2 \cdot 2, (\omega^2 \cdot 2) + 1, (\omega^2 \cdot 2) + 2, \ldots$$
$$(\omega^2 \cdot 2) + \omega, (\omega^2 \cdot 2) + (\omega \cdot 2), \ldots$$
$$\omega^3, \ldots$$
$$\omega^4, \ldots$$
$$\vdots$$
$$\omega^\omega, \omega^{\omega\omega}, \omega^{\omega\ldots\omega}, \ldots$$

The sequent to this sequence is usually denoted by ε_0. Accordingly, ω^{ε_0} is the sequent of the sequence $\{\omega, \omega^\omega, \omega^{\omega^\omega}, \ldots\}$.

But if this leaves the mind reeling, the knock-out blow is yet to come. *For all of the ordinals mentioned above belong to denumerable sets, sets whose cardinal number is $\aleph_0$.* Any of these sets may be placed into a one-to-one correspondence with the natural numbers, and so they have the same cardinal $\aleph_0$. Since each ω set has $\aleph_0$ members, this serves to bring out the fact that $\aleph_0 + \aleph_0 = \aleph_0$, but $\omega + \omega \neq \omega$. This is because in cardinal addition we are computing the cardinal number of the union of two sets each having an infinite cardinal number of members, whereas in ordinal addition we are determining the ordinal number of the union of two sets each of which is ordered according to the ordinal ω. One is a number of membership and the other a number of order. Hence, no matter how many infinities of ω order type one may have, the number of elements in the totality is $\aleph_0$, for $\aleph_0 + \aleph_0 + \aleph_0 \ldots = \aleph_0$. Again, this is because a one-to-one correspondence with the natural numbers can be established.

This might lead one quite naturally to conclude that there can be no cardinal number larger than $\aleph_0$, since it swallows up anything added to it. But this is not so. For it can be demonstrated that the set of all real numbers is larger or more powerful than the set of rational numbers. The set of real numbers includes all the rational numbers plus the irrational numbers (numbers like $\sqrt{2}$ which cannot be expressed as a fraction of two integers but is an infinite, non-periodic decimal). Cantor's method of demonstrating that the real numbers are of a greater infinity than the rational numbers consisted first in converting the rational numbers into non-terminating decimals, e.g., $\frac{2}{3} = 0.666\ldots$, $\frac{1}{2} = 0.4999\ldots$, etc. One may then take these decimalised rational numbers plus the irrational numbers and write them in any order on an infinite list; what Cantor wished to show is that there is a number which cannot appear on the list:

$$
\begin{array}{ll}
1 & 0.3\underline{8}602563078 \cdots \\
2 & 0.5\underline{7}350762050 \cdots \\
3 & 0.99\underline{3}56753207 \cdots \\
4 & 0.257\underline{6}3200456 \cdots \\
5 & 0.0000\underline{5}320562 \cdots \\
\vdots &
\end{array}
$$

This is done by constructing a number out of the italicised numerals in the list: from the first number, select the first digit; from the second number, select the second digit, and so on infinitely. In this case we get $0.37365\ldots$. To find a number that cannot be on the list, simply substitute a non-zero numeral for each of the digits in this number; for example: $0.16427\ldots$ or $0.52798\ldots$ or any other substitution as long as the substitution is different from the numeral it replaces. The number so created *cannot possibly be on the list*. For any number on the list, our new number will differ from it in at least one digit: from the first number in the first digit, from the second in the second digit, from the third in the third digit $\ldots$, from the nth in the nth digit. Thus, should someone assert that our number occurs at the trillionth place on the list, we may respond that it cannot because it will differ from the trillionth number in the trillionth digit.

This leads to the conclusion that it is impossible to have a complete list of the real numbers after all. For items on a list can be numbered, but the real numbers, we have seen, cannot be numbered. They are therefore *non-denumerable*. Thus, we have two different sizes of infinity: a denumerable infinity and a non-denumerable infinity. To represent this second magnitude of infinity Cantor assigned the symbol $\aleph_1$.

$\aleph_1$ is the number of all the mathematical points on a line. For the decimal fractions in the above list could all express distances on a line from an end-point zero, and it is therefore impossible to enumerate all the possible distances that a point could be from zero. Therefore, the number of points on a line is non-denumerable. But oddly enough, this means as well that *there is the same number of points in any line, regardless of length.* To demonstrate the equivalence of the set of points in two lines of unequal length, we form an angle with them, and connecting their end-points, we draw parallel lines from one to the other, thus demonstrating a one-to-one correspondence of points between them:

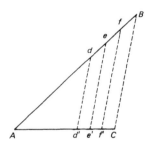

Thus it is proved that there are as many points on a one-inch line as there are in a line the length of a foot, a mile, or a light year. More than that, it may be demonstrated that there are as many points on a line one inch long as there are in a line infinitely long. To prove this we may take the one-inch line, form an angle from it, and place it on the infinite line. By drawing lines from a point midway between the ends of the one-inch line, we may establish a one-to-one correspondence between the two lines:

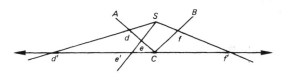

Therefore, regardless of length, two lines always have the same number of points: $\aleph_1$.

But even more curious conclusions follow. For it may be demonstrated that *the number of points in a line is the same as the number of points in a plane*. Take a point whose position on a line is given by some number, say 0·75120386. ... By taking every other digit we can construct two numbers from this: 0·7108 ... and 0·5236. ... Use these two numbers to locate a point on a square by letting one number determine the horizontal distance and the other the vertical distance:

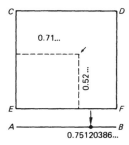

In this way every point on the line will correspond to a point on the square. The process can be reversed by selecting a point on the square which is determined by, say, the numbers 0·4835 ... and 0·9907 ... and combining these numbers to form 0·49893057. ... This number will determine some point on the line. In this way a one-to-one correspondence between the points of a line and a plane is demonstrated. Hard as it is to imagine, the set of points in line *AB*, which is equivalent to one side of the square, is also equivalent to all the points in the planar surface.

And that is not all. For by a similar procedure one may prove that *there are just as many points in a line as there are in a cube*. Simply break the original decimal fraction into three parts; e.g., 0·735106822548312 ... into 0·71853 ... ,

0·30241 . . . , 0·56282 . . . . These numbers can be used to locate a point inside the cube:

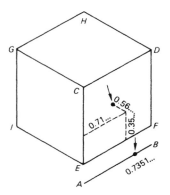

And again any point in the cube can be made to correspond to a point on the line by merging the three decimal fractions into one. Thus, the number of the points in line *AB*, which is equivalent to one edge of the cube, is the same as the number of the points in the entire cube. And when we recall that a one-inch line has as many points as an infinite line and now see that an infinite line would have as many points as an infinite volume, we realise that there is the same number of points in a one-inch line as there is in all of infinite space.

But if this leads one to think that all non-denumerable infinites are of the same size, one would be mistaken. For it can be shown that the set of all real functions in the interval $o < x < 1$ is greater than $\aleph_1$.[25] This is denoted by $\aleph_2$ and is the third transfinite cardinal. It is the number of all possible geometric curves. But even here we do not stop. For it can be shown that the system of transfinite cardinals is infinite, that there is no highest cardinal. For of any set, the set of all the possible subsets of that set has a higher cardinal number than that set.[26] Thus, the set of all the subsets of a set having $\aleph_2$ members would have the cardinal number $\aleph_3$, and the set of all its subsets would have the cardinal $\aleph_4$, and so on infinitely.

But the purely conceptual nature of this system is nowhere clearer than when one begins to perform arithmetic operations with transfinite cardinal numbers. Addition of two infinite cardinals is defined as the union of two infinite sets, and we have already begun to see that the results of transfinite arithmetic will be different from those of finite arithmetic. For example,

$$\aleph_0 + n = \aleph_0$$
$$\aleph_0 + \aleph_0 = \aleph_0$$
$$\aleph_0 + \aleph_0 + \aleph_0 = \aleph_0$$
$$\aleph_1 + n = \aleph_1$$
$$\aleph_1 + \aleph_0 = \aleph_1$$
$$\aleph_1 + \aleph_1 = \aleph_1$$

Multiplication of transfinite cardinals is defined as the cardinal number of the Cartesian product of two infinite sets, that is to say, it is the formation of a third set by taking each element of the first set and associating with it in turn each element of the second set. The cardinal number of the product set is the product of the two cardinal numbers being multiplied. The results are similar to those of addition:

$$n \cdot \aleph_0 = \aleph_0$$
$$\aleph_0 \cdot \aleph_0 = \aleph_0$$
$$n \cdot \aleph_1 = \aleph_1$$
$$\aleph_0 \cdot \aleph_1 = \aleph_1$$
$$\aleph_1 \cdot \aleph_1 = \aleph_1$$

Perhaps the most interesting feature of transfinite cardinal arithmetic, however, is that the inverse operations of addition and multiplication, namely, subtraction and division, cannot be performed. For these operations produce contradictory results. Compare these various attempts at subtraction:

If:	Then:	
$N = \{1, 2, 3, \ldots\}$	$N - N = \{\ \}$ or	$\aleph_0 - \aleph_0 = 0$
$N_1 = \{2, 3, 4, \ldots\}$	$N - N_1 = \{1\}$	$\aleph_0 - \aleph_0 = 1$
$N_2 = \{3, 4, 5, \ldots\}$	$N - N_2 = \{1, 2\}$	$\aleph_0 - \aleph_0 = 2$
$N_n = \{n + 1, n + 2, n + 3, \ldots\}$	$N - N_n = \{1, 2, 3, \ldots, n\}$	$\aleph_0 - \aleph_0 = n$
$G = \{2, 4, 6, \ldots\}$	$N - G = \{1, 3, 5, \ldots\}$	$\aleph_0 - \aleph_0 = \aleph_0$

When one attempts to divide transfinite cardinals, similar inconsistencies occur:

Since:	Then:
$n \cdot \aleph_1 = \aleph_1$	$\aleph_1 \div \aleph_1 = n$
$\aleph_0 \cdot \aleph_1 = \aleph_1$	$\aleph_1 \div \aleph_1 = \aleph_0$
$\aleph_1 \cdot \aleph_1 = \aleph_1$	$\aleph_1 \div \aleph_1 = \aleph_1$

Therefore, the extention of computational operations beyond
the realm of finite cardinals is possible only for the direct
operations— addition and multiplication— not for their inverses.

Cantor's theories reach their dizziest heights when one arrives
at the exponentiation of transfinite cardinals. For finite numbers,
m^n is defined by repeated multiplication of m for n times. The
power of a transfinite cardinal number base is defined the
same way:

$$n \cdot \aleph_0{}^3 \cdot \aleph_1{}^2 = (n) \cdot (\aleph_0 \cdot \aleph_0 \cdot \aleph_0) \cdot (\aleph_1 \cdot \aleph_1) = \aleph_1$$

But when the exponent is itself a transfinite number we achieve
the following results for n (>1), $\aleph_0$, $\aleph_1$, $\aleph_2$:

Exponent n: $m^n < \aleph_0$; $\aleph_0{}^n = \aleph_0$; $\aleph_1{}^n = \aleph_1$; $\aleph_2{}^n = \aleph_2$

Exponent $\aleph_0$: $n^{\aleph_0} = \aleph_0{}^{\aleph_0} = \aleph_1{}^{\aleph_0} = \aleph_1$; $\aleph_2{}^{\aleph_0} = \aleph_2$

Exponent $\aleph_1$: $n^{\aleph_1} = \aleph_0{}^{\aleph_1} = \aleph_1{}^{\aleph_1} = \aleph_2{}^{\aleph_1} = \aleph_2$

Exponent $\aleph_2$: $n^{\aleph_2} > \aleph_2$

With these calculations, the human mind attains heights that
leave the real world far removed (infinitely removed?). Even
more sobering is the fact that such exponentiation can proceed
limitlessly to higher and higher powers of infinity. Indeed, the
transfinite system is greater than the finite. But the transfinite
number system seems almost transformed back into a finite
number system by these operations. For the temptation is to
treat $\aleph_0$, $\aleph_1$, $\aleph_2$, ... like the series of finite numbers all over
again, since the finite human mind cannot even begin to conceive
of such magnitudes.

Now I have no intention whatsoever of trying to drive mathematicians from their Cantorian paradise. While such a system
may be perfectly consistent in the mathematical realm, given
its axioms and conventions, I think that it is intuitively obvious
that such a system could not possibly exist in reality. The
best way to show this is by way of examples that illustrate
the various absurdities that would result if an actual infinite
were to be instantiated in the real world.

For instance, if an actual infinite could exist in reality, then
we could have a library with an actually infinite collection
of books on its shelves. Remember that we are talking not
about a potentially infinite number of books, but about a com-

pleted totality of definite and distinct books that actually exist simultaneously in time and space on these library shelves. Suppose further that there were only two colours of books, black and red, and every other book was the same colour. We would probably not balk if we were told that the number of black books and the number of red books is the same. But would we believe someone who told us that the number of red books in the library is the same as the number of red books *plus* the number of black books? For in the latter collection there are all the red books—just as many as in the former collection, since they are identical—plus an infinite number of black books as well. And if one were to imagine the library to have three different colours of books, or four or five or a hundred different colours of books—can we honestly believe that there are in the total collection of books of all colours no more books than in the collection of a single colour? And if there were an infinite number of colours of books, would we not naturally surmise that there was only one book per colour in the total collection? Would we believe anyone who told us that for each of the infinite colours there is an infinite collection of books and that all these infinities taken together do not increase the total number of books by a single volume over the number contained in the collection of books of one colour?

Suppose further that each book in the library has a number printed on its spine so as to create a one-to-one correspondence with the natural numbers. Because the collection is actually infinite, this means that *every possible* natural number is printed on some book. Therefore, it would be impossible to add another book to this library. For what would be the number of the new book? Clearly there is no number available to assign to it. Every possible number already has a counterpart in reality, for corresponding to every natural number is an already existent book. Therefore, there would be no number for the new book. But this is absurd, since entities that exist in reality can be numbered. It might be suggested that we number the new book 'no 1' and add one to the number of every book thereafter. This is perfectly successful in the mathematical realm, since we accommodate the new number by increasing all the others out to infinity. But in the real world this could not be done. For an actual infinity of objects already exists that completely exhausts the natural number system—every possible number has been instantiated in reality on the spine of a book. Therefore, book no 1 could not be called book no 2, and book no 2 be called book no 3, and so on, to infinity. Only in a potential infinite, where new numbers are created as the collection grows, could such a recount be possible. But in an actual infinite, all the members exist in a determinate, complete whole, and such a re-count would necessitate the creation of a new number. But this is absurd, since every possible natural number has been used up. (If they have not been used up, then the collection is not an actual infinite after all.) Therefore, it is of no help to add the book to the beginning of the series. If it is suggested we call the new book $\omega + 1$ or $\aleph_0 + 1$, this is easily dismissed. It could not be $\omega + 1$, for this has the same cardinal number as ω, and we need a new cardinal number for this book. It could not be $\aleph_0 + 1$, for this reduces to $\aleph_0$, and yet we do have an extra, irreducibly real book on our hands. (Besides, there is no book $\aleph_0$ in the collection, since $\aleph_0$ has no immediate predecessor as books do. The symbol $\aleph_0$ just informs us that the whole collection of books as a determinate totality has a denumerably infinite number of books in it, which we already know *ex hypothesi*.) So it would therefore be impossible to add the new book to the stacks.

The same absurdity is evident in an illustration employed by David Hilbert to exhibit the paradoxical properties of the actual infinite, appropriately dubbed 'Hilbert's Hotel': Let us imagine a hotel with a finite number of rooms, and let us assume that all the rooms are occupied. When a new guest arrives and requests a room, the proprietor apologises, 'Sorry— all the rooms are full.' Now let us imagine a hotel with an infinite number of rooms, and let us assume that again all the rooms are occupied. But this time, when a new guest arrives and asks for a room, the proprietor exclaims, 'But of course!' and shifts the person in room 1 to room 2, the person in room 2 to room 3, the person in room 3 to room 4, and so on. . . . The new guest then moves into room 1, which has now become vacant as a result of these transpositions. But now let us suppose an *infinite* number of new guests arrive, asking for rooms. 'Certainly, certainly!' says the proprietor, and he proceeds to move the person in room 1 into room 2, the person in room 2 into room 4, and the person in room 3 into room 6, the person in room 4 into 8, and so on. . . .

In this way, all the odd-numbered rooms become free, and the infinity of new guests can easily be accommodated in them.[27]

In this story the proprietor thinks that he can get away with his clever business move because he has forgotten that his hotel has an *actually infinite* number of rooms, not a potentially infinite number of rooms, and that *all the rooms are occupied*. The proprietor's action can only work if the hotel is a potential infinite, such that new rooms are created to absorb the influx of guests. For if the hotel has an actually infinite collection of determinate rooms and *all* the rooms are full, then there is no more room.

These illustrations show that if an actual infinite could exist in reality, it would be impossible to add to it. But it obviously is possible to add to, say, a collection of books: just take one page from each of the first hundred books, add a title page, and put it on the shelf. Therefore, an actual infinite cannot exist in the real world.

But suppose we could add to the infinite collection of books. The new book would have the ordinal $\omega + 1$. And yet our collection of books has not increased by a single book. But how can this be? We put the book on the shelf: there is one more book in the collection; we take it off the shelf: there is one less book in the collection. We can see ourselves add and remove the book—are we really to believe that when we add the book there are no more books in the collection and when we remove it there are no less books in the collection? Suppose we add an *infinity* of books to the collection; the ordinal number is now $\omega + \omega$. Are we seriously to believe that there are *no more* books in the collection than before? (How could a collection of books numbered $\{1, 2, 3, \ldots, 1, 2, 3, \ldots\}$ have the same cardinal number as a collection numbered $\{1, 2, 3, \ldots\}$, namely, $\aleph_0$? For $\aleph_0$ is the number of elements in the natural number series, and these are completely used up in the first infinite series of books, there being a one-to-one correspondence between every book and every number.) Suppose we add an infinity of infinite collections to the library $(\omega + \omega^2)$—is there actually not one more single volume in the entire collection than before? Suppose we add ω^ω books— how can one express this in words?—to the collection. Is there not one extra book in the collection? Clearly, something must be amiss here. What is it?—we are trying to take conceptual operations guaranteed by the convention of the principle of correspondence and apply them to the real world of things, and the results are just not believable.

But to continue. Suppose we return to our original collection (though supposedly it never really increased) and decide to loan out some of the books. Suppose book no 1 is loaned out. Is not there now one book fewer in the collection? Suppose book nos 1, 3, 5, ... are loaned out. The collection has been depleted of an infinite number of books, and yet we are told that the number of books remains constant. The cumulative gap created by the missing books would be an infinite distance, yet if we push the books together to close the gaps, all of the infinite shelves will remain *full* (this is Hilbert's Hotel in reverse). If we once more remove every other book from the collection, we again have removed an infinity of books, and yet the number of books in the collection is not depleted. And if we close the gaps between the books, all the shelves will remain full. We could do this infinitely many times, and the collection would never have one book fewer and the shelves would always be completely full. But suppose we were to loan out book nos 4, 5, 6, ... At a single stroke the collection would be virtually wiped out, the shelves emptied, and the infinite library reduced to finitude. And yet, we have removed *exactly the same number* of books this time as when we removed book nos 1, 3, 5, ... Can anyone believe such a library can exist in reality? It may be said that inverse operations cannot be performed with the transfinite numbers—but this qualification applies to the mathematical world only, not the real world. While we may correct the mathematician who attempts inverse operations with transfinite numbers, we cannot in the real world prevent people from checking out what books they please from our library.

All this has been said concerning mere denumerably infinite collections. What a non-denumerable collection would be like is nearly inconceivable. It would perhaps be like saying the pages in our books correspond to the real numbers, while the books correspond to the integers. But this is absurd, for in the real world, one can count pages; but the infinity is supposed to be non-denumerable. Besides, since things in reality occupy some space, however tiny, and since there are an infinity of real numbers between every integer, each of our books would be infinitely thick, so that one book would be as wide as the entire collection of books set side by side! In point of fact, no non-denumerable infinity could exist in reality, since things in reality can be numbered. The examples of non-denumerable infinites like mathematical points and functions have no real existence. (More of this later.) Needless to say, then, the infinites possessing even greater power than these also could not exist in reality.

These examples serve to illustrate that the real existence of an actual infinite would be absurd. Again, I must underline the fact that what I have said in no way attempts to undermine the theoretical system bequeathed by Cantor to modern mathematics. Indeed, some of the most eager enthusiasts of the system of transfinite mathematics are only too ready to agree that these theories have no relation to the real world. Thus, Hilbert, who exuberantly extolled Cantor's greatness, nevertheless held that the Cantorian paradise from which he refused to be driven exists only in the ideal world invented by the mathematician; he concludes,

> . . . the infinite is nowhere to be found in reality. It neither exists in nature nor provides a legitimate basis for rational thought—a remarkable harmony between being and thought. . . .
>
> The role that remains for the infinite to play is solely that of an idea—if one means by an idea, in Kant's terminology, a concept of reason which transcends all experience and which completes the concrete as a totality—that of an idea which we may unhesitatingly trust within the framework erected by our theory.[28]

Our case against the existence of the actual infinite says nothing about the use of the idea of the infinite in conceptual mathematical systems.

To return here to a point alluded to earlier, the only mathematicians who would feel uneasy with what I have contended thus far would be those who regard mathematical entities in a Platonistic way, as somehow part of the real world. The question we are raising here is, what is the ontological status of sets?[29] The question is similar to the medieval debate over the existence of universals, and the schools of thought divide along pretty much the same lines: Platonism, nominalism, and conceptualism.

1. *Platonism*, or realism, maintains that corresponding to every well-defined condition there exists a set, or class, comprised of those entities that fulfil this condition and which is an entity in its own right, having an ontological status similar to that of its members. Mathematics is a science of the discovery, not creation, of numbers and their properties, which exist independently of the activity of the mathematician's mind. This viewpoint finds expression in the school of *logicism*, as represented by Frege and Russell, which attempted to reduce the laws of the mathematics of number to logic alone. According to the Platonistic perspective, Cantor's transfinite numbers do exist as a part of reality, and the existence of the actual infinite is guaranteed by the infinity of the natural number series and other mathematical examples of infinite sets.

2. *Nominalism* holds that there are no abstract entities such as numbers or sets, but that only individuals exist. Much of the task of nominalism consists in re-phrasing the language of mathematics in terms of individual entities alone instead of classes or sets. But even these individual mathematical entities are not regarded as having any real existence. When it comes to Cantorian analysis of the infinite, nominalists are only too glad to jettison the whole system as a mathematical fiction.

3. *Conceptualism* contends that abstract entities such as numbers and sets are created by and exist in the mind only, and have no independent status in the real world. A well-defined condition produces a corresponding set, but this set has mental existence only—the mathematician *creates* his mathematical entities; he does not discover them. The most important modern school of conceptualistic persuasion is *intuitionism*, as represented by Kronecker and Brouwer, which argues that only those mathematical entities claim ideal existence which can be constructed by our intuitive activity of counting. Proofs involving an infinite number of steps—such as Cantor's proof of non-denumerable infinites—are ruled out of court because the mind cannot actually construct such sets. Constructible entities have a conceptual existence; non-constructible entities cannot even claim that. When applied to Cantor's theories, conceptualism could accord

purely ideal existence, but not real existence, to the actual infinite, or, if it has an intuitionistic slant, it could deny any sort of existence whatsoever to the actual infinite, since it is non-constructible.

Arising out of the debate between these three schools of thought came a fourth perspective, that of *formalism*. The adherents of this position eschew all ontological questions concerning mathematical entities and maintain that mathematical systems are nothing but formalised systems having no counterparts in reality. Mathematical calculations are merely marks on paper, symbols without content, and the only condition for these is consistency. Mathematical existence is freedom from contradiction. Mathematical calculations may have utility in the real world—but that does not give the formalised systems any literal significance. Formalism's attitude toward Cantor's work is exemplified in the attitude of one of its most famous representatives, Hilbert, who regarded Cantor's system as a consistent mathematical system that carries no ontological implications.

It is highly significant that three of the four schools of thought on the question of the ontological status of mathematical entities ascribe no real existence to these entities. For the nominalist, the conceptualist, and the formalist, the mathematical validity of the Cantorian system implies no commitment to the existence of the actual infinite in the real world. Thus, the mathematical instances of the actual infinite—such as the natural number series, the set of mathematical points on a line, or the set of all functions between zero and one—have nothing to say about the real existence of the actual infinite. Only for the Platonist-realist, who accepts the independent status of mathematical entities in the real world, do Cantor's theories have ontological implications for the real world. This means that our argument against the real existence of the actual infinite would contradict Cantor's work only if the Platonist-realist position on the ontological status of numbers and sets were proven to be the correct one, for our argument would be compatible with any of the other three.

And, in fact, the Platonist-realist view is not tenable. It has been decisively discredited by the irresolvable antinomies to which naive Cantorian set theory gives rise.[30] Just at the moment when the resistance of the mathematical world to his system seemed to be dissolving, Cantor discovered in 1895 the first of several logical antinomies within his system. Not published immediately, the antinomy was also discerned in 1897 by Burali-Forti, whose name it bears. Cantor discovered a second antinomy in 1899—though it was not published until 1932—which bears his name. But Cantor did not regard these contradictions as having much significance and never abandoned a naive view of his set theories. In 1902 the severest blow to Cantor's system was dealt with the publication by Russell of a third antinomy at the very roots of set theory. This antinomy, named after Russell, forced a major reworking of modern set theory and so undermined the Platonist-realist view of sets.

1. *Burali-Forti's antinomy* is also known as the antinomy of the set of all ordinals. Very simply, the antinomy states that if every set has an ordinal number, then the set of all ordinal numbers would also have to have an ordinal number. But then the ordinal number would itself have to be in the set, thus requiring a larger orginal number. Thus, there could be no ordinal number for the set of all ordinals.

2. *Cantor's antinomy* springs out of Cantor's theorem that the set of all subsets of any given set has a cardinal number greater than the set itself has. This means that the set of all sets has a power set—a set containing all the subsets of itself—that has a greater cardinal than the set itself, which is contradictory, since the original set was declared to be the set of *all* sets.

3. *Russell's antinomy* proceeds on the assumption that it is meaningful to ask whether a set is a member of itself. Some sets are clearly not members of themselves. For example, the set of all pigs is not itself a pig, and, hence, it is not a member of itself. But some sets appear to be members of themselves; for example, the set of all things mentioned in this chapter is itself mentioned in this chapter and so would seem to be a member of itself. But what about the set of all sets that are not members of themselves—is it a member of itself? Denoting this set by S, we discover that if S is a member of itself, then it cannot be in S, for S includes only sets that are *not* members of themselves. But if S is not a member of itself, then, since it fulfils the condition for being in S, it is a member

of itself. Thus, we reach the contradictory conclusion that S is a member of S if S is not a member of S.

In the face of these antinomies, set theory either had to be abandoned or radically revised. Not being of the quitting sort, mathematicians and philosophers pursued primarily three courses of possible revision: logicism, axiomatisation, and intuitionism.[31] Logicism sought to circumvent the antinomies by use of the theory of types, which asserted that all the entities referred to in set theory are arranged in a hierarchy of types, with each entity belonging to a certain level. At the lowest level are individuals, that is, entities which are not sets. Above this level are sets which contain the individuals of the lower level as members. Above these are sets whose members are the sets of the second level, and so forth. A set may only have members that are from the level immediately below it, and to speak of any set not fulfilling this condition is strictly nonsensical. In this way the antinomies could not arise because no set could be a member of itself.

Axiomatisation chose a different course: it sought to restrict the concept of set in such a way that the paradoxical sets could not arise. This was accomplished by abandoning Cantor's naive definition of set as any collection fulfilling a condition and adopting instead a system based on seven or eight axioms which do not attempt a definition of 'set', but rather delimit the behaviour of sets so that sets like the set of all ordinals cannot appear in the system.

Intuitionism tended to welcome the antinomies, for they exposed the weakness of non-intuitionistic mathematics with its nonconstructible sets. Only those sets can be granted mathematical existence which are constructible; therefore, sets such as the power set of the set of all cardinals cannot exist, since it is not constructible. The antinomies are actually helpful in that they aid in defining the scope of human mathematical creativity and thus the realm of mathematical entities.

All this strikes at the heart of the Platonist-realist thesis that numbers and sets are component parts of independently existing reality. The logical antinomies in naive set theory are fatal to this thesis because if numbers and sets do exist extra-mentally, then such sets as are encountered in the antinomies seem inevitable. There is no reason for denying that the set of all ordinals or the power set of all cardinals should exist. On this basis, Stephen Barker scores the logicist theory of types as without foundation:

> ... Russell's avowed philosophy was that of realism, and realism offers no philosophical rationale for rejecting impredicative definitions [definitions which, in defining a thing, refer to some totality to which the thing being defined belongs]. If a set has independent reality, then why may not members of the set be defined by reference to the set itself?[32]

Logicism, therefore, was not a very convincing revision of the Platonist-realist position and failed to generate much support, as contrasted with the axiomatic method. Therefore, the Platonist-realist view of numbers and sets as independently existing entities awaiting discovery is exposed as inadequate by the antinomies of naive set theory. If it could be proved that the Platonist-realist view of the ontological status of mathematical entities is correct and that such a view could escape the logical antinomies implicit in naive set theory, then our argument that an actual infinite cannot exist in reality would stand opposed to Cantor's analysis. But as it is, either axiomatisation or intuitionistic reform seem much more plausible alternatives. And under either of these two views, the world which Cantor created is clearly a purely theoretical one: in the one case deduced from presumed axioms just as a Euclidean or a non-Euclidean geometry might be deduced without reference to the real world, and in the other case mentally constructed within the bounds of the mind's finite operations. Thus, out of the four schools of thought concerning the ontological status of sets—Platonism, nominalism, conceptualism, and formalism— only the first is rendered untenable by the antinomies. All the others could acceptably escape these contradictions of naive set theory, and any of them are compatible with our case against the real existence of the actual infinite. Therefore, the Cantorian theory of the actual infinite does not imply that an actual infinite can really exist; indeed, we have seen that this theory itself makes it intuitively obvious that such a conceptual system cannot be instantiated in the real world.

Up to this point we have assumed that the Cantorian analysis of the actual infinite is correct, but it should now be noted that one important school of mathematicians, the intuitionists, do not regard it as so. Their contention is significant, for although the school of intuitionists is not large, it numbers among its members some of the most brilliant mathematicians of the past few generations from several nations. We have seen that the root presupposition of intuitionism is that the basis of mathematics is found in the pure intuitition of counting. Thus, constructibility by actual operations becomes the prerequisite of any true mathematical operation. Since an actual infinite cannot be constructed by the human mind, it follows that the infinite is not a well-defined totality. And not being well-defined, the actual infinite cannot be said to exist in the mathematical realm. Thus, both Kronecker and Brouwer deny that the natural number series is a complete and determinate ideal totality. The natural number series is only an indefinite series, surpassing each limit it reaches. In other words, only the existence of the potential infinite is granted, and intuitionism is thus the heir of the Aristotelian tradition of basing mathematics on the potential infinite. This sort of infinite causes no problems for mathematics because any statement about a potential infinite can be translated into a statement about a finite but extendable entity.

So the Cantorian analysis of the actual infinite is far from unchallenged among mathematicians. If the intuitionists are correct, then not only the real existence but even the conceptual existence of the actual infinite is inadmissible. And why not?— for it is consistent to conceive of the natural number series as a potential infinite, never arriving at infinity, but increasing according to a rule, that of adding one, so that new numbers are created, not discovered, by the mind. One cannot help but wonder if the resistance to intuitionism among many mathematicians is not due more to a stubborn refusal to abandon the Cantorian paradise than to the inadequacy of intuitionistic theories. Of course, intuitionists have no doubt generated opposition to their theories by arguing, for example, that the law of excluded middle does not hold for certain operations (because they concern entities that are not well-defined and are thus insusceptible to determination of their truth value), but it would seem that their view of the infinite as potential and not actual is of itself significant, apart from what might be considered 'objectionable' tenets. If the Platonist-realist view of the ontolo-

gical status of numbers is discarded, then there does not appear
to be any *proof* that the number series is a mathematical instance
of an actual infinite—usually this seems to be just taken for
granted.[33] But there appears to be no necessity for regarding
it as such. If, then, the number series is conceived of as a
potential infinite, the case against the real existence of the
actual infinite would be even stronger, since there would not
only be no real instances of such an entity but no mathematical
instances either.

Finally we may, at the risk of going out on a limb, venture
an opinion as to *why* it is that an actual infinite cannot exist
in reality without entailing the various absurdities described.
It seems to me that the surd problem in instantiating an actual
infinite in the real world lies in Cantor's principle of correspondence. The principle asserts that if a one-to-one correspondence
between the elements of two sets can be established, the sets
are equivalent. This principle is simply adopted in set theory
as a convention; for how could it be proved? One may cite
empirical examples of the successful use of the principle for
comparing finite real collections such as eggs and apples, beads
and coins, persons and seats; but it would be impossible to
conduct such an empirical proof for infinite collections. Therefore, in the mathematical realm equivalent sets are simply *defined*
as sets having a one-to-one correspondence. The principle is
simply a convention adopted for use in the mathematical system
created by the mathematician. This is why, given this principle,
Cantor can consistently assert, for example, that $\omega + \omega$ has
a cardinal number of $\aleph_0$, which, we have argued, is not a
condition realisable in the real world. For given the principle
of correspondence, the set $\{1, 2, 3, \ldots\}$ *is* equivalent to the
set $\{1, 2, 3, \ldots, 1, 2, 3, \ldots\}$, odd as this appears. This
is also why Cantor can consistently maintain that a proper
subset of an infinite set is equivalent to the whole set. For
given the principle of correspondence, the set $\{\ldots -3, -2,
-1, 0, 1, 2, 3, \ldots\}$ *is* equivalent to the set $\{1, 2, 3, \ldots\}$,
strange as this may seem.

Should someone naively object to Cantor's system on the
basis that in it the whole is not greater than a part, mathematicians will remind him that Euclid's maxim holds only for finite
magnitudes, not infinite ones. But surely the question that then
needs to be asked is, how does one know that the principle

of correspondence does not also hold only for finite collections, but not for infinite ones? Here the mathematician can only say that it is simply defined as doing so. For all the finite examples in the world cannot justify the extrapolation of this principle to the infinite; its proveability is precisely the same as Euclid's maxim. One can show that both of these principles hold true for finite collections, but neither can be proved to be true for infinite collections. Moreover, it is clear that they cannot *both* be true for infinite collections, since they are, in this case, converse principles: one asserts that the whole is greater than a part, while the other maintains that the whole is not greater than a part. But which principle is to be sacrificed? Both seem to be intuitively obvious principles in themselves, and both result in counter-intuitive situations when either is applied to the actual infinite. The most reasonable approach to the matter seems to be to regard both principles as valid in reality and the existence of an actual infinite as impossible.

In summary, we have argued in support of the first premiss of our syllogism: (1) that the existence of an actual infinite would entail various absurdities; (2) that the Cantorian analysis of the actual infinite may represent a consistent mathematical system, but that this carries with it no ontological import for the existence of an actual infinite in the real world; and (3) that even the mathematical existence of the actual infinite has not gone unchallenged and therefore cannot be taken for granted, which would then apply doubly so to the real existence of the actual infinite. Therefore, we conclude that an actual infinite cannot exist.

The second premiss states that an infinite temporal regress of events is an actual infinite. By 'event' we mean 'that which happens'. Thus, the second premiss is concerned with change, and it asserts that if the series or sequence of changes in time is infinite, then these events considered collectively constitute an actual infinite. The point seems obvious enough, for if there has been a sequence composed of an infinite number of events stretching back into the past, then the set of all events would be an actually infinite set.[34]

But manifest as this may be to us, it was not always considered so. The point somehow eluded Aristotle himself, as well as his scholastic progeny, who regarded the past sequence of events as a potential infinite. Aristotle contended that since things in time come to exist sequentially, an actual infinite never exists at any one moment; only the present thing actually exists.[35] Similarly, Aquinas, after confessing the impossibility of the existence of an actual infinite, nevertheless proceeded to assert that the existence of an infinite regress of past events is possible.[36] This is because the series of past events does not exist in actuality. Past events do not now exist and hence do not constitute an infinite number of actually existing things. The series is only potentially infinite, not actually infinite, in that it is constantly increasing by addition of new events. But surely this analysis is inadequate. The fact that the events do not exist simultaneously is wholly irrelevant to the issue at hand; the fact remains that since past events, as determinate parts of reality, are definite and distinct and can be numbered, they can be conceptually collected into a totality. Therefore, if the temporal sequence of events is infinite, the set of all past events will be an actual infinite. It is interesting that at least one prominent Thomist agrees that Aquinas and Aristotle fail to carry their case; thus Fernand Van Steenberghen states,

> For him [Aristotle] an infinity in act is impossible; now a universe eternal in the past implies an infinite series in act, since the past is *acquired*, is *realized*; that this realization has been successive does not suppress the fact that the infinite series is *accomplished* and constitutes quite definitely an infinite series in act.[37]

Accordingly, Van Steenberghen maintains that Aquinas clearly contradicts himself by adhering to both the possibility of an infinite temporal regress of events and to the impossibility of an infinite multitude.[38] Aquinas's own example of the blacksmith working from eternity who uses one hammer after another as each one breaks furnishes a good example of an actual infinite. For the set of all hammers employed by the smith is an actual infinite. In the same way, the set of all events in an infinite temporal regress of events is an actual infinite.

The point raised by Aristotle and Aquinas serves to bring out an important feature of past events that is not shared by future events, namely their actuality. For past events have really existed; they have taken place in the real world, while future events have not, since they have not occurred. In no sense does the future actually exist—we must not be fooled by Minkowski diagrams of four-dimensional spacetime depicting the world line of some entity into thinking that future events somehow subsist further down the line, waiting for us to arrive at them. As P. J. Zwart rightly urges, Minkowski spacetime is only a diagrammatical method of displaying the relations of an object to time and space; the fact that we can mark out the future world line of an object in no way implies that these future events actually exist.[39] Only the sequence of past events can count as an actual infinity.

The importance of this difference between future and past events becomes evident when we turn to questions concerning the actual infinite. For clearly, past events are actual in a way in which future events are not. In the real sense, the set of all events from any point into the future is not an actual infinite at all, but a potential infinite. It is an indefinite collection of events, always finite and always increasing. But the series of past events is an actual infinite, for at any point in the past the series of prior events remains infinite and actual.

Because the series of past events is an actual infinite, all the absurdities attending the real existence of an actual infinite apply to it. In fact, far from alleviating these absurdities, as Aristotle and Aquinas would have us believe, the sequential nature of the temporal series of events actually intensifies them. For example, we argued that it would be impossible to add to a really existent actual infinite, but the series of past events is being increased daily. Or so it appears. For if Cantor's system were descriptive of reality, the number of events that have occurred up to the present is no greater than the number that have occurred *at any point in the past.* This brings to mind Russell's account of Tristram Shandy, who, in the novel by Sterne, writes his autobiography so slowly that it takes him a whole year to record the events of a single day. Were he mortal, he would never finish, asserts Russell, but if he were immortal, then the entire book could be completed, since by the method of correspondence each day would correspond to each year, and both are infinite.[40] Such an assertion is wholly untenable, since the future is in reality a potential infinite only. Though he write forever, Tristram Shandy would only get farther and farther behind so that instead of finishing his autobiography, he will progressively approach a state in which he would be *infinitely* far behind. But he would never reach such a state because the years and hence the days of his life would always be finite in number though indefinitely increasing.[41] Russell has confounded the actual infinite status which past events possess (if an infinite temporal regress exists) with the merely potential infinite status belonging to future events. But let us turn the story about: suppose Tristram Shandy has been writing from eternity past at the rate of one day per year. Would he now be penning his final page? Here we discern the bankruptcy of the principle of correspondence in the world of the real. For according to that principle, Russell's conclusion would be correct: a one-to-one correspondence between days and years could be established so that given an actual infinite number of years, the book will be completed. But such a conclusion is clearly ridiculous, for Tristram Shandy could not yet have written *today's* events down. In reality he could never finish, for every day of writing generates another year of work. But if the principle of correspondence were descriptive of the real world, he should have finished—which is impossible. Here the reader may be reminded of the argument of al-Ghāzāli concerning the concentric spheres which revolved such that the innermost sphere completed one rotation in a year while the outermost sphere required thousands of years to complete a single rotation. If the sequence of past events is infinite, then which sphere has completed the most rotations? According to Cantor, if his system were descriptive of reality, the number of revolutions would be equal, for they could be placed in a one-to-one correspondence. But this is simply unbelievable, since every revolution of the great sphere generated thousands of revolutions in the little sphere, and the longer they revolved the greater the disparity grew.

But now a deeper absurdity bursts into view.[42] For if the series of past events is an actual infinite, then we may ask, why did Tristram Shandy not finish his autobiography yesterday-or the day before, since by then an infinite series of events had already elapsed? No matter how far along the series of past events one regresses, Tristram Shandy would have already completed his autobiography. Therefore, at no point in the infinite series of past events could he be finishing the book. We could never look over Tristram Shandy's shoulder to see

if he were now writing the last page. For at any point an
actual infinite sequence of events would have transpired and
the book would have already been completed. Thus, at no
time in eternity will we find Tristram Shandy writing, which
is absurd, since we supposed him to be writing from eternity.
And at no point will he finish the book, which is equally
absurd, because for the book to be completed he must at some
point have finished. What the Tristram Shandy story really
tells us is that an actually infinite temporal regress is absurd.
Therefore, in demonstrating that an infinite temporal regress
of events is an actual infinite, we not only find that the absurdities pertaining to the existence of an actual infinite apply to
it, but also that these absurdities are actually heightened because
of the sequential character of the series.

Since an actual infinite cannot exist and an infinite temporal
regress of events is an actual infinite, we may conclude that
an infinite temporal regress of events cannot exist. This conclusion alone will be sufficient to convince most people that the
universe had a beginning, since the universe is not separate
from the temporal series of events. But for the sake of complete-
ness, we may add another argument to eliminate the possibility
suggested by al-'Allāf that the temporal sequence of events had
a beginning, but that the universe did not, that is to say,
the temporal series of events was preceded by an eternal, quiescent universe, absolutely still. The first event occurred when
motion arose in the universe; this was then followed by other
events, and the temporal series of events was generated. There
are thus two possibilities: since an infinite temporal regress
of events cannot exist, then either (1) the universe began to
exist or (2) the finite temporal regress of events was preceded
by an eternal, absolutely quiescent universe. Accordingly we
may argue as follows:

1. Either the universe began to exist or the finite temporal
   regress of events was preceded by an eternal, absolutely
   quiescent universe.
2. The finite temporal regress of events was not preceded by
   an eternal, absolutely quiescent universe.
3. Therefore the universe began to exist.

The first premiss is true in the light of the foregoing argument, which eliminated the possibility of an infinite temporal regress of events. This means that the sequence of events is finite and had a beginning.[43] Either this was an absolute beginning of the universe itself or only a relative beginning of events within an utterly immobile universe. Hence the second premise, which eliminates one of these disjuncts, is clearly the key premiss.

We may offer two arguments in support of the second premiss, a philosophical argument and an empirical argument. First we shall examine the philosophical argument, which begins by positing a disjunction. The first event to arise in the absolutely still and eternal universe was either caused or not. Consider the first disjunct, that it was caused. Either the necessary and sufficient conditions giving rise to this first event were eternally present or not. But if these determinate conditions were eternally present, then their effect would also be eternally present—which makes the existence of a *first* event impossible. On the other hand, if the necessary and sufficient conditions for the first event were not eternally present in the universe, then these determinate conditions themselves had to arise in the universe, and we have only succeeded in pushing the temporal regress of events back one more event into the past. But we have already proved that the temporal regress of events cannot be actually infinite because an actual infinite cannot exist. So one must stop at a first event whose determinate conditions did not themselves arise but always existed. But this has already been shown to be impossible. Therefore, the first event to arise in the universe could not be caused. But that forces us over to the second disjunct, that the first event was uncaused. While this is logically possible, it does not seem very reasonable. For this means that this event occurred entirely without determinate conditions for its happening. The universe existed in a static, absolutely immobile state from eternity and then inexplicably, without any conditions whatsoever, a first event occurred. Such a theory seems inherently implausible, as P. J. Zwart observes:

> This leaves us with the alternative of a universe filled with matter in some form or other, this matter being completely in equilibrium, that is to say, its state remaining exactly the same, without even the slightest change, until at some moment . . . suddenly an event occurs. Matter being presumably not uniformly diffused throughout the universe

(this would be contrary to the discontinuous nature of matter as we know it) it would have to be present in the form of one piece, for if there were more parts than one they would move towards each other under the force of gravitation, and the universe would not be in a state of complete rest. ... the universe would have to consist of one tremendous lump of matter, having of course a temperature of o°K (the absolute zero), because only at that temperature the particles may be considered to be at rest. Outside this lump of matter there would be nothing, no light, no radiation, only total emptiness ... this first event would have to be completely uncaused. Obviously it would not have a proximate cause, as it was the first event which occurred. ... But it also could not have any fundamental causes, for if there had been a combination of factors which was sufficient to bring about that first event this combination would have existed always, for the situation before that first event remained exactly the same. So there must have been some reason why this event occurred only when it did and not before. That is to say, there must have been a proximate cause. But a proximate cause proved to be impossible, so the first event must obviously have been totally uncaused. There is absolutely no reason why this event occurred; its occurrence is a complete mystery.[44]

For this reason Zwart rejects the alternative. The possibility of an event's occurring without the necessary and sufficient conditions for its occurrence is not very plausible, and such a picture of the universe is singularly unconvincing. Therefore, if the necessary and sufficient conditions for the occurrence of the first event did not exist from eternity, the first event would never occur; but if the necessary and sufficient conditions for the first event did exist from eternity, then the first event would have occurred from eternity, that is to say, there would have been no first event. Had the universe once been eternally and absolutely quiescent, then it never would have awakened from its sleep of death. But since it obviously is not quiescent, we may conclude that the finite temporal regress of events was not preceded by an eternal, absolutely quiescent universe.

Second, such a picture of the universe is at any rate empirically untenable. For an absolutely quiescent universe would have to exist at the temperature of absolute zero, since heat is the result of motion and there can be no motion in the universe which we envisage. But such a model of the universe is at once disqualified, since it is physically impossible to reach absolute zero. Quite simply, an absolutely quiescent universe is physically impossible: there will always be some heat and some motion and hence some events. Moreover, matter existing in a state of self-collapse caused by gravitation would be anything but cold—it would be a volatile furnace with temperatures exceeding billions of degrees Kelvin, as in the big bang model. Hence, an absolutely quiescent universe is doubly impossible. But even if such a state of absolute rest were attainable, how could a first event ever occur? Frozen into lifeless and absolute immobility, the universe would remain forever still, for no interactions of any sort could ever take place. An event would never occur. But events have occurred, and therefore we know that the universe never lay in such a state. Because an utterly immobile universe is empirically untenable on at least three grounds, we can conclude that the finite temporal regress of events was not preceded by an eternal, absolutely quiescent universe.

Therefore, we conclude: the universe began to exist. And this is the second premiss of our original syllogism which we set out to prove. To recapitulate: since an actual infinite cannot exist and an infinite temporal regress of events is an actual infinite, we can be sure that an infinite temporal regress of events cannot exist, that is to say, the temporal regress of events is finite. If the temporal regress of events is finite, then either the universe began to exist or the finite temporal regress of events was preceded by an eternal, absolutely quiescent universe. But the finite temporal regress of events could not have been preceded by an eternal, absolutely quiescent universe. Therefore, since the temporal regress of events is finite, the universe began to exist.

Second Philosophical Argument

We may now turn to our second philosophical argument in support of the premiss that the universe began to exist, the argument from the impossibility of the formation of an actual infinite by successive addition. The argument may be exhibited in this way:

1. The temporal series of events is a collection formed by successive addition.
2. A collection formed by successive addition cannot be an actual infinite.
3. Therefore the temporal series of events cannot be an actual infinite.

Here we do not assume that an actual infinite cannot exist. Even if an actual infinite can exist, the temporal series of events cannot be one, since an actual infinite cannot be formed by successive addition, as the temporal series of events is.

The first premiss seems obvious enough. First, the collection of all past events prior to any given point is not a collection whose members all co-exist. Rather it is a collection that is instantiated sequentially or *successively* in time, one event following upon the heels of another. Second, nor is the series formed by subtraction or division but by *addition* of one element after another. This elementary point merits underscoring since neglect of it can lead to confusion.[45] For although we may *think* of the past by subtracting events from the present, as when we say an event occurred ten years ago, it is nonetheless clear that the series of events is *formed* by addition of one event after another. We must be careful not to confuse the realms of thought and reality. Even the expression 'temporal regress' can be misleading, for the events themselves are not regressing in time; our thoughts regress in time as we mentally survey past events. But the series of events is itself progressing in time, that is to say, the collection of all past events grows progressively larger with each passing day. Nor is the series of events a continuum from which events are formed by division. We are speaking in this argument primarily of events, definite and distinct happenings, that occur in time; we are not speaking of time itself, which is at least mentally infinitely divisible. Neither subtraction nor division accounts for the sequential formation of the collection of past events. Therefore, the temporal series of events is a collection formed by successive addition.

The second premiss asserts that a collection formed by successive addition cannot be an actual infinite. Sometimes this is

described as the impossibility of counting to infinity. For each
new element added to the collection can be counted as it
is added. It is important to understand exactly *why* it is impossible to form an actual infinite by successive addition. The
reason is that for every element one adds, one can always
add one more. Therefore, one can never arrive at infinity.
What one constructs is a potential infinite only, an indefinite
collection that grows and grows as each new element is added.
Another way of seeing the point is by recalling that $\aleph_0$ has
no immediate predecessor. Therefore one can never reach $\aleph_0$
by successive addition or counting, since this would involve
passing through an immediate predecessor to $\aleph_0$. *Notice that
the argument has nothing to do with any time factor.* Sometimes
it is wrongly alleged that the reason an actual infinite cannot
be formed by successive addition is because there is not enough
time.[46] But this is wholly beside the point. Regardless of the
time involved an actual infinite cannot be completed by successive addition due to the very nature of the actual infinite
itself. No matter how many elements one has added, one can
always add one more. A potential infinite cannot be turned
into an actual infinite by any amount of successive addition;
they are conceptually distinct. To illustrate: suppose we imagine
a man running through empty space on a path of stone slabs,
a path constructed such that when the man's foot strikes the
last slab, another appears immediately in front of him. It is
clear that even if the man runs for eternity, he will never
run across all the slabs. For every time his foot strikes the
last slab, a new one appears in front of him, *ad infinitum.* The
traditional cognomen for this is the impossibility of traversing
the infinite. The impossibility of such a traversal has nothing
at all to do with the amount of time available: it is of the
essence of the infinite that it cannot be completed by successive
addition. As Russell himself states, '. . . classes which are infinite
are given all at once by the defining properties of their
members, so that there is no question of "completion" or
of "successive synthesis".'[47] The only way in which an actual
infinite could come to exist in the real world would be to
be instantiated in reality all at once, simply given in a moment.
To try to progressively instantiate an actual infinite in the
real world would be hopeless, for one could always add one
more element. Thus, for example, if our library of infinite

books were to exist in the real world, it would have to be instantaneously created *ex nihilo* by the divine fiat, 'Let there be . . . !' But even God could not instantiate the infinite library volume by volume, one at a time. No reflection on His omnipotence, for such a successive completion of an actual infinite is absurd.

The only way a collection to which members are being successively added could be actually infinite would be for it to have an infinite 'core' to which additions are being made. But then it would not be a collection *formed* by successive addition, for there would always exist a surd infinite, itself not formed successively but simply given, to which a finite number of successive additions have been made. But clearly the temporal series of events cannot be so characterised, for it is by nature successively formed throughout. Thus, prior to any arbitrarily designated point in the temporal series, one has a collection of past events up to that point which is successively formed and completed and cannot, therefore, be infinite.

Contemporary philosophers have proved impotent to refute this reasoning. John Hospers, himself no friend of philosophical theism, acknowledges that it is insufficient simply to assert that an infinite series of events is possible because an infinite series of integers is possible. For, he asks,

> If an infinite series of events has preceded the present moment, how did we get to the present moment? How could we get to the present moment—where we obviously are now—if the present moment was preceded by an infinite series of events?[48]

Concluding that this difficulty has not yet been overcome and that the issue is still in dispute, Hospers passes on to other forms of the cosmological argument, leaving this one unrefuted. Similarly William L. Rowe, after expositing Bonaventure's argument for creation, comments rather weakly, 'It is difficult to show exactly what is wrong with this argument,' and with that remark moves on without further ado to discuss the Leibnizian argument.[49] But contemporary thinkers have discussed more fully two other philosophical puzzles that embody issues closely related to the present argument: Zeno's paradoxes of motion and the thesis of Kant's first antinomy of pure reason. In order to keep this chapter to a reasonable length, I have chosen to discuss these issues fully in Appendixes 1 and 2. The reader is referred to those discussions at this juncture.

There is one additional issue that I would like to comment on at this point, however, and that is whether our argument necessitates a beginning to time itself. Some persons might be prone to reject the argument if they thought it involved a beginning to time, which they regard as an impossibility.[50] The answer to this problem is: it all depends. If a person believes that time exists apart from events such that if there were no events there would still be time, then our argument does not entail *prima facie* a beginning to time. On the other hand, if one accepts that time cannot exist apart from events, then a beginning of events would entail a beginning of time as well.

There are a few modern authors who hold to the independent status of time apart from events, and they are thus the heirs of the Newtonian conception of absolute time. Swinburne argues that time, like space, is of logical necessity unbounded.[51] For every instant of time must be preceded and succeeded by another instant of time. The physical universe itself may have had a beginning—but this can only be true if there is a period of time before the beginning during which the universe did not exist. Since time is unbounded, it is of logical necessity infinite. Since prior to and after every period of time there is more time and since the same instant of time never recurs, time must have gone on and will go on forever. Although space would not exist without physical objects, time would. But, he adds, without physical objects, time could not be measured: one could not distinguish an hour from a day in a period of time without objects.[52] Therefore, Newton's claims about Absolute Time were correct.[53] To say that the universe began to exist on such a time scale would simply be to say that a finite time ago there were no physical objects.[54]

J. R. Lucas also contends that time could neither begin nor end.[55] He notes that if time is defined in a relational manner, then if there were an absolutely stationary universe prior to the first event, we would have to say that time did not exist until the first event occurred. At the beginning of time no past tense statements could be made, since there was no past. Yet it is obvious that certain statements, such as,

'The stars were moving', is a meaningful, though in this case false, statement that could be made about the state of the universe prior to the first event. Lucas does not deny that the universe may have had a beginning, but he, like Swinburne, argues that in such a case time would precede the beginning of the universe and that it would be undifferentiated.[56] Without a world there would be no metric to impose upon time.

A variant on the above view is expressed by Lawrence Sklar, whose theories of time are heavily influenced by relativity theory. He interprets Minkowski spacetime in a literalistic way, asserting that future events 'have determinate reality' and future objects are 'real existents'.[57] Accordingly, he regards time and space as inextricably bound up together in spacetime.[58] This would seem to imply that if the universe had an absolute beginning *ex nihilo*, then time would also have a beginning; but that if the universe had only a relative beginning from a prior quiescent state, then time would not have a beginning. Ian Hinckfuss also argues that if the universe were frozen into immobility, there would still be time because temporal duration and measurement are not dependent upon the continuous operation of a clock throughout that time.[59]

Presumably to such thinkers the beginning of the temporal series of events would not entail a beginning to time itself. On the other hand, those who adhere to a relational view of time generally take the beginning of events to be synonymous with the beginning of time itself. Zwart, for example, asserts,

> According to the relational theory the passage of time consists in the happening of events. So the question whether time is finite or infinite may be reduced to the question whether the series of events is finite or infinite.[60]

It might be asserted that even on the relational view of time there can be time prior to the first event because one may abstract from individual events to consider the whole universe as a sort of event which occurs at its creation. There would thus be a before and an after with regard to this event: no universe/universe. And a relation of before and after is the primitive relation of which time consists.[61] On the other hand, this level of abstraction may be illegitimate and may presuppose a time above time. For prior to the universe's beginning, if there was *nothing* at all, not even space, then it would certainly seem to be true that there was no time either. For suppose the universe never came to exist—would there still be time? But if the universe does come to exist *ex nihilo*, how could we say this first event has an effect on reality (but of course there was no reality!) before it ever occurred, especially when its occurrence is a contingent matter? We might want to say that time does not exist until an event occurs, but when the event does occur, there is a sort of retroactive effect causing past time to spring into being. But this seems to confuse once more our mental ability to think back in time with the progressive, uni-directional nature of time itself. Though we can, after creation, *think* of nothingness one hour before the first event, in terms of reality, there was no such moment. For there was just nothing, and creation was only a future contingent. When the first event occurred, the first moment of time began.

These are difficult conundrums and it is at least an open question as to whether a beginning of events necessitates a beginning of time. Therefore, we need to ask whether there is any absurdity in supposing that time had a beginning. Certainly Aristotle, Kemp Smith, and Swinburne think so, for all three argue that any instant of time implies a prior instant. Thus, there could be no first instant of time. Within a Newtonian understanding of time this argument, even if sound, would not impair our argument that the universe had a beginning *in* time instead of *with* time. But, in fact, it does seem plausible to contend on a relational view of time that a first instant could exist, since apart from events no time exists. Stuart Hackett argues,

Time is merely a relation among objects that are apprehended in an order of succession or that objectively exist in such an order: time is a form of perceptual experience and of objective processes in the external (to the mind) world. Thus the fact that time is a relation among objects or experiences of a successive character *voids* the objection that the beginning of the world implies an antecedent void time: for time, as such a relation of succession among experiences or objective processes, has no existence whatever apart from these experiences or processes themselves.[62]

Therefore, if nothing existed and then something existed, there is no absurdity in speaking of this as the first moment of time. Brian Ellis notes that because we speak of 'before creation' or 'prior to the first event', we tend to think that a beginning of time is impossible.[63] But Ellis draws a very instructive analogy between this sort of speech and talk of temperatures below absolute zero. When a physicist says there are no temperatures lower than absolute zero, the use of 'lower than' does not presuppose there actually are such temperatures, but only that we can conceive it in our minds. In the same way, to say there was a time when the universe did not exist does not imply there was such a time, but only that we can mentally conceive of such a time. To say there is no time before the first event is like saying there is no temperature below $-273°C$. Both express limits beyond which only the mind can travel. Whitrow remarks in this connection that many people have difficulty imagining a beginning to time because they think of it as a boundary similar to a boundary of space.[64] We reject the latter because we could presumably cross the boundary and find space on the other side. But the case with time is different because we cannot travel freely in time as in space. If time coexists with events, then an origin of time merely implies a beginning of the universe. The first moment of time is not a self-contradictory concept.

There does not appear to be, therefore, any absurdity in the notion of a beginning of time. The idea of a 'time before time' is a mental construction only, a product of the imagination. In reality there seems to be no impossibility in having time arise concomitantly with the universe *ex nihilo*. Thus, our argument for the beginning of the universe does not entail an untenable picture of time. Whether one wants to say the universe arises in an absolute, undifferentiated time or that it comes into existence with time, one may consistently maintain that the temporal series of events had a beginning.

In summary, then, we have argued in support of our second premiss: (1) the formation of an actual infinite by successive addition is impossible because one can always add one more; (2) the Zeno paradoxes show that absurdities would result if an actual infinite could be so formed (Appendix 1); and (3) Kant's first antinomy cogently argues that the present event could never arise if the temporal series of past events were infinite (Appendix 2). Hence, we may conclude that a collection formed by successive addition cannot be an actual infinite. Since the temporal series of events is a collection formed by successive addition, we conclude: therefore, the temporal series of events cannot be an actual infinite. This means, of course, that the temporal series of events is finite and had a beginning. To secure an *absolute* beginning for the universe we would need to reintroduce the philosophical and empirical arguments against an absolutely quiescent universe that we expounded in the first proof. Rather than repeat ourselves, I refer the reader to that discussion. Therefore, since either the universe began to exist or the finite temporal regress of events was preceded by an eternal, absolutely quiescent universe, and since the latter is impossible, we conclude, therefore, the universe began to exist. This is, again, the second premiss in our cosmological argument.

This completes the philosophical case in support of the second premiss. We have argued that the impossibility of the existence of an actual infinite implies that the universe began to exist and that even if an actual infinite could exist, the inability of this infinite to be formed by successive addition implies that the universe began to exist. We may now turn to the empirical confirmation of this argument.

EMPIRICAL CONFIRMATION

Some persons may be sceptical about philosophical arguments concerning the universe—what has been characterised as 'armchair cosmology'. They distrust metaphysical arguments, considering them to be misguided attempts to legislate for reality what can and cannot be. They are liable to be more impressed by empirical facts than by abstract arguments and are apt to ask for scientific evidence that the universe began to exist. I shall now present such evidence, which is drawn from remarkable discoveries made within the last twenty years in what is undoubtedly one of the most exciting and rapidly developing areas of scientific research: astronomy and astrophysics. With astounding rapidity, one breakthrough has come upon the heels of another so that now the prevailing cosmological view among scientists is that the universe did have a beginning. Our empirical

argument is divided into two parts: (1) the argument from
the expansion of the universe and (2) the argument from thermodynamics. To put the empirical evidence into a proper frame-
work, I shall argue that a model of the universe in which
the universe has an absolute beginning is not only logically
consistent but also 'fits the facts' of experience.

First Empirical Confirmation

First, we shall consider the argument from the expansion of
the universe.[65] When Einstein formulated his relativity theories,
he assumed that (1) the universe is homogeneous and isotropic,
so that it appears the same in any direction from any place
and (2) the universe is in a steady state, with a constant mean
mass density and a constant curvature of space. But finding
that his original general relativity theory would not permit
a model consistent with these two conditions, he was forced
to add to his gravitational field equations the cosmological
constant Λ in order to counter-balance the gravitational effect
of matter and so ensure a static model of the universe. Another
solution to Einstein's difficulty was noted by de Sitter, who
observed that in an empty universe the conditions and field
equations would be satisfied. The model is static because there
is no matter. But should particles of matter be introduced,
the Λ factor would cause them to be repulsed from each other,
thus leading to an expanding universe. Such a model of an
expanding universe became known as an Einstein–de Sitter
model, and it serves as a special limiting case for a luxuriant
jungle of expanding universe models that have grown up since
then. Such models were derived independently by Friedmann
and Lemaître; they posited an expanding universe which began
in a state of high density. At the same time that this purely
theoretical work was going on, observational cosmology spear-
headed by Hubble was progressing toward the same sort of
picture of the real universe. Slipher had noted in 1926 that
the optical spectra of the light from distant galaxies were shifted
toward the red end of the spectrum. This was thought to
be the result of the Doppler effect, which displaces the spectral
lines in radiation received from a source because of the relative
motion of the source in the line of sight.[66] When a source
is moving toward an observer, there is a blueshift in the spectral

lines; when the source is receding, a redshift occurs. Hubble demonstrated in 1929 that not only are all measured galaxies receding, but that their velocity of recession is proportional to their distance from us.[67] On what has become known as a Hubble diagram, he plotted the apparent magnitude, or measure of luminosity, of galaxies against their redshifts. Taking magnitude as a measure of distance, Hubble concluded that redshift and distance are linearly related: the greater the distance the greater the source's redshift. This is known as Hubble's law. Since redshift is indicative of velocity, the Hubble diagram showed that the further sources are from us the faster they are receding, so that a source twice as far away from us as another source is receding twice as fast. The constant expressing the ratio between the recession velocities of galaxies and their distance from us is known as the Hubble constant and is abbreviated H_0.

But not only was it found that the universe is expanding, but also that it is expanding isotropically; it is the same in all directions. No matter where in the sky a galaxy is measured, the ratio of its velocity to its distance is the same. Hence, the relational aspects of the universe do not vary:

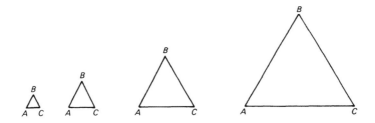

If A, B, and C are three galaxies, then as the universe expands, they will recede from each other, but their relations remain constant. The work of Hubble and his colleagues appeared to establish conclusively that the universe is expanding, just as the theoretical models had predicted. This dramatic harmony of theory and observation was hailed by many as one of the greatest successful predictions in the history of science, and Einstein promptly urged that his original static model of the universe be discarded, along with the cosmological constant which he had introduced.

If the universe is expanding, then the obvious question next to be asked was, how long? The simplest model of the universe would be one in which the recessional velocity of the galaxies would remain unchanged through time. In this case the expansion would have been going on for the time it would take any given galaxy at its present velocity to reach its present position, or, in other words, by the inverse of the Hubble constant. This is called the Hubble time and is the time elapsed from the beginning of the expansion until the present. The staggering implication of this is that by thus extrapolating back into the past, we come to a point in time at which *the entire known universe was contracted into an arbitrarily great density*; if one extrapolates the motion of the galaxies into the past as far as possible, one reaches a state of contraction of *infinite density*. If the velocity of the galaxies has remained unchanged, then one Hubble time ago, the universe began to expand from a state of infinite density in what has come to be called the 'big bang'.

Hubble's original estimate of the Hubble time was two billion years. This, however, conflicted sharply with the age of stellar objects and particularly of the earth itself as given by radioactive decay dating methods. Clearly, either the simplest models of the expanding universe were wrong or the value of H_0 was incorrect. New big bang models were devised, and an alternative model to the big bang theory was broached: the steady state model, expounded in 1948 by Bondi, Gold, and Hoyle.[68] The steady state model also involved an expanding universe, but not a big bang. Instead, it proposed that the gaps left between receding galaxies were filled by matter which was drawn into being *ex nihilo*. The universe was thus infinitely old and in a steady state, new matter continually arising in the space vacated by the receding stellar systems. Much of the rationale for these new models was removed, however, when various inaccuracies in the measurement of luminosity and distance of galaxies were discovered. All these affected the estimates of H_0, whose value was brought more and more into conformity with the results of other dating procedures.

Perhaps the greatest triumph for the big bang model of the universe came in 1965 with the discovery by Penzias and Wilson of a microwave background radiation that permeates the entire universe.[69] In 1946 Gamow had predicted the existence of such a background radiation from purely theoretical considerations of the physics of the early phases of a big bang universe. The earliest phase of the universe has been characterised as a 'primeval fireball', with a temperature in excess of 10^{12}°K.[70] During this phase, called the hadron era, which represents the first one hundred thousandth (10^{-5}) of a second after the big bang, the temperatures were so high that matter could not exist in a structured form—the universe was filled with nuclear particles that were in equilibrium with the field of radiation, that is to say, particles interacted to form photons and *vice versa*. When the temperature had dropped to about 10^{12}°K, the universe entered a phase called the lepton era, which lasted from about one ten thousandth (10^{-4}) of a second after the big bang to ten seconds after the big bang. Before the temperature reached 10^{11}°K, the density was low enough to allow neutrinos and antineutrinos to cease interacting with photons and to maintain independent existence.[71] At this point the universe consisted mostly of photons, electrons ($e-$), positrons ($e+$), neutrinos, antineutrinos, and a trace of protons and neutrons. As the temperature dropped to about 10^9°K, all the positrons were annihilated by combination with electrons, whose number exceeded that of the positrons. This marks the beginning of the radiation era, which lasts from ten seconds until 10^{12} seconds after the big bang. Protons and neutrons combined to form helium; most of the present helium in the universe was synthesised at that time. All the neutrons were used up in this process, so that the universe consisted of protons and helium nuclei together with the electrons that made up an ionised gas; photons and neutrinos were also present. As the universe expanded, the temperature continued to drop until at about 3000°K the nuclei and the electrons of the ionised gas re-combined to form an unionised gas. This marked the beginning of the matter era, around 10^{13} seconds after the big bang. The photons emitted during this recombination are what we detect as the microwave background today. From far beyond the faintest galaxies perceptible comes this low frequency radiation, bathing the whole universe. This radiation field has the spectral characteristics of the thermal radiation emitted by a blackbody, that is, an ideal body which is a perfect emitter of radiation. Its amazing isotropy—it varies only about one part in a thousand—supports the conclusion that this cosmic radiation is indeed the relic of an early era of the universe in which the universe was very hot and very dense. Due to the expansion of the universe, this radiation is Doppler shifted into the microwave region of the spectrum and cooled to about $2.76°K$. Gamow, nearly twenty years before its discovery, had predicted $5°K$. The agreement between the predictions based on Gamow's theoretical model and the observations of Penzias and Wilson constitutes powerful evidence in favour of the big bang cosmology. It was the second time that this model of the universe was successfully corroborated by empirical confirmation of theoretical predictions.

But when did the big bang occur? Estimates of the date of this event are dependent upon two factors: the value of H_0 and the effect of gravity in slowing down the galaxies' recessional velocity. During the 1970s scientists have closed in upon accurate estimations of these two values in what Allan Sandage, who has pioneered the drive, has described as a thirty-year 'search for two numbers'.[72] During the past several years, in a very important series of articles, Sandage and Tammann have described their steady progress toward a determination of these figures.[73] In order accurately to determine H_0, more precise distance estimates had to be first obtained for galaxies sufficiently remote to have significant expansion velocities. This was accomplished in three progressive steps, moving from regions of ionised hydrogen in the interstellar space of nearby galaxies to intermediate, isolated galaxies and finally to remote galaxies that are distant enough to permit reliable determination of the Hubble constant. They found the distances calculated to be greater than Hubble's estimates by a factor of ten. The first indications of an accurate Hubble constant were given by estimates obtained for the Virgo cluster, a cluster of about 2500 galaxies at a distance of 19.5 ± 0.8 Mpc.[74] The value of H_0 for this cluster is 57.0 ± 6 km s^{-1} Mpc^{-1}. (Or, in other words, the cluster is receding at about 57 kilometres per second for every megaparsec it is distant.) When Sandage and Tammann combined these results with individual red shifts, they obtained a local Hubble constant of 57.0 ± 3 km s^{-1} Mpc^{-1}, which was the same as that for the Virgo cluster alone. The final results obtained from the remotest galaxies yields a global value for the Hubble constant very close to the local value: $H_0 = 55.0 \pm 5$ km s^{-1} Mpc^{-1}. This result is the most precise determination to date. The inverse of the Hubble constant gives the Hubble time (H_0^{-1}): 17.7×10^9. Thus, assuming that acceleration is constant, the universe began about eighteen billion years ago in a primordial cataclysmic event.

But the acceleration has undoubtedly not been constant. For the mutual gravitational attraction of the galaxies acts as a restraint on their acceleration from each other. As the universe expands the gravitational effect of matter will cause deceleration of the receding galaxies. Thus, in the past, galaxies must have been moving faster than they are now. Neglecting the decelerating effect of gravity leads to an overestimate of the age of the universe. Only if the acceleration of the galaxies has been constant would the big bang be exactly one Hubble time ago; if there has been a deceleration, then the universe actually began less than a Hubble time ago. Thus, in order to determine more accurately the date of the big bang we need to know the value of the deceleration of the expansion; this is called the deceleration parameter and is symbolised q_0. Since q_0 is a measure of the density of the universe (since it is the density that determines the deceleration), I shall reserve a discussion of the value of q_0 until later. For now I shall simply report that when the value of q_0 is taken into account, the age of the universe is reduced to about 15 billion years.[75]

Thus, according to the big bang model, the universe began with a great explosion from a state of infinite density about 15 billion years ago. Four prominent scientists describe that event in these words:

> ... the universe began from a state of infinite density about one Hubble time ago. Space and time were created in that event and so was all the matter in the universe. It is not meaningful to ask what happened before the big bang; it is somewhat like asking what is north of the North Pole. Similarly, it is not sensible to ask where the big bang took place. The point-universe was not an object isolated in space; it was the entire universe, and so the only answer can be that the big bang happened everywhere.[76]

This event that marked the inception of the universe becomes all the more remarkable when one reflects that a condition of 'infinite density' is precisely equivalent to 'nothing'. There can be no object in the real world that possesses infinite density, for if it had any mass at all, it would not be *infinitely* dense.[77] As Hoyle points out, the steady state model requires the creation of matter from nothing, but so does the big bang; this is because as one follows the expansion back in time, one reaches a time at which the universe was 'shrunk down to nothing at all'.[78]

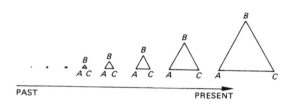

PAST   PRESENT

This is the state of 'infinite density'. What a literal application of the big bang model really requires, therefore, is *creatio ex nihilo*. Of course, one is always at liberty to interrupt this backward extrapolation at any point and maintain that the universe began at t_1, for example. But this seems rather arbitrary, and it raises some very difficult problems. For instance, if the big bang occurred in a super dense pellet existing from eternity, then why did the big bang occur only 15 billion years ago? Why did the pellet of matter wait for all eternity to explode? Indeed, would it be even physically possible for the universe to exist in such a volatile and unstable state for longer than a few hundred thousandths of a second? Or again, if it be alternatively suggested that prior to the big bang there was a contraction of gas which collapsed and then exploded, one may ask how the gas came to be scattered in the first place. For it could not have existed in such a state from eternity, since gravitational attraction would have brought it together. These difficulties all conspire to preclude an arbitrary interruption of the extrapolation back to the absolute origin of the universe.[79] A literal application of the big bang model in which the universe originates in an explosion from a state of infinite density, that is, from nothing, provides a simple, consistent, and empirically sound construction of how the universe began.[80]

Some are unhappy about a theory of the origin of the universe which implies a beginning *ex nihilo*. But if one denies such an origin, then one is left with two alternatives; a steady state model or an oscillating model.

Hoyle, the perennial champion of the steady state model, recoils at the notion of the origin of the universe from nothing (we shall see why later):

> According to our observations and calculations, this was the situation some 15,000 million years ago. This most peculiar situation is taken by many astronomers to represent the *origin of the universe*. The universe is supposed to have begun at this particular time. From where? The usual answer, surely an unsatisfactory one, is: from nothing! The elucidation of this puzzle forms the most important problem of present day astronomy, indeed, one of the most important problems of all science.[81]

He elsewhere admits that the steady state model sought to bypass the conceptual problems involved in the origin of the universe.[82] But the steady state theory has taken a pretty heavy hammering since it was proposed in 1948, and even Hoyle seems ready to throw in the towel. The model had always had something of an *ad hoc* character about it, being devised after the data concerning redshifts had been discovered rather than predicting the data from a theoretical model.[83] A second strike against the steady state model was that a count of radio sources indicates that there were once more radio sources in the universe than there are at present, the radio waves from these ancient sources forming a radio background radiation throughout the universe.[84] Since the steady state model predicts a universe that is at all times the same, the discovery of these radio sources of past eras tended to count against the model. But the real nails in the coffin for the steady state model came in 1965 with the discovery of the microwave background radiation. The radiation background appears to be a vestige of a very hot and very dense state of the universe. But in the steady state model no such state could exist, since the state of the universe has not changed from eternity. Thus, Hoyle, 'after ten years or more of attempting to "tough it out"', admits that the classic steady state model ought to be abandoned because of its inability to account for the microwave background:

> If it were not for the existence of the microwave background, ... the steady state model might reasonably be judged to stand well at the present time. The origin of the microwave background can be explained satisfactorily in terms of the 'big bang' cosmologies. ... No such explanation can be given in the steady state model. ... For the large-scale features of the universe, one epoch cannot be different from another epoch. ...
>
> How, then, in the steady state model can we explain the existence of the microwave background? ... Many radio sources are known which generate such waves. So why should not the sources—i.e., discrete objects like radiogalaxies and QSO's—be responsible for the background? The difficulty with this apparently straightforward approach to the problem is that the known sources ... fail to give an adequate intensity, particularly at the high-frequency end of the background. The only possible recourse would be to postulate the existence of a very large number of *undetected sources*, sources of very low intrinsic emission. ... There would need to be about 10^{14} such weak sources, which is about 100,000 times the total number of visible galaxies. Most astronomers find it unpalatable to assume the existence, not just of a new class of source, but of a class with a very great number of members.[85]

But this does not mean Hoyle is ready to embrace the big bang model: he has proposed a new type of steady state model which attempts to explain the microwave background.[86] In this model Hoyle contends that the universe itself is not expanding, but that the atoms in the universe are expanding. The light from distant galaxies is red shifted because it comes from smaller atoms, thus giving the illusion of motion. The microwave background comes from sources that existed before $\tau = 0$ in a sort of mirror universe to our own, which would approach zero mass at $\tau = 0$. Hoyle will undoubtedly remain something of a maverick in all this, however, for even should his new theory manage to construct alternative explanations of certain features of the universe, it has nothing of positive empirical value to commend it. One gets the impression that Hoyle is not so much trying to explain the results of observational cosmology as trying to explain them away. His is a theoretical model in retreat like the pre-Copernican geo-centric cosmologies, and even should he succeed in establishing a model that explains all the phenomena, it would only make his model a bare possibility, but in no way one having any weight of probability. One must remember that even the Ptolemaic system was not rejected because it could not explain the motions of heavenly bodies; it was mainly that, what with its epicycles on top of epicycles, it was just no longer convincing—it had died the death of a thousand qualifications. Hoyle's attempts at revision generate the same sort of lack of confidence in his theories; he seems to be more interested in 'saving the phenomena' than in supplying the most probable model of the universe.

Why, then, does he persist in so doggedly opposing the big bang model of the universe? We have seen that, according to Hoyle's own admission, the steady state model sought to bypass the conceptual difficulties of the origin of the universe. But why would a man who proposes a theory requiring the continuous generation of matter *ex nihilo* have conceptual difficulties with the beginning of the universe from nothing? I get the strong impression that it is because Hoyle, unlike the vast majority of scientists, realises the metaphysical and theological implications of such a beginning, and he recoils from these implications. Hoyle appears to have a strong philosophical, almost religious, streak, and he looks to the universe itself as a sort of God surrogate:

> If you ask, 'Why investigate the structure of matter, of galaxies, of the universe?' the answer is no different in principle from the motives of the builders of Stonehenge. The motive is religious, ironically, more truly religious than the crude ritualistic survivals from the Stone Age that pass for religion in our modern communities. . . . It is to the structurally elegant and beautiful laws which govern the world that the modern scientist looks in his religious impulses. Discovering deeper levels of significance in these laws has the same religious meaning to the modern scientist that eclipses of the Sun and Moon had to Stone-Age man.[87]

The big bang model tends to undermine such religious vener-
ation of the universe itself. Hoyle realises that an absolute
beginning of the universe points beyond the universe to a reality
more ultimate than itself, since to say it simply sprang into
being for no reason out of nothing is 'unsatisfactory'.[88] But
this opens the door to theism and threatens the sort of pantheistic
sentiments expressed above. This Hoyle simply will not have;
in his text on astronomy and cosmology, he writes with regard
to the absolute beginning of the universe:

> Many people are happy to accept this position. . . . The
> abrupt beginning is regarded as *meta*physical—i.e., *outside*
> physics. The physical laws are therefore considered to break
> down at $\tau = 0$, *and to do so inherently.* To many people this
> thought process seems highly satisfactory because a 'some-
> thing' outside physics can then be introduced at $\tau = 0$. By
> a semantic manoeuvre, the word 'something' is then replaced
> by 'god', except that the first letter becomes a capital, God,
> in order to warn us that we must not carry the enquiry
> any further.[89]

Hence, Hoyle inveighs against those who import 'metaphysical
intrusions' into the world.[90] It is this desire to avoid the intrusion
of theism, in my opinion, that largely accounts for Hoyle's
adherence to steady state models beyond the limits of plausibility.[91] In a sense, Hoyle's own philosophical streak is partly
to blame for the intrusion of metaphysical considerations into
cosmology, for the majority of scientists who adhere to a big
bang model of the universe probably see no theistic implications
in it whatsoever. Thus, when I asked Dr Tinsley of Yale what
relevance the model had to the question of the existence of
God, she replied,

> I don't see that all this has any bearing on the question. . . .
>   I asked your . . . question to a group of my colleagues,
> and their initial reactions were the same as mine—no rele-
> vance.[92]

It is Hoyle the philosopher, not Hoyle the scientist, who cannot
adhere to the big bang model of the universe. The scientific
evidence points to a beginning of the universe, not a steady

state universe. The only motivation for adhering to the steady
state model today is philosophical. As Webster remarks, the
steady state model seeks to sidestep the issues of a beginning
of time and the universe.[93] Hoyle is, I think, more astute than
his colleagues in realising that there *are* philosophical questions
involved in the origin of the universe, but the desire to avoid
these questions cannot change the drift of empirical fact, which
increasingly discredits the steady state model. According to
Ivan King, 'The steady state theory has now been laid to rest,
as a result of clearcut observations of how things have changed
systematically with time. . . .'[94] It serves now as 'an example
of the lengths to which a philosophical system can stretch itself,
in the absence of a sufficiently clear factual picture'.[95]

The other model of the universe which attempts to escape
the necessity of an absolute beginning is the oscillating model.
John Gribbin comments,

> The biggest problem with the Big Bang theory of the
> origin of the Universe is philosophical—perhaps even theologi-
> cal—what was there before the bang? This problem alone
> was sufficient to give a great initial impetus to the Steady
> State theory; but with that theory now sadly in conflict
> with the observations, the best way round this initial difficulty
> is provided by a model in which the universe expands from
> a singularity, collapses back again, and repeats the cycle
> indefinitely.[96]

It is only within the last three or four years that such a model
has been rendered untenable by further advances in observational cosmology. In 1974 four of the world's leading astronomers
concluded on the combined weight of several different lines
of evidence that the universe is open, that is, will continue
to expand forever, contrary to the oscillating hypothesis.[97] The
key consideration is whether the density of the universe is great
enough to overcome by gravitational attraction the recessional
velocity of the galaxies and so pull the universe back together
again. As I indicated earlier, the velocity of the galaxies is
not constant, but is decelerating due to the force of gravity.
But if their velocity is great enough, they will continue to
recede forever, though at progressively slower speeds, just as
a rocket reaching escape velocity will leave the earth's atmos-

phere and continue into space, though its speed will be slowed by the pull of the earth's gravity. In the latter case, the determining factor as to whether the speed is great enough to escape the tug of the earth's gravity is the mass of the earth. In the same way the crucial factor in whether the universe will expand forever is the average density of the universe. If the amount of matter per cubic volume is more than some critical value, then the gravitational force of matter will eventually overcome the velocity of the receding galaxies, and the universe is closed. The galaxies would reach the limit of their expansion, and then in an accelerating contraction they would rush together again. The critical density of the universe is estimated to be around 5×10^{-30} grams per cubic centimeter or about three hydrogen atoms per cubic meter. The ratio of the actual density to the critical density is called the density parameter and is designated by Ω. If $\Omega > 1$, then the universe is closed; if $\Omega < 1$, then the universe is open; and if $\Omega = 1$, then the universe is expanding precisely at escape velocity, and the universe is open.

There are several possible methods of determining whether the universe is open or closed. First, *one may seek to establish directly a value for* q_0. Since the deceleration parameter is a measure of the density of the universe, a determination of q_0 will yield the value of Ω. If $q_0 \leq \frac{1}{2}$, then $\Omega \leq 1$, and the universe is open. If $q_0 > \frac{1}{2}$, then $\Omega > 1$, and the universe is closed. Unfortunately, the value of q_0 cannot be determined by direct observation because the deceleration of any galaxy's velocity would be negligible within the span of a human lifetime. But it is possible to measure the velocities of very remote galaxies and compare them with the velocities of nearer galaxies. Because the light from the remote galaxies has taken billions of years to reach us, as we look at these galaxies, it is just as though we were looking back in time to the state of these systems as they were in the remote past. Galaxies nearer to us are more representative of the present, since the light from them is 'younger'. By comparing the Doppler shifts of these galaxies, scientists can determine whether galaxies are today moving significantly slower than they were in the past. If the velocity of expansion was greater in the past, then at extreme distances the velocity of the galaxies should be greater than that predicted by Hubble's law. Distance estimates are, however, difficult to

ascertain with precision. The distance of galaxies must be estimated on the basis of their apparent magnitude. Presumably
the faintest galaxies are furthest away. But because galaxies
are not all of the same intrinsic luminosity, it is possible for
a fainter source to be actually closer than a brighter source.
Fortunately, such individual anomalies tend to be ironed out
when a sufficiently large sampling is taken because the discrepancies cancel each other out. Another factor that needs to be
taken into account is the change of luminosity of stars in the
course of their evolution. The light from the stars of an isolated
galaxy probably declines a few percentage points every billion
years, which means that galaxies were brighter in the past.
If one were to neglect this decline in luminosity, one would
conclude that the galaxies are closer than they really are, since
the light received from them originates from a time when they
were brighter. Thus, the distances would be underestimated,
and consequently the value of q_0 would be overestimated—the
galaxies would not have decelerated as much as it appears.
According to Gott, Gunn, Schramm, and Tinsley, the best
observable results, taking into account the decline in luminosity,
suggest a value for q_0 that is closer to 0 than to $\frac{1}{2}$, and, therefore,
the universe is open. They hasten to add, however, that these
results are very uncertain and that therefore one cannot conclude
from this test alone that $q_0 < \frac{1}{2}$. But very large values for q_0,
such as $q_0 = 2$, do appear to be excluded.

Second, *one may determine the age of the universe.* If there were
no deceleration, then the age of the universe would equal one
Hubble time. But if the expansion is decelerating, then a comparison of the universe's true age with the Hubble time should
enable one to calculate the amount of deceleration and thus
determine q_0. There are two possible methods in estimating
the universe's age, both yielding lower limits only since they
measure objects in the universe which were formed later than
the big bang. (1) One may determine the age of the oldest
stars. These are found in the globular clusters within our own
galaxy. These formations are tightly packed, symmetrical groups
of thousands of very old stars, whose ages have been estimated
between eight and sixteen billion years old.[98] (2) One may
measure the abundance of certain heavy elements. Radioactive elements such as ^{232}Th and ^{187}Re are thought to have
been formed in supernovas, which have probably been exploding

since the formation of the galaxy. Dating of these elements by radioactive decay methods provides an estimate of their age and hence the age of the galaxy. These indicate an age between six and twenty billion years.[99] If the two ages are to be consistent, they suggest a date for the big bang of between eight and eighteen billion years ago. Unfortunately, these estimates are so generous that it is not possible to determine from them whether the universe is open or closed.

Third, *one may measure the average density of matter in the universe in order to determine directly* Ω. This may be accomplished in two ways. (1) One may count the galaxies in a given volume of space, multiply by the masses of the galaxies, and divide by the volume. The masses of galaxies may be estimated by their observed gravitational effects upon one another. Estimates of the masses of a great many galaxies in different counts of large volumes of space indicate that if all the mass in the universe is associated with galaxies then Ω can be only about 0·04, and the universe is definitely open. Even if the uncertainty is of a factor of three such that $\Omega = 0·12$, this is still far below the density needed to halt the expansion. (2) One may compare the behaviour of distant galaxies with the behaviour of those in the local supercluster of galaxies of which our own galaxy is a member. The average density of galaxies in the local supercluster is two and a half times greater than that in the universe as a whole. If all mass is associated with galaxies, then the average density of the matter in the supercluster must be two and a half times greater than that outside it. Because of the greater density of the supercluster, nearby galaxies should be decelerated. If Ω is small, the greater deceleration would be imperceptible; but if Ω is large, there ought to be a significant difference. In fact, the difference is undetectable. Therefore, Ω must be very small, no larger than 0·1. These estimates indicate that the galaxies themselves cannot close the universe.

It might be objected that substantial amounts of matter are not, in fact, associated with the galaxies, but exist in the form of intercluster gas, dust, and other material. However, there appears to be no evidence to substantiate this. If the galaxies condensed from a smoothly distributed gas, then they would eventually have pulled in the extraneous material as well. It might be contended that the missing mass needed to close the universe consists of some uniformly distributed medium with enough internal pressure not to be affected by the galaxies' gravitation. But this is untenable, according to Gott and his collaborators, because then the galaxies would have been prevented from forming in the first place.

Fourth, *one may measure the amount of deuterium in the universe in order to discover* Ω. Within a few minutes after the big bang, subatomic particles begin to interact to form the lighter elements. The simplest of these is deuterium, which is formed by the synthesis of one proton and one neutron.[100] Deuterium nuclei would then combine to form helium, which is composed of two protons and two neutrons. The proportion of deuterium to helium is closely related to the density of the universe at that time. If the universe possessed a great density, most or all of the deuterium would have been converted into helium. But, in fact, this was not the case, for in the present universe deuterium is abundant, 4×10^{-31} grams per cubic centimeter in nearby interstellar space. For any value of the Hubble time between thirteen and nineteen billion years, a value of Ω as great as 1 is inconsistent with the deuterium abundance.

This argument assumes that no deuterium has been synthesised since the big bang. It has been suggested by Hoyle and Fowler that deuterium could possibly be synthesised in shocks in the envelopes of supernovae.[101] But according to Gott and his colleagues, this possible production of 'deuterium ex machina' 'cannot be taken seriously' because the amounts of boron and beryllium also produced would be greater than their observed abundance ratios to deuterium.[102] According to Audouze and Tinsley, even if all observed B and Be were produced by supernovae shocks—which is unlikely—the amount of D produced is still much less than that observed.[103] Therefore, the present abundance of deuterium is probably due to primordial factors.

These four constraints—the deceleration parameter, the age of the universe, the density of galaxies, and the abundance of deuterium—all combine to point to a value of Ω between 0·04 and 0·09, a value well below that required to close the universe. And it is noteworthy that two other observations are consistent with this range of values. (1) The age of globular cluster stars is extremely sensitive to the primordial helium abundance, which is, in turn, dependent upon the density of the universe. The age of the stars is determined by nucleochronology is consistent with the age required by the helium abundance in a universe of $\Omega < 1$. (2) These constraints require a Hubble time between thirteen and twenty billion years. This is consistent with the estimates both of Sandage and Tammann and of Kirschner and Kwan, who employed a method completely independent of all steps in the classic approach of the former team.[104] The evidence straightforwardly interpreted therefore suggests a universe which will expand forever and is potentially infinite in extent.

Since the time Gott, Gunn, Schramm, and Tinsley first broached their case for an open universe, developments in this fast-moving field of science have confirmed their conclusions. Perhaps most striking is the work of Sandage and Tammann to home in on accurate values for H_0 and q_0, which served as only the most general of constraints for Gott and his colleagues. We have seen that Sandage and Tammann determined $H_0 = 55 \pm 5$ km s^{-1} Mpc^{-1}. The best way to determine q_0, they contend, is deriving the age of the universe from other sources.[105] The oldest known objects in the universe, the halo globular clusters, are estimated to have an age of $14 \pm 1 \times 10^9$ years, which serves as an upper limit for q_0. But one must allow additional time for the collapse of the galaxy in question and for the formation of the protogalaxy out of the pregalactic gas; this pushes the origin of the universe back a billion years to fifteen billion years ago. From this data it may be determined what the value of q_0 is:

q_0	T_0 ($H_0 = 55$)
0·000	17·73
0·025	16·58
0·100	15·00
0·200	13·81
0·300	12·98
0·500	11·83
0·600	10·12

If the universe is at least fifteen billion years old, then q_0 is no greater than 0·1, which is far below the $q_0 < \frac{1}{2}$ needed to guarantee an open universe. This means, Sandage and Tammann conclude, that *the universe has happened only once and that the expansion will never stop.*[106] In a later article, Sandage reviews six methods for determining q_0: (1) direct measurement of the deceleration by comparison of nearby to remote galaxies' redshifts; (2) comparison of the Hubble time with the age of events in the early universe to give an accurate estimate of T_0; (3) attempts to determine the average density of the universe by dynamical arguments concerning the infall of matter into clusters yielding the observed X-ray flux; (4) comparison of the observed deuterium abundance with the calculated production of D in the big bang as a function of density; (5) summing up the density of galaxies, and (6) use of local velocity perturbations to measure the effect of gravity on the expansion.[107] Utilising the last method, Sandage derives a value for $q_0 < 0.28 \pm 0.09$. This accords closely with the results obtained by all the other five methods and suggests, according to Sandange, (1) that the deceleration is almost negligible, (2) the universe is open, and (3) the expansion will not reverse.[108] It has even been suggested by Gunn and Tinsley that far from decelerating, the expansion may actually be accelerating.[109] Thus, the case for an open universe has been considerably strengthened by more precise calculations of q_0.

A value of $\Omega < 1$ is confirmed by Gott and Rees in their analysis of galaxy formation.[110] If galaxies evolved from primordial density fluctuations, then the data fit much better with a model in which $\Omega = 0.1$ than a model in which $\Omega = 1.0$. Elsewhere Turner and Gott also argue that it is much easier to maintain a stable population of galaxies in an open cosmology.[111] If the universe were closed, the population would be unstable, tending to the formation of more galactic clusters. In another study Gott and Turner estimate the mean luminosity density of galaxies and their characteristic mass to light ratio and from these attempt to discover the contribution Ω_G of galaxies to the critical density.[112] They calculate $\Omega_G = 0.08$ and report, '... our conclusion is an old one: if the $\Lambda = 0$ Friedmann world model applies and if galaxies and their environs contain more than a small fraction of all matter, the Universe is open by a wide margin.'[113] An independent confirmation of Gott and his colleagues' estimates of Ω is reported by Fall, who calculates $0.01 \lesssim \Omega \lesssim 0.05$.[114] He supports the view that the density of matter must be low in order that inhomogeneities do not disrupt the recessional expansion of galaxies more than is observed. The universe is therefore open by a large margin, he concludes. The calculations of Eichler and Solinger as to the amount of unseen matter in the universe in the form of burned out stars and black holes confirm the previous estimates that it is not sufficient to close the universe.[115]

The researches of Epstein and Petrosian confirm that the abundance of deuterium points to an open universe.[116] They note that the deuterium abundance would have to be less than one-fifth of the observed lower limit in order for the universe to be closed. If the universe is to be closed then either (1) our galaxy was formed out of especially deuterium-rich matter or (2) much deuterium-deficient matter (including black holes) is preferentially excluded from the interstellar gas. The former possibility is unlikely because in the more dense regions, which would presumably be the sites for galaxy formation, deuterium is underabundant. As to the latter possibility, either the black holes formed prior to or subsequent to nucleosynthesis of the elements. If prior, they could not affect deuterium production, and the abundance of deuterium is characteristic of diffuse matter. If subsequent, the higher density regions are deficient in deuterium and so would enhance its abundance in the remaining gas. These considerations weigh against the possibility of a closed universe. According to Epstein and Petrosian, the mass density of the universe is at least a factor of three below the critical density needed to close it. Audouze asserts that arguments from the nucleosynthesis of elements like helium and deuterium actually constitute the best indicators in favour of an open universe.[117]

The evidence therefore appears to preclude an oscillating model of the universe, since such a model requires a universe of closure density. A model in which the universe begins at a singularity and expands indefinitely seems to be the model that best fits the facts. Adherents of the oscillating model might retreat to the position (though none to my knowledge have done so) that the current expansion is the last of a prior series of expansions, each of which was finite and ended in contraction. But besides being unable to explain how the universe could jump from a finite expansion to a potentially infinite expansion, this model would seem to be only a theoretical, not a real, possibility; as Tinsley comments with regard to oscillatory models:

... even though the mathematics says that the universe oscillates, there is no known physics to reverse the collapse and bounce back to a new expansion. The physics seems to say that those models start from the big bang, expand, collapse, then end.[118]

In such a case one does not escape the necessity of an absolute beginning of the universe.

In summary, we have seen that (1) the scientific evidence related to the expansion of the universe points to an absolute beginning of the universe about fifteen billion years ago; (2) the steady state model of the universe cannot account for certain features of observational cosmology, and (3) the oscillating model of the universe violates several constraints of observational cosmology which indicate that the universe is open. Therefore, we conclude that the universe began to exist.

Second Empirical Confirmation

We may now turn to our second empirical argument in support of our second premiss, the argument from thermodynamics. About the middle of the nineteenth century, several physicists sought to formulate a scientific law that would bring under a general rule all the various irreversible processes encountered in the world. The result of their efforts is now known as the second law of thermodynamics.[119] First formulated by Clausius, it stated that heat of itself only flows from a point of high temperature toward a point of low temperature; the reverse is never possible without compensation. But heat is only an instance of an even more general tendency toward levelling in nature; the same is true, for example, of gases and electricity. As Zwart points out, without this general tendency toward levelling, life would be completely impossible. Because of such levelling, the air in the room never suddenly separates into oxygen at one end and nitrogen at the other. It is also why when we step into our bath we may be confident that the water will be pleasantly warm instead of frozen at one end and boiling at the other. It is easy to see why life would not be possible in a world where the second law of thermodynamics did not hold true.

Ludwig Boltzmann developed the second law further by showing that this tendency toward levelling is founded on the tendency of any system to pass from a less probable to a more probable state. According to Boltzmann, the probability of a state is a function of its order: more ordered states are less probable, and less ordered states are more probable. The most probable state is therefore a totally disordered state, that is, a state which is completely undifferentiated. Thus, the second law could be formulated: all systems have the tendency to pass from a more ordered to a less ordered state.

A third important step in the development of the second law was the realisation that disorder is connected with entropy: the greater the disorder the greater the entropy. This yields a third formulation of the law: all systems have the tendency to pass from a state of lower entropy into a state of higher entropy. Only two obstacles could prevent such a transition: (1) since the law concerns probabilities, it is conceivably possible for the transition to be avoided, and (2) the system could leak energy to its surroundings. But in the first case, these logical possibilities are inconsequential in macroscopic systems. It is theoretically possible for the bath to be boiling at one end and frozen at the other, but this is a practical impossibility. In the second case, a further stipulation must be introduced: the system must be closed. This leads to a fourth formulation of the second law: spontaneously proceeding processes in closed systems are always attended by an increase in entropy. The law in this form is virtually certain. To illustrate: the probability of all molecules in one litre of gas occupying 99.99% of the volume and consequently only one tenth of a millilitre being completely empty of molecules is about $1 : 10^{10^{20}}$. If one made a thousand observations a second, it would take $10^{10^{20}-11}$ years to observe one such unequal distribution. The number 11 pales into insignificance beside 10^{20}, so that it does not matter if one made a million or a billion observations per second: the chance of coming across the state in question is not measurably increased for all that. For all practical purposes, therefore, the second law of thermodynamics may be regarded as absolutely certain.[120]

Our interest in the second law concerns what happens when it is applied to the universe as a whole. For by definition the universe is a closed system, since it is all there is.[121] No energy leakage or input is possible. What this seems to imply is that eventually the universe and all its processes will, so to speak, 'run down', and the entire universe will slowly grind to a halt and reach equilibrium. Zwart describes such a state:

> . . . according to the second law the whole universe must eventually reach a state of maximum entropy. It will then be in thermodynamical equilibrium; everywhere the situation will be exactly the same, with the same composition, the same temperature, the same pressure etc., etc. There will be no objects any more, but the universe will consist of one vast gas of uniform composition. Because it is in complete equilibrium, absolutely nothing will happen any more. The only way in which a process can begin in a system in equilibrium is through an action from the outside, but an action from the outside is of course impossible if the system in question is the whole universe. So in this future state of maximal entropy, the universe would be in absolute rest and complete darkness, and nothing could disturb the dead silence. Even if there would by chance occur a small deviation from the state of absolute equalization it would of itself rapidly vanish again. Because almost all energy would have been degraded, i.e. converted into kinetic energy of the existing particles (heat), this supposedly future state of the universe, which will also be its last state, is called the heat death of the universe.[122]

Since the universe is a gigantic but nonetheless closed system, eventually all the energy in it will become evenly distributed, and it will die. But if this is so, then why, if the universe has always existed, has it not reached a state of maximum entropy? Certainly not for lack of time—it has had eternity to achieve its state of equal energy distribution. The present state of disequilibrium points to the fact that the processes in the universe have not been going on forever, that at some point in the finite past the universe was in a state of arbitrarily low entropy and that it has been 'running down' since then.[123] In short, the present state of disequilibrium points to a beginning of the universe. It was apparently Newton who first noticed this fact, and he took it as evidence that the universe had a Creator.[124]

But while the argument seems to work well within a Newtonian world system, the introduction by Einstein of general relativity and the rise of relativistic cosmological models have altered the situation somewhat. For if the universe is expanding and open, then there seems to be no chance of an even distribution of matter. And if the universe is expanding but closed, then gravitational pull would also prevent such an even distribution. Indeed, gravity is the key factor in determining the nature of thermodynamic processes on a cosmological scale, as P. C. W. Davies points out: 'The origin of *all* thermodynamic irreversibility in the real universe depends ultimately on gravitation.'[125] Therefore, in order to discover if the universe will suffer heat death in an irreversible thermodynamic process, we must inquire into the effect of gravity on relativistic world models.

Suppose, then, we select a model in which the universe is expanding and open—what is the thermodynamic future of such a universe? Since the force of gravity is not sufficient to overcome the recessional velocity of the universe, it will simply go on expanding forever. And as it does, it will grow cooler and cooler until it dies in a kind of heat death peculiar to this model. Davies explains,

> Recalling the discussion of the Friedmann cosmological models . . . , it is evident that conventional cosmology will permit two possible ends to the present condition of the universe. Either the whole universe will be returned to a very hot high-density phase once again, or it will continue to expand and cool forever. In the laboratory an isolated system soon reaches a state of equilibrium from which no perceptible change occurs over time scales of usual interest. . . .
>
> In the case of the whole universe the process relaxation times are very much longer than those of laboratory processes, but a straightforward application of the laws of thermodynamics leads to the inevitable conclusion that eventually, if the expansion continues, equilibrium will prevail throughout, and the entire universe will reach a final state from which no change will occur. This particular outcome is known as the *heat death* of the universe.[126]

But, Davies adds, the precise nature of this heat death differs from that of the laboratory case. In the heat death of the universe, the stellar nuclear fuels will be exhausted, and all starlight will cease. The end of a star will be a white dwarf, a neutron star, or a black hole. Of these only the black hole represents the cosmological final state of matter. Within the galaxies, a slow accretion of surrounding material by black holes will occur. Interstellar collisions will bring about the end of many stars in this fashion. The entropy of intergalactic gas and radiation will also continue to increase by ionic recombination and photon absorption. The universe will tend toward a state of maximum entropy, though this may never be fully actualised, since in some models there will be some uncollapsed matter and unrecombined ions and some radiation will not be absorbed. Tinsley describes the final state of such a world, a universe in ruins:

> ... if the universe has a low density, its death will be cold. It will expand forever, at a slower and slower rate. Galaxies, in time, will turn all of their residual gas into stars, and the stars will burn out. Our own sun will become a cold, dead remnant, floating among the corpses of other stars in an increasingly isolated Milky Way.[127]

Far from escaping a heat death, then, the expanding open model of the universe implicitly contains a stark form of it.

Suppose on the other hand that the force of gravitation is sufficient to reverse the expansion and cause the universe to contract upon itself. This, too, will involve a heat death of the universe, though of a sharply different nature from that of the open model. Tinsley describes such a death:

> In one projection, if the average density of matter in the universe is great enough, the mutual gravitational attraction between bodies will eventually slow the expansion to a halt. The universe will then contract and collapse into a hot fireball ... there is no known physical mechanism ... that could reverse a catastrophic big crunch. Apparently, if the universe becomes dense enough, it is in for a hot death.[128]

So if the force of gravity is sufficiently strong to close the universe, then the end of the universe will come in a fiery death from which it will never re-emerge.

Therefore, relativistic world models have substantially the
same end as the Newtonian world model: heat death either
cold or hot. It is clear that if the universe and its processes
have existed for infinite time, then the universe should now
exist in some form of heat death. Since it does not, but is
still in a process of disequilibrium, it must have had a beginning
a finite number of years ago.

But yet one more model seeks to escape this conclusion:
an oscillating model of the universe. In this model every expansion is followed by a contraction, and vice versa:

Such a universe has neither beginning nor end, and, as Richard
Tolman points out, it is therefore not fated to a heat death.[129]
Under classical theories, says Tolman, the expansions and con-
tractions would have to cease eventually, but relativity theory
leads to a perpetually expanding and contracting model.[130]

Now we have already observed that there are no known
physical laws that could ever reverse a cosmic contraction,
so the model is a hypothetical possibility only. Davies further
notes that the model appears to be inconsistent with general
relativity theory because the extremity of each contraction would
produce a singularity, making it impossible to trace physical
continuity of the universe through the extremities of each cycle.
Davies has a mind to press this objection, but because so many
authors have speculated about such a model, he is generous
and does not take this objection 'as seriously as we perhaps
should'.[131] But at any rate, for our purposes the decisive consideration is that the thermodynamic properties of the oscillating
model imply the very beginning of the universe that the model
seeks to avoid. This is implied in Tolman's own calculations,
as the renowned Russian scientists Novikov and Zel'dovich
point out:

> If, in spite of these difficulties, bounce can occur, one
> has to consider two possibilities: an open universe, in which
> reversal occurs just once . . . , and a closed universe in which

it occurs repeatedly. The second possibility suggests the appealing picture of a cyclic universe, persisting indefinitely into the past and the future. However, there is a flaw in this picture. As Tolman (1934) pointed out long ago . . . , every cycle involves irreversible generation of entropy . . . hence, the maximum radius must increase from cycle to cycle. . . . *The multicycle model therefore has an infinite future, but only a finite past.*[132]

The cycles of an oscillating universe are therefore diagrammed:

What this means, as Gribbin observes, is that the oscillating model still implies an origin of the universe prior to the smallest cycle.[133] So even on this model, thermodynamic considerations impel us to conclude that the universe had a beginning.

So whether one considers a Newtonian model of the universe, an open model, a closed model, or even an oscillating model of the universe, thermodynamic considerations suggest in every case that the universe began to exist. Against this conclusion two stock objections are commonly urged. Swinburne employs them both: (1) the argument works only if the universe is spatially finite, and (2) since the law expresses statistical probability only, then in an eternally closed system entropy may at any point be decreasing rather than increasing.[134] Each objection bears examination.

Grünbaum suggests two reasons why the second law of thermodynamics does not apply to a spatially infinite universe.[135] (1) Entropy becomes indefinable in a universe comprised of an actually infinite number of particles, since the particles could assume an infinite variety of complexions. (2) If the universe is spatially infinite but contains a finite number of particles, then in order to reach maximum entropy the particles would have to be evenly distributed throughout all of infinite space, which is impossible. Neither of these objections can be sustained: (1) An actually infinite material universe is untenable both philosophically and empirically. Philosophically, a universe comprised of an infinite number of particles would involve all the absurdities entailed in the existence of an actual infinite. Empirically, there is no evidence that the material universe must be infinite; indeed, the expansion hypothesis holds that it may not.[136] Therefore, this objection may not concern the real universe and be only hypothetical. But even if the material universe were infinite, the objection fails. For if the indefinability of entropy means simply that we can no longer measure it in an infinite universe, then the inadequacy of our methods of measuring entropy can hardly prevent entropy from increasing. But furthermore, the notion of heat death need not involve the concept of entropy at all. We may simply speak of the entire universe's arriving at a state of equilibrium. As Davies remarks,

> . . . if each individual region of the universe reaches equilibrium, then the whole universe will be in equilibrium. Because the heat death really only involves the concept of equilibrium rather than entropy explicitly, I do not see a problem here.[137]

Thus, given infinite time, even an actually infinite material universe would run down and exist at an equilibrium state. (2) The second objection is more descriptive of a type of universe which is at all times finite and only potentially infinite spatially. The objection assumes that for equilibrium to be achieved, the finite particles must be evenly scattered throughout space, which is simply false. Indeed, we have argued that as the universe expands, the finite particles of matter will recede farther and farther into the dark recesses of space, and the universe will suffer a cold death. So even if space itself were infinite (in that the material universe could expand indefinitely), thermodynamic considerations would still apply to the material universe in space. As a potentially infinite but at all times finite closed system, the universe would slowly 'wind down' until it reached equilibrium. Because it is not now in such a state, it must have had a beginning a finite time ago.

The second major objection to our argument is that the present disequilibrium may be nothing more than a fluctuation from a state of equilibrium at which the universe normally exists. But here the objectors seem to have lost all sense of proportion. For while fluctuations from a state of equilibrium are physically important for micro-systems containing a few particles, when one comes to macro-systems, such fluctuations are negligible. Schlegel comments: 'The fluctuation which would give any pronounced entropy decrease to an isolated macro-system is, because of its extremely slight probability, only of interest as a theoretical possibility.'[138] But furthermore, even if such theoretical possibilities were actualised, they would be so small as to be imperceptible. As Zwart explains, the entropy in a closed system decreases on the average as much as it increases, but this concerns only small fluctuations around the state of equilibrium.[139] The original process which led to the state of equilibrium is never reversed. Zwart describes as 'totally incorrect' diagrams purporting to show fluctuations from thermodynamic equilibrium which look somewhat like a patient's cardiogram.[140] These give

> ... a completely distorted picture of the situation, going even as far as showing fluctuations of fluctuations. In view of the fact that even the original fluctuations are too small to be perceptible this is of course absurd.[141]

Actually, the line of the graph would run absolutely straight. According to Zwart, proponents of this objection have lost sight of the difference between fluctuations and processes. A process is determinate and determinable, but a fluctuation is not. A process is a change of state, a transition from one state to another. But fluctuations belong to one and the same state; they are part of that state. Thus, fluctuations in a universe of maximum entropy, or heat death, would be inconsequential. Finding the universe in a state of disequilibrium, what are we to conclude? According to Davies, there are three options, only one of which is viable: either (1) we are in a colossal fluctuation from the normal state of equilibrium; (2) the steady state model is correct (i.e., the universe is not closed after all), or (3) the big bang model is correct (i.e., the universe began to exist a finite number of years ago). As for the first alternative,

> The conjecture can be faulted on several grounds. First, a fluctuation which produced the *present* low entropy condition

of the universe is overwhelmingly more likely than one which produced a still *lower* entropy condition in the past. . . . Yet there are non-thermodynamic reasons why we know that the entropy of the universe was lower in the past than it is now; for example, when distant galaxies are observed they are seen as they were many millions of years ago in a condition of thermodynamic disequilibrium. Another objection . . . is that a fluctuation just on the size of the solar system would be sufficient to ensure the existence of life on Earth, and such a fluctuation is *far* more probable than one of cosmic proportions.[142]

The second alternative fares no better:

In recent years mounting observational evidence in astronomy, in particular the discovery of the cosmic microwave background radiation (which appears to demand an earlier dense state), has led to the almost complete abandonment of the steady-state theory.[143]

Therefore, the third alternative must be affirmed:

In the absence of continual creation of matter, it is necessary to consider the 'big bang' type of event. . . . Because of the finite age of these models, the entire universe can be regarded as a sort of gigantic branch system, which was created in a low entropy state at $t = 0$ and is in the process of running through its course to equilibrium. . . . As in the case of branch systems, the initial low entropy condition of the universe is not attributed to a fluctuation from an earlier equilibrium state, because the universe simply did not exist prior to this creation event. However, unlike the situation with branch systems, it is not possible to account for the low entropy initial state of the universe as due to interaction with the outside world, because the universe *is* the whole world.[144]

Thus, the present disequilibrium indicates that the universe has not existed forever, but began to exist at a low state of entropy a finite number of years ago. Thus, one is forced to accept the conclusion, uncomfortable as this may appear from a scientific point of view, that '... the negative entropy in the universe was simply "put in" at the creation as an initial condition'.[145]

In summary, then, we have argued that (1) thermodynamic considerations point to an origin of the universe a finite number of years ago; (2) these considerations hold true whether we adopt Newtonian or relativistic world models, and (3) traditional objections to this argument are invalid on various counts. Because a universe existing for infinite time could not now be in the present state of disequilibrium, we conclude, therefore, that the universe began to exist.

This concludes our empirical support for our second premiss. I have argued that scientific evidence concerning the expansion of the universe and the thermodynamic properties of closed systems indicates that the universe is finite in duration, beginning to exist about fifteen billion years ago. This is a truly remarkable confirmation of the conclusion to which philosophical argument alone led us. In support of our second premiss, then, we have maintained four distinct arguments, two philosophical and two empirical: (1) the argument from the impossibility of the existence of an actual infinite, (2) the argument from the impossibility of the formation of an actual infinite by successive addition; (3) the argument from the expansion of the universe, and (4) the argument from thermodynamics. In the light of these considerations, I think we are amply justified in concluding our second premiss: the universe began to exist.

First Premiss: Everything that Begins to Exist Has a Cause of Its Existence

We may now return to a consideration of our first premiss, that everything that begins to exist has a cause of its existence. The phrase 'cause of its existence' needs clarification. Here I do not mean sustaining or conserving cause, but creating cause. We are not looking here for any continual ground of being, but for something that brings about the inception of existence of another thing. Applied to the universe, we are asking, was the beginning of the universe caused or uncaused? In this book I do not propose to construct an elaborate defence of this first premiss. Not only do considerations of time and space (in their practical, not philosophical, sense!) preclude such, but I think it to be somewhat unnecessary as well. For the first premiss is so intuitively obvious, especially when applied to the universe, that probably no one in his right mind *really* believes it to be false. Even Hume himself confessed that his academic denial of the principle's demonstrability could not eradicate his belief that it was nonetheless true.[146] Indeed the idea that anything, especially the whole universe, could pop into existence uncaused is so repugnant that most thinkers intuitively recognise that the universe's beginning to exist entirely uncaused out of nothing is incapable of sincere affirmation. For, as Anthony Kenny emphasises,

According to the big bang theory, the whole matter of the universe began to exist at a particular time in the remote past. A proponent of such a theory, at least if he is an atheist, must believe that the matter of the universe came from nothing and by nothing.[147]

Now this is a pretty hard pill to swallow. Thus Broad, after asserting that the universe either (1) had no beginning and is temporally infinite, (2) had no first event but is temporally finite, being analogous to the series . . . $\frac{1}{8}$, $\frac{1}{4}$, $\frac{1}{2}$, or (3) had a first event and is temporally finite, makes this very interesting comment:

> Now . . . I find no difficulty in supposing that the world's history had no beginning and that its duration backwards from its present phase is infinite. Nor do I find any insuperable difficulty in supposing that the world's history had no beginning, but that its duration backwards from its present phase does not exceed a certain finite limiting value. But I must confess that I have a very great difficulty in supposing that there was a first phase in the world's history, *i.e.*, a phase immediately before which there existed neither matter, nor minds, nor anything else.
> . . . I suspect that my difficulty about a first event or phase in the world's history is due to the fact that, whatever I may *say* when I am trying to give Hume a run for his money, I can not really *believe in* anything beginning to exist without being *caused* (in the old-fashioned sense of *produced* or *generated*) by something else which existed before and up to the moment when the entity in question began to exist.
> . . . I . . . find it impossible to give up the principle; and with that confession of the intellectual impotence of old age I must leave this topic.[148]

It seems that old age had actually brought a measure of insight to Broad, for while his first two alternatives are untenable in the light of our arguments in favour of the second premiss, his reasoning concerning the third alternative is entirely correct. That the universe began to exist is true enough, but that it should begin to exist utterly uncaused out of nothing is too incredible to be believed. And Broad is not alone in this; for example, in the Maimonidean–Thomist argument that a necessary being must exist or else given infinite time nothing

would exist, virtually no one ever questions the premiss that
if in the past nothing existed then nothing would exist now.
That something should spring into existence out of nothing
is so counter-intuitive that to attack Maimonides and Aquinas
at this point seems to colour one's intellectual integrity. The
old principle *ex nihilo nihil fit* appears to be so manifestly true
that a sincere denial of this axiom is well-nigh impossible.[149]
Reluctant to fly in the face of this principle, many philosophers
find it easier to believe that the universe must be temporally
infinite. Thus, Zwart, after arguing that a beginning of time
and the universe are logically possible, writes,

> Nevertheless, I do think it inconceivable that time could
> have a beginning. . . . A first event would have to be preceded
> . . . by timelessness; a state of the universe in which nothing
> whatsoever happens. This state of timelessness does not seem
> logically impossible in itself; for instance, if the universe
> were absolutely empty nothing would, obviously, happen in
> it, and consequently it would be timeless. It is of course
> a moot point whether such a universe would deserve the
> name of universe at all. But more important is the fact
> that it seems quite inconceivable that our universe, as we
> now know it, could have sprung from such an absolute void.
> . . . If there is anything we find inconceivable it is that
> something could arise from nothing. . . . Change to us can
> only be change of state; there must be a fundamental some-
> thing (generally called matter) which remains identical. There-
> fore a conversion of nothing into something . . . seems to
> us utterly out of the question. . . .[150]

Zwart is correct in so far as he goes: it *is* inconceivable that
the universe should spring into being out of nothing. But the
answer is not to embrace the equally inconceivable position
that the universe and its temporal series of events is infinite.
The most plausible solution to the problem of the origin of
the universe is that the universe was *created*, that is to say,
it was caused to exist. In terms of sheer 'believability', it
is much more plausible to believe that the universe has an
efficient cause of its existence than to believe that it has existed
for infinite time or sprang into being out of nothing. But,

in fact, we are not dependent upon an appeal to mere 'believability', for we have already shown that both philosophical and empirical reasoning preclude a temporally infinite universe. The alternatives, then, are two: either the universe was caused to exist or else it sprang into existence wholly uncaused out of nothing a finite number of years ago. The first alternative appears eminently more reasonable.

It has been contended, however, that the second alternative is equally plausible. Thus, Hume writes,

> . . . as all distinct ideas are separable from each other, and as the ideas of cause and effect are evidently distinct, 'twill be easy for us to conceive any object to be non-existent this moment, and existent the next, without conjoining to it the distinct idea of a cause or productive principle. The separation, therefore, of the idea of a cause from that of a beginning of existence, is plainly possible for the imagination; and consequently the actual separation of these objects is so far possible, that it implies no contradiction or absurdity; and is therefore incapable of being refuted by any reasoning from mere ideas; without which 'tis impossible to demonstrate the necessity of a cause.[151]

What this argument amounts to, as Anscombe points out, is that because we can imagine something's coming into existence without a cause, it is possible that something really can come into existence without a cause.[152] But, she continues,

> The trouble about it is that it is very unconvincing. For if I say I can imagine a rabbit coming into being without a parent rabbit, well and good: I imagine a rabbit coming into being, and our observing that there is no parent rabbit about. But what am I to imagine if I imagine a rabbit coming into being without a cause? Well, I just imagine a rabbit coming into being. That this *is* the imagination of a rabbit coming into being without a cause is nothing but, as it were, the *title* of the picture. Indeed I can form an image and give my picture that title. But from my being about to do *that*, nothing whatever follows about what is possible to suppose 'without contradiction or absurdity' as holding in reality.[153]

What is true of rabbits is equally true of the universe. We can in our mind's eye picture the universe springing into existence uncaused, but the fact that we can construct and label such a mental picture does not mean the origin of the universe could have really come about in this way. As F. C. Copleston puts it, '. . . even if one can imagine first a blank, as it were, and then X existing, it by no means follows necessarily that X can begin to exist without an extrinsic cause.'[154] All Hume has really shown is that the principle 'everything that begins to exist has a cause of its existence' is not analytic and that its denial, therefore, does not involve a contradiction or a *logical* absurdity. But just because we can imagine something's beginning to exist without a cause it does not mean this could ever occur in reality. There are other absurdities than logical ones. And for the universe to spring into being uncaused out of nothing seems intuitively to be really, if not logically, absurd. Therefore, of the two alternatives presenting themselves, namely that the universe has a cause of its existence or the universe came into existence uncaused, the first is inherently more plausible.

Although we have declined an elaborate defence of the principle that everything that begins to exist has a cause of its existence, two possible lines of support might be elucidated.

1. *The argument from empirical facts:* The causal proposition could be defended as an empirical generalisation based on the widest sampling of experience. The empirical evidence in support of the proposition is absolutely overwhelming, so much so that Humean empiricists could demand no stronger evidence in support of any synthetic statement. To reject the causal proposition is therefore completely arbitrary. Although this argument from empirical facts is not apt to impress philosophers, it is nevertheless undoubtedly true that the reason we—and they—accept the principle in our everyday lives is precisely for this very reason, because it is repeatedly confirmed in our experience. Constantly verified and never falsified, the causal proposition may be taken as an empirical generalisation enjoying the strongest support experience affords.

2. *The argument from the* a priori *category of causality:* Hackett formulates a neo-Kantian epistemology and defends the validity of the causal principle as the expression of the operation of

a mental *a priori* category of causality which the mind brings to experience.[155] Kant had argued that knowledge is a synthesis of two factors: the sense data of experience and the *a priori* categorical structure of the mind. The categories are primitive forms of thought which the mind must possess in order to make logical judgements without which intelligible experience would be impossible. Kant attempted to compile a list of these categories by correlating a category with each of the types of logical judgement; the category associated with the hypothetical judgement type is the category of causality. Kant argued that these categories are not simply psychological dispositions in which we think, but that they are objectively valid mental structures which the mind brings *a priori* to experience. For without them no object of knowledge could be thought; if the mind does not come to experience with the *a priori* forms of thought, thought could never arise. Therefore, the categories must be objectively real. Kant made two crucial limitations on the operation of the categories: (1) the categories have no application beyond the realm of sense data, and (2) the categories furnish knowledge of appearances only, but not of things in themselves.

Hackett makes three critical alterations in Kant's formulation of a categorical epistemology.[156] First, the number of the categories must be reduced. It is universally recognised that Kant's tables of categories and logical judgement types are highly artificial; accordingly, Hackett eliminates the categories of totality and limitation and equates the category of existence to that of substance. The remaining categories he regards as validly derived. Second, the categories have application beyond the realm of sense data. Kant's position is self-refuting: for if the categories are restricted in operation to the realm of sense data alone, then no knowledge of the categories themselves would be possible, since they are characterised by the very absence of sense data. Yet we do possess speculative knowledge of the categories; therefore, they cannot be restricted to the realm of sense experience. Third, the categories do furnish knowledge of things in themselves. For either things in themselves exist or they do not. If they do not, we are reduced to solipsism. Besides the obvious problems of solipsism, the crucial point is this: since the categories do apply to the phenomena and these are all that exist, it follows that the categories do give a knowledge of reality in itself. But suppose things in themselves do exist (as Kant undoubtedly believed); then it becomes impossible to deny that the categories provide knowledge of things in themselves. For at least the categories of reality and causality must apply to them (since they cause the phenomena which we apprehend), unless one is willing to relapse into solipsism. Thus, to assert, 'No knowledge of the noumena is possible' is self-refuting, since it itself purports to be an item of knowledge about the noumena. This means, concludes Hackett, that the categories are both forms of thought and forms of things—thought and reality are structured homogeneously.

How can it be shown that the *a priori* categories are objective structural features of the mind? Hackett sums up his positive defence:

> ... either the categories are thus *a priori* or they are derived from experience. But an experiential derivation of the categories is impossible because only by their means can an object be thought in the first place. Since the categories are preconditions of all possible knowledge, they cannot have been derived from an experience of particular objects: the very first experience would be unintelligible without a structure of the mind to analyze it. . . .
>
> After all either thought starts with some general principles with which the mind is initially equipped, or it cannot start at all. Thought consists of ideas and judgments, as we have seen: and the very first act of judging presupposes that the thinker has a structure of thought in terms of which subject and predicate may be united according to certain relations.[157]

The argument, which is basically Kant's, is not that without the categories we could not experience sensations much as an animal does, but that self-conscious thought could not arise unless the human mind were structured so that it could.

Since the categories are objective features of both thought and reality and since causality is one of these categories, the causal relation must hold in the real world, and the causal principle would be a synthetic *a priori* proposition. It is *a priori* because it is universal and necessary, being a precondition of thought itself. But it is synthetic because the concept of an event does not entail the concept of being caused. Hackett's attempt to thus found the causal principle on an *a priori* mental category merits further investigation outside the scope of this book; for, as Bella Milmed observes, although much of Kant's work is obsolete,

> . . . surely most if not all of his categories are still recognizable as relevant to the interpretation of the empirical world; and the increased flexibility of logic means that it should be easier to find logical foundations for such categories, avoiding those of Kant's derivation that appear strained. Moreover, some of the most important of his derivations, e.g., those of substance and causality, do not appear strained at all.[158]

These two arguments suggest possible ways of defending the principle that everything that begins to exist has a cause of its existence. But probably most people do not really need convincing. In summary, we have contended that (1) it is intuitively obvious that anything that begins to exist, especially the entire universe, must have a cause of its existence; (2) Hume's attempt to show the universe could have sprung uncaused out of nothing fails to show this to be a *real* possibility, and (3) the causal principle could be more elaborately defended in two ways. Therefore, we conclude our first premiss: everything that begins to exist has a cause of its existence.

Conclusion: The Universe Has a Cause of Its Existence

Since everything that begins to exist has a cause of its existence, and since the universe began to exist, we conclude, therefore, the universe has a cause of its existence. We ought to ponder long and hard over this truly remarkable conclusion, for it means that transcending the entire universe there exists a cause which brought the universe into being *ex nihilo*. If our discussion has been more than a mere academic exercise, this conclusion ought to stagger us, ought to fill us with a sense of awe and wonder at the knowledge that our whole universe was caused to exist by *something* beyond it and greater than it.[159] For it is no secret that one of the most important conceptions of what theists mean by 'God' is Creator of heaven and earth.

But even more: we may plausibly argue that the cause of the universe is a personal being. Here we may pick up again the threads of the argument discussed in relation to Kant's first antinomy. There Kant argued in the antithesis that the universe could not have had a beginning in time. He asserted,

> For let us assume that it has a beginning. Since the beginning is an existence which is preceded by a time in which the thing is not, there must have been a preceding time in which the world was not, *i.e.* an empty time. Now no coming to be of a thing is possible in an empty time, because no part of such a time possesses, as compared with any other, a distinguishing condition of existence rather than of non-exis-

tence; and this applies whether the thing is supposed to arise of itself or through some other cause. In the world many series of things can, indeed, begin; but 'the world itself cannot have a beginning, and is therefore infinite in respect of past time.[160]

Now Kant's argument is to a large degree cogent. He is not arguing that there is any inherent absurdity in the notion of a void time, as is sometimes thought. Rather he is contending that prior to the existence of the universe no moment is distinguishable from another and, therefore, no condition exists at one moment rather than another which would account for the universe's beginning to exist at that moment rather than earlier or later.[161] Whitrow refutes Kant's antithesis by arguing that on a relational view of time, time begins with the first event, and therefore the question of why the universe did not begin earlier or later cannot arise.[162] But this only partly solves the problem, for it works only if the beginning of the universe is *uncaused*. If the beginning of the universe is uncaused, then whenever it springs into being is irrelevant, since its beginning is wholly unrelated to determinate conditions. Thus, if it springs into being in Newtonian absolute time, no distinguishing condition of one moment from another is necessary. And if it comes into existence with relational time, no problem arises because no conditions are necessary prior to the beginning of time. But what if the beginning of the universe is *caused*? Here Whitrow's response is of no avail. For either the necessary and sufficient conditions for the production of the first event are present from eternity or not. If they are, then the effect will exist from eternity, that is to say, the universe will be eternal. But if they are not, then the first event could never occur, since the necessary and sufficient conditions for the production of the first event could never arise. Kant may be assuming that the first event must have been caused, since he speaks of conditions for its existence. The antithesis of the first antinomy, which like the thesis echoes so clearly the arguments of the *mutakallimūn*, really asks, why did the universe begin to exist when it did instead of existing from eternity? The answer to Kant's conundrum was carefully explained by al-Ghāzali and enshrined in the Islamic principle of determination. According to that principle, when two different states of affairs are equally possible and one results, this realisation of one rather than the other must be the result of the action of a personal agent who freely chooses one rather than the other. Thus, Ghazāli argues that while it is true that no mechanical cause existing from eternity could create the universe in time, such a production of a temporal effect from an eternal cause is possible if and only if the cause is a personal agent who wills from eternity to create a temporally finite effect. For while a mechanically operating set of necessary and sufficient conditions would either produce the effect from eternity or not at all, a personal being may freely choose to create at any time wholly apart from any distinguishing conditions of one moment from another. For it is the very function of will to distinguish like from like. Thus, on a Newtonian view of time, a personal being could choose from eternity to create the universe at any moment he pleased.[163] On a relational view of time, he could will timelessly to create and that creation would mark the inception of time.[164] Thus, Kant's antithesis, far from disproving the beginning of the universe, actually provides a dramatic illumination of the nature of the cause of the universe; for if the universe began to exist, and if the universe is caused, then the cause of the universe must be a personal being who freely chooses to create the world.

This forces us to re-examine our discussion as to whether a beginning of the universe involves a beginning of time. For prior to the first event, the Creator of the universe exists. Would his existence necessitate the presence of time prior to creation? Lucas argues that a personal God could not be timeless and that if God is eternal, then time must be infinite as well.[165] But Hackett argues convincingly that a personal God need not experience a temporal succession of mental states. He could apprehend the whole content of the temporal series in a single eternal intuition, just as I analogously apprehend all the parts of a circle in a single sensory intuition. God could know the content of all knowledge—past, present, and future—in a simultaneous and eternal intuition.[166] Therefore, the fact that the Creator is personal does not necessitate the presence of time prior to creation. Sturch argues that in order to avoid an infinite temporal regress of states of consciousness, God's knowledge must be timeless.[167] On a Newtonian view of time, this would not necessitate a beginning of time, but it would on a relational view. Prior to the first event, the creation, God would exist changelessly and eternally. But what about subsequent to the first event? If God sustains any relations to the world, does not this imply that He exists in time? Although Aquinas argues that God remains timeless after creation because He sustains no *real* relation to the world, Aquinas's solution is singularly unconvincing.[168] For his solution is system-dependent upon a peculiar understanding of relation as an accident inhering in a substance. Abandon these Aristotelian categories and it seems foolish to say God is not really related to the world as Creator to creature. If God is related to the world, then it seems most reasonable to maintain that God is timeless prior to creation and in time subsequent to creation. This occurs not because of any change in God but because He is suddenly related to changing things. As Swinburne explains,

> . . . since God coexists with the world and in the world there is change, surely there is a case for saying that God continues to exist for an end-less time, rather than that he is timeless. In general that which remains the same while other things change is not said to be outside time, but to continue through time.[169]

Thus, on a relational view of time, God would exist timelessly and independently prior to creation: at creation, which He has willed from eternity to appear temporally, time begins, and God subjects Himself to time by being related to changing things. On the other hand, the Newtonian would say God exists in absolute time changelessly and independently prior to creation, and that creation simply marks the first event in time.[170]

We have thus concluded to a personal Creator of the universe who exists changelessly and independently prior to creation and in time subsequent to creation. This is a central core of what theists mean by 'God'. Further than this we shall not go. The *kalām* cosmological argument leads us to a personal Creator of the universe, but as to whether this Creator is omniscient, good, perfect, and so forth, we shall not inquire.[171] These questions are logically posterior to the question of His existence.[172] But if our argument is sound and a personal Creator of the universe really does exist, then surely it is incumbent upon us to inquire whether He has specially revealed Himself to man in some way that we might know Him more fully or whether, like Aristotle's unmoved mover, He remains aloof and detached from the world that He has made.

Notes

1. Aristotle *Physica* 3. 5. 204b1–206a8.
2. Simon Van Den Bergh, Notes to *Tahafut al-Tahafut* [*The Incoherence of the Incoherence*], 2 vols., by Averroës (London: Luzac & Co., 1954), 2: 8.
3. Aristotle *Physica* 3. 6. 206a15–20. For a good discussion, consult David Bostock, 'Aristotle, Zeno, and the Potential Infinite', *Proceedings of the Aristotelian Society* 73 (1972–3): 37–57. To argue that there can be a potential infinite but no actual infinite does not commit one to the self-contradictory position that there are possibilities that cannot be actualised. (W. D. Hart, 'The Potential Infinite', *Proceedings of the Aristotelian Society* 76 [1976]: 247–64.)
4. Abraham Robinson, 'The Metaphysics of the Calculus', in *The Philosophy of Mathematics*, ed. Jaakko Hintikka, Oxford Readings in Philosophy (London: Oxford University Press, 1969), pp. 156, 159. On some interesting medieval precedents for Cantor's work, see E. J. Ashworth, 'An Early Fifteenth-Century Discussion of Infinite Sets', *Notre Dame Journal of Formal Logic* 18 (1977): 232–4. On Leibniz's view of infinitesimal terms as useful fictions, see John Earman, 'Infinities, Infinitesimals, and Indivisibles: The Leibnizian Labyrinth', *Studia Leibnitiana* 7 (1975): 236–51.
5. Karl Friedrich Gauss and Heinrich Christian Schumacher, *Briefwechsel*, 6 vols., ed. C. A. F. Peters (Altona: Esch, 1860–65), 2: 269.
6. Bernard Bolzano, *Paradoxes of the Infinite*, trans. Fr. Prihonsky with an Introduction by Donald A. Steele (London: Routledge & Kegan Paul, 1950), pp. 81–4.
7. Ibid., pp. 95–6. Despite the one-to-one correspondence, Bolzano insisted that two infinites so matched might nevertheless be non-equivalent.
8. Richard Dedekind, 'The Nature and Meaning of Numbers', in Richard Dedekind, *Essays on the Theory of Numbers*, trans. Wooster Woodruff Beman (New York: Dover Publications, 1963), p. 63.
9. For an exposition and defence of Cantor's system, see Robert James Bunn, 'Infinite Sets and Numbers' (Ph.D. dissertation, University of British Columbia, 1975).

10. Georg Cantor, *Contributions to the Founding of the Theory of Transfinite Numbers*, trans. with an Introduction by Philip E. B. Jourdain (New York: Dover Publications, 1915), pp. 55–6.

11. Ibid., p. 108.

12. David Hilbert, 'On the Infinite', in *Philosophy of Mathematics*, ed. with an Introduction by Paul Benacerraf and Hilary Putnam (Englewood Cliffs, N.J.: Prentice-Hall, 1964), pp. 139, 141.

13. Ibid., p. 139. Fraenkel adds,

In almost all branches of mathematics, especially in analysis (for instance, in the theory of series and in calculus, also called 'infinitesimal calculus'), the term 'infinite' occurs frequently. However, mostly this infinite is but a *façon de parler* . . . ; the statement

$$\lim_{n \to \infty} \frac{1}{n} = 0$$

asserts nothing about infinity (as the ominous sign ∞ seems to suggest) but is just an abbreviation for the sentence: $1/n$ can be made to approach zero as closely as desired by sufficiently increasing the positive integer n. In contrast herewith the set of all integers is infinite (infinitely comprehensive) in a sense which is 'actual' (proper) and not only 'potential'. (Abraham A. Fraenkel, *Abstract Set Theory*, 2d rev. ed. [Amsterdam: North-Holland Publishing Co., 1961], pp. 5–6.) See also Antonio Moreno, 'Calculus and Infinitesimals: A Philosophical Evaluation', *Angelicum* 52 (1975): 228–45.

14. Fraenkel, *Theory*, p. 10.

15. Ibid., p. 29.

16. Ibid., p. 28.

17. For example, R. L. Sturch dismisses the *kalām* argumentation against the existence of an actual infinite with one sentence: '. . . the result of applying Cantorian theory to [these] paradoxes is to resolve them. . . .' (R. L. Sturch, 'The Cosmological Argument' [Ph.D. thesis, Oxford University, 1970], p. 79.) W. I. Matson similarly asserts that since there is no logical inconsistency in an infinite series of numbers, there is no logical inconsistency in an infinite series of events, and therefore the first cause argument is incurably fallacious. (Wallace I Matson, *The Existence of God* [Ithaca, N.Y.: Cornell University Press, 1965], pp. 58–60.) Matson fails to understand that the *kalām* argument holds that the existence of an actual infinite is really, not logically, impossible. That there is a difference can be seen in the fact that God's non-existence, if He exists, is logically, but not really, possible; if He does not exist, His existence is then logically, but not really, possible. Analogously, the existence of an actual infinite is really impossible, even if it may not involve logical contradiction.

18. Bolzano, *Paradoxes*, p. 84. See also Dedekind, 'Numbers', p. 64. These thinkers pointed to the set of all true propositions or the set of all objects of thought as examples of infinite sets, since by self-reference an infinite series is generated. But clearly such sets do not exist in the real world, and they may be considered to be potential infinites only.

19. Bolzano, *Paradoxes*, p. 101. Cantor also believed that his discoveries concerning the nature of infinity might be of great service to religion in

understanding the infinity of God and even carried on a fascinating correspondence with Pope Leo XIII to this effect. (See Joseph W. Dauben, 'Georg Cantor and Pope Leo XIII: Mathematics, Theology, and the Infinite', *Journal of the History of Ideas*, 38 [1977]: 85–108.)

20. Robinson, 'Calculus', p. 163. Cantor did think the number of atoms in the universe might be denumerably infinite.

21. Fraenkel, *Theory*, p. 240.

22. B. Rotman and G. T. Kneebone, *The Theory of Sets and Transfinite Numbers* (London: Oldbourne, 1966), p. 61. Thus, when one selects from an infinite set an infinite subset, the actual possibility of such an operation is not implied. 'The conception of an infinite sequence of choices (or of any other acts) ... is a mathematical fiction—an idealization of what is imaginable only in finite cases.' (Ibid., p. 60.)

23. Alexander Abian, *The Theory of Sets and Transfinite Arithmetic* (Philadelphia and London: W. B. Saunders Co., 1965), p. 68.

24. Pamela M. Huby, 'Kant or Cantor? That the Universe, if Real, Must Be Finite in Both Space and Time', *Philosophy* 46 (1971): 130.

25. Consult Joseph Breuer, *Introduction to the Theory of Sets*, trans. Howard F. Fehr (Englewood Cliffs, N.J.: Prentice-Hall, 1958), pp. 35–6.

26. For example, the cardinal of $\{1, 2, 3\}$ is 3, but the cardinal of its power-set (the set of all its subsets)
$$\{\{1\}, \{2\}, \{3\}, \{1, 2, 3\}, \{1, 2\}, \{1, 3\}, \{2, 3\}\}$$
is 7.

27. This story is recorded in an entertaining work by George Gamow, *One, Two, Three, ... Infinity* (London: Macmillan & Co., 1946), p. 17.

28. Hilbert, 'Infinite', p. 151.

29. For a good discussion of this issue, consult Abraham A. Fraenkel, Yehoshua Bar-Hillel, and Azriel Levy, *Foundations of Set Theory*, 2d rev. ed. (Amsterdam and London: North-Holland Publishing Co., 1973), pp. 331–45; Stephen F. Barker, *Philosophy of Mathematics*, Foundations of Philosophy Series (Englewood Cliffs, N.J.: Prentice-Hall, 1964), pp. 69–91.

30. For a thorough discussion of these, consult Fraenkel, Bar-Hillel, and Levy, *Foundations*, pp. 1–14; Barker, *Philosophy*, pp. 82–5.

31. An in-depth discussion of each of these reforms may be found in Fraenkel, Bar-Hillel, and Levy, *Foundations*, pp. 154–209, 15–153, 210–74; see also Barker, *Philosophy*, 85–91.

32. Barker, *Philosophy*, p. 87. Barker himself adopts a syncretistic view, arguing that because transfinite arithmetic and the set theory from which it is deduced cannot be regarded as statements about counting, these parts of mathematics ought to be regarded as 'games with marks', albeit games 'of great intellectual interest'. (Ibid., p. 103.)

33. James Thomson, after dismissing Bolzano and Dedekind's examples of actual infinity as having 'an air of artificiality', points to the natural numbers as an actual infinite:

If we agree to start counting at 0, then each number is the number of those less than itself, and if every number has a successor, no number in the class can be the number of the class. If we wish to say that every class has a number (a cardinality), we must say that there is at least one infinite number, the number of the class of inductive numbers. . . . (*Encyclopedia of Philosophy*, s.v. 'Infinity in Mathematics and Logic', by James Thomson.)

But why must we say that every class has a number? If the class of natural numbers is a potential infinite, increasing just as Thomson describes, then it is indefinite and cannot be said to possess an actually infinite number of elements. See Hermann Weyl, 'Mathematics and Logic', *American Mathematical Monthly* 53 (1946): 2–13. That a potential infinite need not imply an actual infinite, as Cantor contended, is argued by Hart, 'Potential Infinite', pp. 254–64.

34. It might be protested that we need not bring in the notion of actual infinity when speaking of past events; we may simply say that the series of temporal events is beginningless. This does not appear to be counter-intuitive and avoids the problems of the actual infinite. But such an escape route is easily barred: for it is in analysing what a beginningless series of events involves that the absurdities become manifest. As G. E. Moore indicates, if we grant that events really occur in time, then only two alternatives are possible: either there was a first event or there has been an actually infinite series of events prior to the present one. For if there was no first event, then there must have been an event prior to any given event; since this one also could not be first, there must be an event prior to it, and so on *ad infinitum*. (George Edward Moore, *Some Main Problems of Philosophy*, Muirhead Library of Philosophy [London: George Allen & Unwin, 1953; New York: Macmillan Co., 1953], pp. 174–5.) Therefore, a beginningless series involves the existence of an actual infinite.

35. Aristotle *Physica* 3. 6. 206a25–206b1.

36. Thomas Aquinas *Summa theologiae* 1a. 7. 4.

37. F. Van Steenberghen, 'Le "processus in infinitum" dans les trois premières "voies" de saint Thomas', *Revista Portuguesa de Filosofia* 30 (1974): 128. Another Thomist of the same judgement is Lucien Roy, 'Note philosophique sur l'idée de commencement dans la création', *Sciences Ecclesiastiques* 1 (1949): 223.

38. Van Steenberghen, '"processus"', p. 129.

39. P. J. Zwart, *About Time* (Amsterdam and Oxford: North Holland Publishing Co., 1976), p. 179.

40. Bertrand russell, *The Principles of Mathematics*, 2d ed. (London: George Allen & Unwin, 1937), pp. 358–9. Remarkably, even Fraenkel appears to agree with Russell on this score, though a mathematician of his status ought to be acquainted with the difference between a potential and an actual infinite. (Fraenkel, *Theory*, p. 30.)

41. Russell's fallacy is also discerned by G. J. Whitrow, *The Natural Philosophy of Time* (London and Edinburgh: Thomas Nelson & Sons, 1961), p. 149. Whitrow argues that Russell presupposes the incompletable series of events in question may be regarded as a whole, when in fact it is not legitimate to consider the events of Tristram Shandy's life as a completed infinite set, since the author could never catch up with himself.

42. See a similar argument in David A. Conway, 'Possibility and Infinite

Time: A Logical Paradox in St. Thomas' Third Way', *International Philosophical Quarterly*, 14 (1974): 201-8.

43. D. H. Sanford objects: 'Arguments which try to force a choice between an infinite series and a series with a definite first member overlook a third possibility.' (D. H. Sanford, 'Infinity and Vagueness', *Philosophical Review* 84 [1975]: 534.) This is that the series is finite but has no first member because the series's beginning tails away into a condition of vagueness which makes it impossible to specify membership in the series and thus designate a first member. For example, in a series of men each a millimetre taller than his predecessor, one cannot specify exactly where in the series the distinction between 'short' men and 'non-short' men ought to be made, since only a mere millimetre separates each man. Similarly, the temporal series of events may gradually shade off into a primordial 'chaos' in which time correlation was impossible. (Ibid., p. 528.) One could then say that the series of past events was finite, but that nevertheless there was no precisely first event. Sanford's article is intensely interesting because he obviously feels keenly the difficulties involved in affirming that the temporal series of past events is actually infinite, but he cannot bring himself to believe that there was therefore a first event, a thesis which, he says, has never been 'explicitly affirmed' by anyone. (Ibid., p. 527.) Therefore he is constrained to forge a third way which is not, unfortunately, very compelling. For a universe in which events occur must be a temporal universe, since the occurrence of any event will take some time (however short) in which to happen; the notion of a non-temporal event is a self-contradiction. Now in such a universe, these temporal events must be correlated with each other, for while it makes sense to say that *processes* in time proceed at different rates in different parts of the universe (a familiar correlate of relativity theory), it makes no sense to assert that time itself goes faster or slower in different parts of the universe, since this commits the well-known fallacy of speaking of the flow or passage of time. The only way one might conceivably have different 'times' would be by positing in the past two or more juxtaposed, unrelated universes from which our universe evolved. But this is impossible since, as Sanford himself points out, '. . . there is no process by which contiguous spatial or temporal intervals can be rendered non-contiguous'. (Ibid., p. 529.) Therefore the events in our universe's past must have been temporally interrelated, such that if the series of events is finite, there must have been a first event. Wholly apart from this, one may ask if the primordial events were causally connected or not. If not, then Sanford has not explained how things could come into being uncaused (the rather facile use of the word 'chaos' explains nothing). If they are causally related, then one automatically has temporal series and the problem of whether they can be infinite arises all over again. Finally, even if a so-called chaos could exist in which things come into and go out of existence uncaused, it could never evolve into a temporal series lacking a first event. The moment one event occurred after another, there would automatically be a first event (viz., the event that happened just before). The problem with the analogy of the series of men is that while there are degrees of height, there do not appear to be degrees of temporal relatedness. Therefore, if the series of past events is not infinite, it must be finite and have a temporally first event. And

waiving all theoretical considerations, Sanford's third way is at any rate empirically untenable, for it contradicts what Zel'dovich and Novikov call the 'firmly established' hot universe theory in which the universe expands from a singular state in the past. (Ia. B. Zel'dovich and I. D. Novikov, 'Contemporary Trends in Cosmology', *Soviet Studies in Philosophy* 14 [1976]: 37.) This model not only ensures the existence of universal time, reckoned according to the expansion and thermodynamic properties of the entire universe, from the origin of the universe several billion years ago until now, but also of physical and causal continuity of the series of past events back to the point of singularity. Sanford's gradual evolution from chaos to temporal series is confuted by the facts of current cosmology, of which he is admittedly unaware. (Sanford, 'Infinity', p. 534.)

44. Zwart, *Time*, pp. 239–40.

45. For example, William James distinguishes between a 'standing' infinity and a 'growing' infinity, by which he means an infinity that is simply given and an infinity formed by successive addition. He acknowledges that a growing infinity can never be completed and that the infinite cannot be traversed, but he holds that past time is nevertheless infinite because it is a standing infinity. (William James, *Some Problems of Philosophy* [London: Longman, Green, & Co., 1911], pp. 167–70, 182.) But this is clearly wrong-headed, for the past was formed precisely by successive addition and was never simply given. Thus, if it is infinite, it is an example of a growing infinite that has been completed, an actual infinite which has been traversed.

46. For example, Russell declares, '. . . when Kant says that an infinite series can "never" be completed by successive synthesis, all that he has even conceivably a right to say is that it cannot be completed *in a finite time*.' (Bertrand Russell, *Our Knowledge of the External World*, 2d ed. [New York: W. W. Norton & Co., 1929], p. 171.) Cf. Matson: 'This . . . begs the question, since it is only impossible to run through an infinite series in a finite time.' (Matson, *God*, p. 60.)

47. Ibid., p. 170. But suppose someone objects that the man in question has been running from eternity past: if his foot strikes a stone every second and there are in eternity past an infinite number of seconds, will he not have completed his course successfully? In one sense, yes; *if* an infinite number of seconds could elapse, then an infinite number of stones could be traversed. But this only pushes the issue one step backwards: how can an infinite number of seconds elapse? One does not eliminate the problem of forming an infinite collection by successive addition by superimposing another collection on top of the first; for if one is possible, both are possible, and if one is absurd, both are absurd. Since *any* collection formed by successive addition cannot be infinite, an infinite number of seconds cannot have elapsed. This means that time either had a beginning or that measured time was preceded by an undifferentiated time.

48. John Hospers, *An Introduction to Philosophical Analysis*, 2d ed. (London: Routledge & Kegan Paul, 1967), p. 434. Hosper's own statement of the argument is defective, for he argues that it would take infinite time to get through an infinite series, and this is the same as never getting through. It is not the same, of course, but the argument has nothing to do with

the amount of time allowed: it is *inherently* impossible to form an actual infinite by successive addition.

49. William L. Rowe, *The Cosmological Argument* (Princeton, N.J.: Princeton University Press, 1975), p. 122.

50. For example, Moore rejects the thesis of Kant's first antinomy because he believes there cannot be a first moment in time; there must always be time before time. (Moore, *Problems*, p. 176.)

51. R. G. Swinburne, *Space and Time* (London: Macmillan, 1968), pp. 207–8.

52. Ibid., p. 209.

53. Ibid., p. 245.

54. Ibid., p. 296.

55. J. R. Lucas, *A Treatise on Time and Space* (London: Methuen & Co., 1973), pp. 10–11.

56. Ibid., pp. 311–12.

57. Lawrence Sklar, *Space, Time, and Spacetime* (Berkeley and Los Angeles: University of California Press, 1974), p. 274.

58. Ibid., p. 297.

59. Ian Hinckfuss, *The Existence of Space and Time* (Oxford: Clarendon Press, 1975), pp. 72–3.

60. Zwart, *Time*, p. 237.

61. Ibid., p. 36. '... *time is the generalized relation of before-and-after extended to all events.*' (Ibid., p. 43.)

62. Stuart C. Hackett, *The Resurrection of Theism* (Chicago: Moody Press, 1957), p. 263.

63. Brian Ellis, 'Has the Universe a Beginning in Time?' *Australasian Journal of Philosophy* 33 (1955): 33.

64. G. J. Whitrow, *What is Time?* (London: Thames & Hudson, 1972), pp. 146–7.

65. For an introduction to scientific cosmology, see P. J. E. Peebles, *Physical Cosmology*, Princeton Series in Physics (Princeton, N.J.: Princeton University Press, 1971); D. W. Sciama, *Modern Cosmology* (Cambridge: Cambridge University Press, 1971); J. D. North, *Measure of the Universe* (Oxford: Clarendon Press, 1965); and S. Weinberg, *Gravitation and Cosmology* (New York: Wiley, 1972).

66. There has been some controversy over the value of redshifts as distance indicators. (For a synopsis of the debate, consult George B. Field, Halton Arp, and John N. Bahcall, *The Redshift Controversy*, Frontiers in Physics [Reading, Mass.: W. A. Benjamin, 1973]. A lucid history of the dispute may also be found in Daniel Weedman, 'Seyfert Galaxies, Quasars and Redshifts', *Quarterly Journal of the Royal Astronomical Society* 17 [1976]: 227–62.) Pointing to various discrepancies in the redshift data, especially those from quasi-stellar objects (QSO's), some have argued that some other factor may account for the observed redshifts. But the weight of the evidence supports the expansion hypothesis. Bahcall enumerates six observational tests which the theory of redshifts as distance indicators has passed, as well as three successful predictions of the theory. (Field, Arp, and Bahcall, *Redshift*, pp. 77–9, 108.) According to Lang and his colleagues, the uncertainty concerning QSO redshifts is due to small sampling and that the QSO slope, when corrected, is comparable

to that of galaxies. (Kenneth R. Lang, Steven D. Lord, James M. Johanson, and Paul D. Savage, 'The Composite Hubble Diagram', *Astrophysical Journal* 202 [1975]: 583–90.) The discrepancies of redshifts among closely related stars, moreover, do not suffice to overturn the Doppler effect theory, according to P. C. Joss, D. A. Smith, and A. B. Solinger, 'On Apparent Associations among Astronomical Objects', *Astronomy and Astrophysics* 47 (1976): 461–2. See also D. Wills and R. L. Ricklefs, 'On the Redshift Distribution of Quasi-stellar Objects', *Monthly Notices of the Royal Astronomical Society* 175 (1976): 65p–70p; M. Rowan-Robinson, 'Quasars and the Cosmological Distance Scale', *Nature* 262 (1976): 97–101; Richard F. Green and Douglas O. Richstone, 'On the Reality of Periodicities in the Redshift Distribution of Emission-line Objects', *Astrophysical Journal* 208 (1976): 639–45. In the early fall of 1976 an international astronomical conference held in Paris devoted itself largely to a debate of the redshift controversy. The results of this important conference will be published in the *Proceedings of the International Astronomical Union* 37 and the *Centre National de la Recherche Scientifique Colloque International* 263, edited by J. Heidmann and B. E. Westerlund, but they were not yet available at the time of writing. According to Peebles, there is no serious competitor to the expansion hypothesis, and he lists seven points in favour of an expanding universe: (1) the redshifts from galaxies, (2) the frequency shifts of radio lines, (3) the fact that Hubble's law fits a homogeneous and isotropic universe, (4) the harmony of theory and observation, (5) the fact that the Hubble time coincides with the age of the stars and the elements, (6) the presence of the blackbody background radiation, and (7) the fact that relativistic corrections to stellar magnitudes brings these into harmony with the theory. (Peebles, *Cosmology*, pp. 25–7.) Most of these points will be explained later, but this seems the best place to list them all.

67. Edwin Hubble, 'A Relation Between Distance and Radial Velocity Among Extra-galactic Nebulae', *Proceedings of the National Academy of Sciences* 15 (1929): 168–73.

68. H. Bondi and T. Gold, 'The Steady-State Theory of the Expanding Universe', *Monthly Notices of the Royal Astronomical Society* 108 (1948): 252–75; F. Hoyle, 'A New Model for the Expanding Universe', *Monthly Notices of the Royal Astronomical Society* 108 (1948): 372–82.

69. A. A. Penzias and R. W. Wilson, 'A Measurement of Excess Antenna Temperature at 4080 Mc/s', *Astrophysical Journal* 142 (1965): 419–21; see also R. H. Dicke, P. J. E. Peebles, P. G. Roll, and D. T. Wilkinson, 'Cosmic Black-Body Radiation', *Astrophysical Journal* 142 (1965): 414–19.

70. For a good synopsis of phases of the early universe, see E. R. Harrison, 'Standard Model of the Early Universe', *Annual Review of Astronomy and Astrophysics* 11 (1973): 155–86.

71. A neutrino is a stable, subatomic particle that has no charge and zero mass when at rest (which it never is, since it is travelling at the speed of light as long as it exists).

72. Allan R. Sandage, 'Cosmology: A Search for Two Numbers', *Physics Today*, February 1970, p. 34.

73. Allan Sandage and G. A. Tammann, 'Steps Toward the Hubble Constant. I. Calibration of the Linear Sizes of Extragalactic H_{II} Regions', *Astro-*

physical Journal 190 (1974): 525–38; Allan Sandage and G. A. Tammann, 'Steps Toward the Hubble Constant. II. The Brightest Stars in the Late-Type Spiral Galaxies', *Astrophysical Journal* 191 (1974): 603–21; Allan Sandage and G. A. Tammann, 'Steps Toward the Hubble Constant. III. The Distance and Stellar Content of the MIOI Group of Galaxies', *Astrophysical Journal* 194 (1974): 223–43; Allan Sandage and G. A. Tammann, 'Steps Toward the Hubble Constant. IV. Distances to 39 Galaxies in the General Field Leading to a Calibration of the Galaxy Luminosity Classes and a First Hint of the Value of H_0', *Astrophysical Journal* 194 (1974): 559–68; Allan Sandage and G. A. Tammann, 'Steps Toward the Hubble Constant. V. The Hubble Constant from Nearby Galaxies and the Regularity of the Local Velocity Field', *Astrophysical Journal* 196 (1975): 313–28; Allan Sandage and G. A. Tammann, 'Steps Toward the Hubble Constant. IV. The Hubble Constant Determined from Redshifts and Magnitudes of Remote Sc I Galaxies: the Value of q_0', *Astrophysical Journal* 197 (1975): 265–80.

74. Mpc is the abbreviation for megaparsec. A parsec is equal to 3·26 light years. Mega is a prefix meaning 10^6.

75. Sandage and Tammann, 'Steps Toward the Hubble Constant. VI', p. 277.

76. J. Richard Gott III, James E. Gunn, David N. Schramm, and Beatrice M. Tinsley, 'Will the Universe Expand Forever?' *Scientific American*, March 1976, p. 65.

77. It is sometimes erroneously asserted that black holes are infinitely dense; I have even seen them described in one popular magazine as infinitely dense and hence literally nothing! In reality a black hole (so called because light cannot escape its gravitational field, thus causing it to appear only as a dark area) is simply a region whose radius becomes smaller than $2GM/c^2$ (G = gravitational constant; M = mass; c = speed of light), and its density can be quite small if the mass is large.

78. Fred Hoyle, *From Stonehenge to Modern Cosmology* (San Francisco: W. H. Freeman & Co., 1972), p. 36; Fred Hoyle, *Astronomy and Cosmology: A Modern Course* (San Francisco: W. H. Freeman & Co., 1975), p. 658.

79. In the words of Zel'dovich and Novikov:

Quite recently the question has been discussed as to whether singularity, infinite density of matter at the onset of the expansion, actually exists. Perhaps singularity is characteristic only of an ideal, homogeneous, isotropic model. ... *Today it has been rigorously shown that singularity did exist in the real universe*, even if early stages of expansion differed sharply from homogeneous, isotropic expansion. (Zel'dovich and Novikov, 'Trends', pp. 46–7 [My italics].)

80. Michael Scriven protests sharply against those who claim that empirical science can determine whether or not the universe is temporally finite. He asks, how do we know what is the basic stuff of the universe? Perhaps it is something our instruments cannot detect. So how can we determine whether and when the universe began? Perhaps prior to the big bang was a stable state whose duration cannot be measured. So science can never determine whether or not the universe began to exist. (Michael Scriven,

'The Age of the Universe', *British Journal for the Philosophy of Science* 5 [1954]: 181–90.) But J. H. Bird rightly takes Scriven to task for violating the spirit of scientific inquiry. Sceptical arguments against cosmology simply revive the old objections against induction, Bird asserts, and are futile and pointless. Scriven would require apodeictic certainty from scientists, which was not possible in this sort of enterprise. (J. H. Bird, 'The Beginning of the Universe', *The Aristotelian Society* 40 [1966]: 139–50.) Scriven demands absolute verifiability from cosmologists, which is impossible, while he himself proposes hypotheses which are entirely unfalsifiable. Besides, in our argument, the empirical evidence is simply confirmatory of a conclusion already reached by pure philosophical argument; it shows, if you will, a harmony between theory and observation. Even Swinburne admits that if there were better evidence for a creation theory of the universe, which he did not think there was at the time of his writing, then '. . . the popularisers would be right in claiming that the evidence showed that the Universe had a beginning a finite time ago'. (Swinburne, 'Beginning', p. 136.) In the more than a decade that has passed since Swinburne wrote, the evidence in favour of creation has accumulated to such an extent that it appears that the 'popularisers' are right after all.

81. Fred Hoyle, *Astronomy Today* (London: Heinemann, 1975), p. 165.

82. Fred Hoyle, 'The Origin of the Universe', *Quarterly Journal of the Royal Astronomical Society* 14 (1973): 278.

83. Peebles, *Cosmology*, p. 25.

84. Adrian Webster, 'The Cosmic Background Radiation,' *Scientific American*, August 1974, pp. 26–8; M. S. Longair, 'Radioastronomy and Cosmology', *Nature* 263 (1976): 372–4.

85. Hoyle, *Astronomy and Cosmology*, p. 680.

86. Ibid., pp. 686–90; Fred Hoyle, 'On the Origin of the Micro-wave Background', *Astrophysical Journal* 196 (1975): 661–70.

87. Hoyle, *Stonehenge*, p. 2. Hugo Meynell reports, 'In his contribution to a symposium, [*Religion and the Scientists*, ed. Mervyn Stockwood, p. 56.] Hoyle says that he believes in a God in the sense of an intelligence at work in nature, but then he qualifies this by saying that he means by 'God' the universe itself rather than some being who transcends the universe.' (Hugo Meynell, *God and the World: the Coherence of Christian Theism* [London: SPCK, 1971], pp. 18–19.)

88. Hoyle, *Astronomy*, p. 165.

89. Hoyle, *Astronomy and Cosmology*, pp. 684–5.

90. Ibid., p. 685.

91. Noting that the steady state theory failed to secure 'a single piece of experimental verification', Jaki points out that the theory's exponents often had 'overtly anti-theological, or rather anti-Christian motivations' for propounding this cosmological model. (Stanley L. Jaki, *Science and Creation* [Edinburgh and London: Scottish Academic Press, 1974], p. 347.)

92. Beatrice M. Tinsley, personal letter.

93. Webster, 'Radiation', p. 28.

94. Ivan R. King, *The Universe Unfolding* (San Francisco: W. H. Freeman, 1976), p. 462.

95. Ibid.

96. John Gribbin, 'Oscillating Universe Bounces Back', *Nature* 259 (1976): 15.

97. J. Richard Gott III, James E. Gunn, David N. Schramm, and Beatrice M. Tinsley, 'An Unbound Universe?' *Astrophysical Journal* 194 (1974): 543-53. The previously cited article by the same authors in the *Scientific American* is a re-write and revision of this article.

98. See Icko Iben, 'Post Main Sequence Evolution of Single Stars', *Annual Review of Astronomy and Astrophysics* 12 (1974): 215-56. See also Icko Iben, Jr., 'Globular Cluster Stars', *Scientific American*, July 1970, pp. 26-39.

99. See David N. Schramm, 'Nucleo-Cosmochronology', *Annual Review of Astronomy and Astrophysics* 12 (1974): 383-406. See also David N. Schramm, 'The Age of the Elements', *Scientific American*, January 1974, pp. 69-77.

100. For a good general review of the deuterium question, see Jay M. Pasachoff and William A. Fowler, 'Deuterium in the Universe', *Scientific American*, May 1974, pp. 108-18.

101. Fred Hoyle and William A. Fowler, 'On the Origin of Deuterium', *Nature* 241 (1973): 384-6.

102. Gott, Gunn, Schramm, and Tinsley, 'Unbound Universe?' p. 548. If deuterium were produced in supernovae, then we would have too much ^7Li, ^9Be, and ^{11}B, according to Richard I. Epstein, W. David Arnett, and David N. Schramm, 'Can Supernovae Produce Deuterium?' *Astrophysical Journal* 190 (1974): L13-16. See also Harrison, 'Early Universe', pp. 166-9; Hubert Reeves, Jean Audouze, William A. Fowler, and David N. Schramm, 'On the Origin of Light Elements', *Astrophysical Journal* 179 (1973): 909-30.

103. Jean Audouze and Beatrice M. Tinsley, 'Galactic Evolution and the Formation of the Light Elements', *Astrophysical Journal* 192 (1974): 487-500.

104. R. P. Kirschner and J. Kwan, cited in Gott, Gunn, Schramm, and Tinsley, 'Unbound Universe?' p. 552.

105. Sandage and Tammann, 'Steps Toward the Hubble Constant. VI', p. 276. Davis and May have reported that they have determined as a result of observations of the 839·4 MHz absorption line in the spectrum of the quasar 3C 286 a redshift accuracy of one part in 10^6; observations over several decades could place 'useful limits on q_0.' (Michael M. Davis and Linda S. May, 'New Observations of the Radio Absorption Line in 3C 286, with Potential Application to the Direct Measurement of Cosmological Deceleration', *Astrophysical Journal* 219 [1978]: 3.) Thus, indirect estimates of q_0 may not be the exclusive possibility in the future.

106. Ibid., p. 278.

107. Allan Sandage, 'The Redshift-Distance Relation. VIII. Magnitudes and Redshifts of Southern Galaxies in Groups: A Further Mapping of the Local Velocity Field and an Estimate of q_0', *Astrophysical Journal* 202 (1975): 563-82.

108. Ibid., p. 579.

109. James E. Gunn and Beatrice M. Tinsley, 'An Accelerating Universe', *Nature* 257 (1975): 454-7. There are complications with this theory, however, and it has been suggested by Ostriker and Tremaine that a counter-evolutionary effect may restore deceleration, though the universe would still be open. (J. P. Ostriker and Scott D. Tremain, 'Another Evolutionary Correction to the Luminosity of Giant Galaxies', *Astrophysical Journal* 202 [1975]:

L113–17.) According to Tinsley,

> ... all these effects are so uncertain that we should stick to the view given in the earlier papers, that estimates of the density constitute the strongest tests for the type of cosmological model, and they point to monotonic expansion from the big bang. The arguments in our paper based on density and age estimates have been strengthened, but not substantially altered, by subsequent developments. (Tinsley, personal letter.)

Cf. Beatrice M. Tinsley, 'The Cosmological Constant and Cosmological Change', *Physics Today* 30 (1977): 32–8.

110. J. Richard Gott III and Martin J. Rees, 'A Theory of Galaxy Formation and Clustering', *Astronomy and Astrophysics* 45 (1975): 365–76.

111. Edwin L. Turner and J. Richard Gott III, 'Evidence for a Spatially Homogeneous Component of the Universe: Single Galaxies', *Astrophysical Journal* 197 (1975): L.89–93.

112. J. Richard Gott III and Edwin L. Turner, 'The Mean Luminosity and Mass Densities in the Universe', *Astrophysical Journal* 209 (1976): 1–5.

113. Ibid., pp. 4, 5. By weighting each galaxy by its luminosity rather than weighting giant and dwarf galaxies equally, Turner and Ostriker determine a mass to light ratio that also yields $\Omega \sim 0 \cdot 08$. (Edwin L. Turner and Jeremiah P. Ostriker, 'The Mass to Light Ratio of Late-Type Binary Galaxies: Luminosity-versus Number-Weighted Averages', *Astrophysical Journal* 217 [1977]: 24–36.)

114. S. Michael Fall, 'The Scale of Galaxy Clustering and the Mean Matter Density of the Universe', *Monthly Notices of the Royal Astronomical Society* 172 (1975): 23p–26p.

115. David Eichler and Alan Solinger, 'The Electromagnetic Background: Limitations on Models of Unseen Matter', *Astrophysical Journal* 203 (1976): 1–5. Field and Perrenod argue further that both observational and theoretical constraints (including limitations of the energy source needed to heat the gas, the observed deuterium abundance, and the lack of evidence for any clumping of gas clouds in intergalactic space, without which they could not persist) combine to make a cosmologically significant amount of hot intergalactic gas uncertain. (George B. Field and Stephen C. Perrenod, 'Constraints on a Dense Hot Intergalactic Medium', *Astrophysical Journal* 215 [1977]: 717–22.)

116. Richard I. Epstein and Vahe Petrosian, 'Effects of Primordial Fluctuations on the Abundances of Light Elements', *Astrophysical Journal* 197 (1975): 281–4. See also Donald G. York and John B. Rogerson, Jr., 'The Abundance of Deuterium Relative to Hydrogen in Interstellar Space', *Astrophysical Journal* 203 (1976): 378–85.

117. Jean Audouze, 'L'universe est-il ouvert ou fermé?' *Recherche* 6 (1975): 462–5. For a good summary of possible mechanisms for deuterium production, see Richard I. Epstein, James M. Lattimer, and David N. Schramm, 'The Origin of Deuterium', *Nature* 263 (1976): 198–202. After exploring the possible production of deuterium by spallation reactions, pregalactic cosmic rays, shock waves in a low density medium, hot explosive events, and disrupted neutron stars, they conclude,

... very severe restrictions can be placed on mechanisms for producing deuterium. In fact it seems unlikely that objects or events which are currently known or inferred to have existed in our Galaxy or in well-observed extra-galactic objects could be capable of producing the observed deuterium abundance. . . .

Big-bang nucleosynthesis . . . requires only the simplest cosmological assumptions and is consistent with all well-established cosmological data. Contrasted to this, post-big-bang deuterium production requires extremely violent and exotic events, the existence of which is certainly doubtful.
. . . Big-bang nucleosynthesis is by far the most reasonable site for the origin of deuterium. (Ibid., pp. 199, 202.)

118. Tinsley, personal letter.
119. The following survey is taken from Zwart, *Time*, pp. 93–116.
120. Zwart summarises and refutes two objections to the second law. (1) *Loschmidt's reversibility objection:* Molecules in motion do not prefer one direction over another. So a certain direction and its opposite are equally probable. The laws which govern the motion of molecules are time symmetric, so that the successive states of a system could be reversed. Therefore, in a closed system every state has the same probability as its opposite, and every process must occur in both directions an equal number of times. (2) *Zermelo's periodicity objection:* Every conceivable state of a system has some probability. So given enough time, every possibility will be realised. And this will occur again and again cyclically, each system passing through the same states exactly as in the previous times.

Against these objections Zwart urges: (1) The objections are contravened by the facts. The entropy of a closed system is never seen to decrease. Observation's universal testimony in support of the second law ought to make us suspect some error in the objections, not in the law itself. (2) All real processes are irreversible, and the reversible processes are just idealisations. In reality entropy will never decrease in a closed system. (3) There are positive errors in the objections. (a) Loschmidt's premiss that a state and its opposite are equally possible is incorrect because every actual state is the result of everything that has happened before in the system. Only by disregarding the system's past history can we say any state and its reverse are equally probable; in reality, given the prior influences, the actual state has a probability of 1 and its reverse a probability of 0. (b) Zermelo's objection is purely theoretical and fails to take into account the fact that before a deviation of the second law could occur, the system would have perished. Thus, before one-tenth of a millilitre in a litre of gas would be empty, the whole solar system would have ceased to exist.

121. Toulmin objects that it does not make sense to ask if the universe is an isolated system because since it is all there is, it cannot be said to be isolated from anything. (Stephen Toulmin, 'Contemporary Scientific Mythology', in *Metaphysical Beliefs*, ed. Alasdair MacIntyre [London: SCM Press, 1957], p. 36.) It is hard to believe Toulmin intends this argument to be taken seriously. For as Sturch points out, when we say a system is closed or isolated, we mean that there is no other system with which the system in question has an interchange of energy; this is obviously the case with

the universe. (Sturch, 'Argument', p. 230.) For a refutation of Toulmin's other objections, see Ibid., pp. 229–34.

122. Zwart, *Time*, p. 136.

123. Richard Schlegel explains,

> If we follow time along the ω series we should eventually come to a state of maximum entropy; for, the ω series has no end, and hence, if it does represent future time, and if the assertion of entropy increase may be applied to the entire universe, the equilibrium state of maximum entropy should be approached. Considerations of this sort have led to a prediction of an ultimately lifeless universe. . . .
>
> This model for the future of the universe . . . presents a difficulty when extrapolation is made in time, along the $*\omega$ series. Now at each earlier time the universe must have had a successively smaller entropy, and, since the $*\omega$ series is also an unending one, one must come to as small an entropy as desired by going far enough back in time. An alternative, that the universe was at some equilibrium state at an earlier time, is hardly tenable, since the universe is clearly not at present in an equilibrium state, and if it had earlier been in one it should have remained so, having then already reached its maximum entropy. It would appear, then, that . . . one must postulate some other mechanism for bringing the universe to an arbitrarily low entropy state at past times. In some way, . . . the universe must have been wound up. (Richard Schlegel, 'Time and Thermo-dynamics', in *Voices*, ed. Fraser, pp. 510–11.)

124. See R. E. D. Clark, *The Universe: Plan or Accident?* 3d ed. (London: Paternoster Press, 1961), p. 19. Clark supports Newton's argument as reasonable.

125. P. C. W. Davies, *The Physics of Time Asymmetry* (London: Surrey University Press, 1974), p. 109.

126. Ibid., p. 185.

127. Beatrice M. Tinsley, 'From Big Bang to Eternity?' *Natural History Magazine*, October 1975, p. 103.

128. Ibid., pp. 102–3.

129. Richard C. Tolman, *Relativity, Thermodynamics, and Cosmology* (Oxford: Clarendon Press, 1934), p. 444.

130. Ibid., pp. 327–9.

131. Davies, *Physics*, p. 188. Novikov and Zel'dovich are less generous, urging technical considerations again the probability of a 'bounce' in a Friedmann model. (I. D. Novikov and Ya. B. Zel'dovich, 'Physical Processes near Cosmological Singularities', *Annual Review of Astronomy and Astrophysics* 11 [1973]: 401.)

132. Novikov and Zel'dovich, 'Processes', pp. 401–2. (My italics.) Russian-speaking readers are also referred to Ya. B. Zel'dovich and I. D. Novikov, *Relativistic Astrophysics* (Moscow: Nauka, 1967) and Ya. B. Zel'dovich and I. D. Novikov, *Structure and Evolution of the Universe* (Moscow: Nauka, 1973). Davies also concludes that the cycles of an oscillating universe will gradually increase, and furnishes a diagram like that of Novikov and Zel'dovich. (Davies, *Physics*, pp. 190–1.) These findings are also confirmed by P. T. Landsberg

and D. Park, 'Entropy in an oscillating universe', *Proceedings of the Royal Society of London* A 346 (1975): 485–95. See also Gribbin, 'Oscillating Universe', pp. 15–16.

133. Gribbin, 'Oscillating Universe', p. 16.

134. Swinburne, *Space and Time*, p. 304.

135. Adolf Grünbaum, *Philosophical Problems of Space and Time*, 2d ed., Boston Studies in the Philosophy of Science, vol. 12 (Dordrecht, Holland and Boston: D. Reidel Publishing Co., 1973), p. 262.

136. W. S. Krogdahl explains,

... the universe has been expanding since the moment of release. Its boundary is therefore as many light years in any direction as there have been years since the expansion began. Present reckoning from the observed distances and velocities of galaxies puts this time at 15 to 20 billion years. Hence no galaxies could yet be more than 15 to 20 billion light years from us. In this sense, the universe is finite. (Wasley S. Krogdahl, 'The Creation of the Universe', *Sky and Telescope* [March 1973]: 143.)

137. P. C. W. Davies, personal letter.

138. Schlegel, 'Time and Thermodynamics', p. 508.

139. Zwart, *Time*, p. 117.

140. Ibid., p. 118.

141. Ibid., pp. 118–19.

142. Davies, *Physics*, pp. 103–4.

143. Ibid., p. 188.

144. Ibid., p. 104.

145. Ibid.

146. Hume wrote,

But allow me to tell you that I never asserted so absurd a Proposition as *that anything might arise without a cause*: I only maintain'd, that our Certainty of the Falshood of that Proposition proceeded neither from Intuition nor Demonstration; but from another Source. (David Hume to John Stewart, February 1754, in *The Letters of David Hume*, 2 vols., ed. J. Y. T. Greig [Oxford: Clarendon Press, 1932], 1: 187.)

147. Anthony Kenny, *The Five Ways: St. Thomas Aquinas' Proofs of God's Existence* (New York: Schocken Books, 1969), p. 66.

The reader may be curious as to what the attitude of scientists is toward the philosophical and theological implications of their own big bang model. That there are such implications seems evident, for as Reeves remarks, 'The problem of the origin involves a certain metaphysical aspect which may be either appealing or revolting.' (Reeves, Audouze, Fowler, and Schramm, 'Origin', p. 912.) But as Albert Einstein once observed, 'The man of science is a poor philosopher.' (Albert Einstein, *Out of My Later Years* [New York: Philosophical Library, 1950], p. 58.) For such implications seem either to escape or not interest most scientists. Hoyle, after explaining that the big bang model cannot inform us as to where the matter came from or why the big bang occurred, comments, 'It is not usual in present day cosmological discussions to seek an answer to this question; the question and its answer are taken to be outside the range of scientific discussion.' (Hoyle, *Astronomy*, p. 166.) Since the big bang was a singularity, no empirical information is available about what preceded it; therefore, most scientists simply ignore the question. But while this may satisfy the scientist, it can never satisfy the philosopher. For while the big bang may describe the origin of the universe, it by no means solves it, as Webster explains,

> Choosing to work backward from the present state of the universe to gain some knowledge of the initial conditions is not at all arbitrary, but it does not suffice to *explain* the initial conditions. Probably the most we can expect from this approach is that we shall be able at least to describe those conditions. (Webster, 'Radiation', p. 31.)

Certain scientists with a more philosophical bent feel the inadequacy of such a solution. Thus, J. V. Narlikar complains,

> Another unsatisfactory feature of the classical cosmological model is the scant attention paid to the question of matter creation. It is assumed that all the present matter (and radiation) in the Universe appeared in its primary form at the time of the 'big bang'. Subsequent to this event matter as a whole is conserved according to the Einstein equations, although it may change its form as the universe evolves. So the question 'How was the matter created in the first place?' is left unanswered. (J. V. Narlikar, 'Singularity and Matter Creation in Cosmological Models', *Nature: Physical Science* 242 [1973]: 135–6.)

Such considerations prompted the various steady state models of Hoyle, Narlikar, and others. But these, too, are inadequate. (See J. M. Barnothy and Beatrice M. Tinsley, 'A Critique of Hoyle and Narlikar's New Cosmology', *Astrophysical Journal* 182 [1973]: 343–9.) The scientific evidence points to a temporal beginning of the universe. As rigorous scientists we may stop there and bar further inquiry, but as philosophers and, we dare say, as men, must we not inquire further until we come to the cause of the beginning of the universe?

148. Broad, 'Antinomies', pp. 9–10.

149. It has been alleged that *creatio ex nihilo* also violates this principle. (Leroy T. Howe, 'God and the Being of the World', *Journal of Religion* 53 [1973]: 411.) But *creatio ex nihilo* asserts only that creation lacks a *material* cause, not an *efficient* cause. In this premiss we are maintaining the necessity of an efficient cause of the universe.

150. Zwart, *Time*, pp. 239–40.

151. Hume, *Treatise*, pp. 79–80.

152. G. E. M. Anscombe, '"Whatever Has a Beginning of Existence Must Have a Cause": Hume's Argument Exposed', *Analysis* 34 (1974): 150.

153. Ibid. See also Kenny, *Five Ways*, pp. 66–8; Aziz Ahmad, 'Causality', *Pakistan Philosophical Journal* 12 (1973): 17–24.

154. Frederick C. Copleston, *A History of Philosophy*, vol. 5: *Hobbes to Hume* (London: Burns, Oates & Washbourne, 1959), p. 287.

155. Hackett, *Theism*, pp. 37–113.

156. Ibid., pp. 46–55.

157. Ibid., p. 57.

158. Bella Milmed, *Kant and Current Philosophical Issues* (New York: New York University Press, 1961), p. 45.

159. Objections to a First Cause of the universe hardly merit refutation. Laird argues that the universe is the 'theatre' of causes but does not itself need a cause. (John Laird, *Theism and Cosmology* [London: George Allen & Unwin, 1940], p. 95.) This is manifestly untrue, since the 'theatre' itself had a beginning, and no doubt did not spring into being uncaused. Hospers and Matson object that the First Cause would also have to have a cause, which is impossible. (Hospers, *Introduction*, p. 431; Matson, *God*, p. 61.) This is incorrect because the causal principle concerns only what *begins* to exist, and God never began to exist, but is eternal. MacIntyre contends that a causal relationship involves two observable events; since God is not observable, the relationship between God and the world cannot be causal. (Alasdair C. MacIntyre, *Difficulties in Christian Belief* [London: SCM Press, 1959], p. 60.) But MacIntyre's stipulation is entirely arbitrary and unwarranted; for unobservable entities such as cosmic rays cause observable effects. And could not an unobservable spirit being like an angel or demon, if there be such, cause observable effects, such as the levitation of an object? Why then could not God cause the world?

The significance of this conclusion may be seen in the fact that it thoroughly undermines the foundation of modern process theology. According to process theologians, God and the universe are co-eternal poles of the one divine being, which develops through the process of inter-relation between these poles. But if our analysis is correct, such an understanding of the universe (to say nothing of God) is both philosophically unsound and empirically unscientific. We have argued that the temporal series of events cannot be infinite; therefore, the universe cannot have been developing co-eternally with God. (And even if it could, then the process of God's development would have already been completed by now.) To retreat to the position that God and the world lay dormant from eternity and began a process of mutual development a finite number of years ago completely removes any rationale for process theology, since according to this school, process and development are essential to God's very nature, and he cannot exist without development. Moreover, such a theology is anti-empirical, for it appears to presuppose some sort of continuous steady-state universe. To try to wed process theology with modern cosmology can only make us smile at the incongruity: a pitiable God, indeed, whose poor body explodes from a point of infinite density and perishes in the cold reaches of outer space! It is ironic that theologians should have developed such a view of God and the universe at precisely the same time that scientists were accumulating evidence that tended to confirm *creatio ex nihilo*.

160. Kant, *Critique*, p. 397.

161. See Gottfried Martin, *Kant's Metaphysics and Theory of Science*, trans. P. G. Lucas (Manchester: Manchester University Press, 1955; reprint ed., Westport, Conn.: Greenwood Press, 1974), p. 48. According to Martin, 'In this empty time before the beginning of the world there was the passage

of time, but no events.' (Ibid.) Accordingly, the antithesis asks why the world began at a certain point in time, when all moments are alike. (Sadik J. al-Azm, *The Origins of Kant's Arguments in the Antinomies* [Oxford: Clarendon Press, 1972], pp. 44–5.)

162. Whitrow, *Time*, p. 566; Whitrow, *Philosophy*, p. 32; G. J. Whitrow, 'The Age of the Universe,' *British Journal for the Philosophy of Science* 5 [1954]: 217.

163. Hospers objects that it makes no sense to speak of God's choosing from eternity to create because choice is always a temporal decision. (Hospers, *Introduction*, p. 433.) The objection is incorrect because choice does not imply changing one's mind, but is simply a determination of the mind to freely execute a certain course of action. Hence, it is perfectly intelligible to speak of God's choosing from eternity.

164. As that wise old man C. D. Broad remarks,

> On this relational view of time the question: 'Why did the world begin when it did, and not at some earlier or later moment?' would reduce to the question: 'Why did the particular event, which in fact had no predecessors, not have predecessors?' ... But I cannot help doubting whether it is a significant question, except in a rather special theistic context; and in that context the only answer is: 'God knows!'. (Broad, 'Antinomies', p. 7.)

More seriously, Sturch argues that God may eternally wish that a temporal world exist; since He is omnipotent, God's wish is done, and a temporal world exists. (R. L. Sturch, 'The Problem of Divine Eternity', *Religious Studies* 10 [1974]: 488–9.) On the question of whether God could have created the universe sooner, see Bas Van Fraassen, *An Introduction to the Philosophy of Time and Space* (New York: Random House, 1970), pp. 24–30.

165. Lucas, *Treatise*, pp. 3, 309.

166. Hackett, *Theism*, pp. 286–7. I think that it is within the context of Trinitarian theology that the personhood and timelessness of God may be most satisfactorily understood. For in the eternal and changeless love relationship between the persons of the Trinity, we see how a truly personal God could exist timelessly, entirely sufficient within Himself. Most writers who object to a timeless, personal God consider God only subsequent to creation as He is related to human persons, but fail to consider God prior to creation. (Eg., Nelson Pike, *God and Timelessness* [London: Routledge & Kegan Paul, 1970], pp. 121–9.) The former would appear to involve God in time, but the latter would not, for if God is tri-personal He has no need of temporal persons with whom to relate in order to enjoy personal relationships—the three persons of the Godhead would experience perfect and eternal communion and love with no necessity to create other persons. Thus, the answer to the question, 'What was God doing prior to creation?' is not the old gibe noted by Augustine: 'He was preparing hell for those who pry into mysteries'; but rather, 'He was enjoying the fullness of divine personal relationships, with an eternal determination for the temporal creation and salvation of human persons.' Why did God so determine? Perhaps to share the joy and love of divine fellowship with persons outside Himself

and so glorify Himself; on the other hand, perhaps we lack sufficient information to answer this question. Once these temporal persons were created, God would then begin to experience temporal personal relationships with them.

167. Sturch, 'Eternity', p. 492.

168. Thomas Aquinas *Summa theologiae* 1a. 13. 7. See also John Donnelly, 'Creatio ex nihilo', in *Logical Analysis and Contemporary Theism*, ed. John Donnelly (New York: Fordham University Press, 1972), pp. 210–11.

169. R. G. Swinburne, 'The Timelessness of God', *Church Quarterly Review* 166 (1965): 331.

170. This serves to effectively rebut the objection of Julian Wolfe to the *kalām* cosmological argument. (Julian Wolfe, 'Infinite Regress and the Cosmological Argument', *International Journal for Philosophy of Religion* 2 [1971]: 246–9. The crucial premiss is, in Wolfe's opinion, that an infinite time cannot elapse. He argues that this is incorrect because prior to causing the first effect, the uncaused cause existed for infinite time. Since the first event did occur, then an infinite time must have elapsed. But in the first place, Wolfe's formulation of the argument is defective, for the contention is that an infinite number of *events* cannot elapse, not that an infinite *time* cannot elapse. The Newtonian could hold that if God is changeless prior to creation, then an undifferentiated, measureless, infinite time could elapse before the first event, but that an infinite temporal series of definite and distinct events could not elapse. Because the argument concerns events, not time, Wolfe's analysis is inapplicable, since prior to creation there were no events at all. Second, if the relationist is correct, then an infinite time does not elapse prior to creation because time begins at creation. God is simply timeless before the first event. As Harris urges, 'A persistent state of affairs which is not contrasted with any series of changes, either internal or external to it . . . , could not be conceived as enduring . . . , because there would be nothing (no lapse) *through* which it could be thought to endure.' (Errol E. Harris, 'Time and Eternity', *Review of Metaphysics* 29 [1976]: 467.)

171. It might be objected that the argument does not prove the existence of a being who is truly and fully God. If the argument is sound, however, then it is true that *a personal Creator of the universe exists*. This remarkable conclusion is in no way diminished just because it has not also been proved that the Creator is all-good, omnipotent, omniscient, and so forth. To complain that such attributes have not also been proved is to show that one has not really appreciated what has been proved. I am reminded of those philosophers who casually dismiss the teleological argument without another thought because, they say, it proves only a designer of the universe, not a Creator. If they really believed that the argument proved that an actual being exists who designed the whole universe, they would be wide-eyed and open-mouthed at such a prospect, instead of complaining that the cosmic architect *may not* be the Creator. Similarly, having proved that a personal Creator of the universe exists, are we now to grumble because we do not know if he is omnipotent or omniscient? Should we not rather turn our theological objections into questions and ask whether the Creator is good, benevolent, and so forth? The theological objection has force only in seminary classrooms in which systematic theology is being discussed; there such a bare-boned

conception of God as the personal Creator of the universe would be inadequate. But the cosmological argument does not pretend to present a full-blown doctrine of God—if it did there would be nothing for the theologian to do. In fact I find the modesty of the *kalām* argument's conclusion one of its appealing features; the argument does not try to prove *too much*. I am very suspicious of marvellous arguments of natural theology which purport to prove from reason alone a whole catalogue of divine attributes. If theologians dogmatically insist, however, that only a being who is proved to be omnipotent, omniscient, and so forth, deserves to be called 'God', then it is of course true that the cosmological argument as I have presented it does not prove the existence of 'God'. I would be perfectly happy to say only that the argument shows that a personal Creator of the universe exists. We must then seek to discover by means of reason or revelation whether the Creator is good, omnipotent, and so forth. But I think I would also question the stipulation that the concept 'God' must include all the divine attributes. For biblically speaking, the concept of God simply as the personal Creator of the universe is an adequate, though not exhaustive, understanding of God. Thus, in drawing the essential difference between God and false gods, Jeremiah writes, '... The gods who did not make the heavens and the earth shall perish from the earth and from under the heavens.' (Jer.10.11) By contrast,

> But the LORD is the true God;
> . . . .
> It is he who made the earth by his power,
>   who established the world by his wisdom,
>   and by his understanding stretched out the heavens.

> (Jer.10.10,12)

In the same way, Isaiah exclaims, 'For thus says the LORD, / who created the heavens / (he is God!). . . .' (Is.45.18) And the Psalmist says,

> Before the mountains were brought forth,
>   or ever thou hadst formed the earth and the world,
>   from everlasting to everlasting thou art God.

> (Ps.90.2)

These and a host of similar passages seem to imply that to be the independent Creator of the universe is to be God. Indeed, when the biblical writers want to assert an attribute of God such as omnipotence or infinity, this is usually done by praising God as the Creator of all things in heaven and on earth. So I think that in proving that a personal Creator of the universe exists, we are justified in calling him God.

172. This is highly significant because it means that our argument cannot be discredited by anti-theistic appeals to the problem of evil. It is a point not often appreciated by philosophers of religion that the problem of evil is logically posterior to the question of theism. The problem of evil cannot disprove the existence of God, but only the goodness of God. Having shown that a personal Creator of the universe does exist, we may now ask, 'Is

He beneficent and good?' We leave that an open question in this thesis. Therefore, the objection of John Hick against what he calls probabilistic theistic arguments (i.e., arguments that claim plausibility rather than apodeictic certainty) does not apply. Hick contends that probability arguments for the existence of God must fail because there are no common scales in which to weigh the theistic and anti-theistic evidences against each other, for example the presence of order in the universe against the presence of evil. (John Hick, *Arguments for the Existence of God*, Philosophy of Religion Series [New York: Herder & Herder, 1971], pp. 30–3.) But such an objection has little force against the argument as we have expounded it. For while ours is what Hick would call a 'probability' argument—since we have not even tried to demonstrate the first premiss, but have appealed to its inherent reasonableness—what probative anti-theistic probabilities could be urged against it? The problem of evil is strictly irrelevant, since it concerns the moral nature, not the existence, of the Creator of the universe. The only probabilities pertinent to the argument are those contained in the argument itself. The anti-theist must attack head-on either the probability that the universe began to exist or the probability that everything that begins to exist has a cause of its existence. For if he grants that these are, in fact, probably true, he will have lost his case, since the main weapon in his arsenal, the problem of evil, is inapplicable. The attractive feature of the argument as we have expounded it is that it leaves the anti-theist a *way of escape*: he can always deny the first premiss and assert that the universe sprang into being uncaused out of nothing. But anti-theists will hardly beat themselves out the back door for this alternative, since it at once exposes them as men interested only in an academic refutation of the proof and not in really discovering the truth about the universe; for even the sceptical Hume considered it absurd that something should come to exist without a cause.

APPENDIX I
The *Kalām* Cosmological Argument and Zeno's Paradoxes

The problem of whether an actual infinite could be formed by successive addition plays a central role in modern philosophical discussions of the Zeno paradoxes. The most important paradoxes for our discussion are the 'Achilles and the Tortoise' and the 'Dichotomy'.[1] The first of these imagines a race between Achilles and a tortoise, in which the tortoise is given a head start. Zeno argues that Achilles will never catch the tortoise because he must run from his starting-point A to the tortoise's original starting point T_0. By the time Achilles reaches T_0, the tortoise will have moved on to T_1. And by the time Achilles reaches T_1, the tortoise will be at T_2, and so on.

$$\begin{array}{llll} \rule{6cm}{0.4pt} & & & \cdots \\ A & T_0 & T_1\ T_2 \end{array}$$

While Achilles will continually narrow the gap, he can never close it, and, hence, he will never overtake the tortoise. The 'Dichotomy' has two versions and makes essentially the same point as the Achilles paradox. In the first version, Achilles could never reach the end of any racecourse, tortoises or not, because before he can traverse the entire distance he must first cover half of it. Before he can cross the remaining half ot the course, he must cover half of the remainder. Before he can cover the remaining quarter of the track, he must cross half of that, and so on.

$$\begin{array}{llll} \rule{6cm}{0.4pt} & & & \\ A & \frac{1}{2} & \frac{3}{4} & \frac{7}{8}\ \cdots \end{array}$$

Again, though Achilles will approach closer and closer to the end of the course, he will never reach it, for a fraction of the distance, however infinitesimal, will always remain. The second version of the 'Dichotomy' asserts that Achilles could never even begin the race at all. For before he could run the entire distance, he must run half. Before he could run half, he must run a quarter, and so on.

$$A \quad \frac{1}{8} \quad \frac{1}{4} \qquad \frac{1}{2}$$

Thus, Achilles could never even move, for before he could move *any* distance, he must have traversed a portion of it already.

Contemporary discussions of the paradoxes have focused on the problem of completing an infinite number of tasks, and in order to demonstrate the absurdity of such a feat, sometimes called a 'super-task', various philosophers have concocted 'infinity machines' which are purported to be able to perform super-tasks.[2] Thus, Max Black, noting that the logical difficulty in the paradoxes is that Achilles is called upon to perform an infinite series of tasks, namely, traversing an infinite number of finite distances, sets out to prove that the notion of 'infinite series of acts' is self-contradictory.[3] To demonstrate this he envisages an infinity machine designed to move an infinite number of marbles from one tray to another. To eliminate the time factor, he imagines that the machine, called Alpha, transfers the first marble in one minute and rests a minute, transfers the second marble in a half-minute and rests a half-minute, transfers the next marble in a quarter-minute and rests a quarter-minute, and so on, until the transfers are but a blur, so rapidly does the machine work. At the end of four minutes the tray formerly containing the infinite number of marbles is empty and the formerly empty tray is now full. But now, says Black, let us envision a second infinity machine Beta which works just like Alpha except that it has only one marble to move and each time it moves the marble, some device returns it to its original tray. Suppose further that Beta works at exactly the same rate as Alpha; each time Alpha moves a marble, Beta moves its marble (which is immediately returned to the original tray to await its next transposition).

This makes it obvious, Black argues, that Alpha cannot really exist. For Beta could never complete an infinite series of transferences, since every time the marble is moved it is returned, and nothing is accomplished. It is like a man trying to plug three holes with two pegs: no matter how fast he goes, he can never fill all the holes, since each move creates a new vacancy. Or again, it is like Hercules trying to cut off the heads of the Hydra, which grows back a head every time one is decapitated. No matter how fast Hercules cuts, it does no good because the heads are always replaced. Therefore, Beta could not complete an infinite number of moves, and since its every movement correlated to those of Alpha, neither could Alpha. Someone might object that if at the end of four minutes, the marble was in the right-hand tray, this is proof that Beta has succeeded. But Black creates a third machine Gamma to discount this possibility. Suppose the device which returns Beta's marble each time is another infinity machine which works just like Beta but in the opposite direction. Whenever Beta moves the marble, Gamma moves it right back again when Beta is resting. Now at the end of four minutes' operation, asks Black, *where is the marble?* Every time Beta moved it Gamma moved it back, and every time Gamma moved it Beta moved it back. So at the end of four minutes, the marble may be on the right or the left or nowhere. The contradiction, Black concludes, lies in the fact that the machine violates the continuity of space and motion. For there would have to be an infinitely fast motion at some point in the transpositions. Therefore, Black states, the notion of an infinite series of acts is self-contradictory. The solution to the Achilles paradox lies in the fact that Achilles does not actually perform an infinite number of tasks; the distance traversed is only conceptually infinitely divisible, but is not infinitely divided in reality.

James Thomson has urged similar considerations.[4] Suppose one has a desk lamp that is switched on and off by the press of a button. If the lamp is originally off and the button is pressed an odd number of times, then the lamp is on, but if an even number of times, the lamp is off. Now suppose one presses the button once in a minute, again in the next half-minute, and so on. At the end of two minutes, *is the lamp on or off?* The lamp must be either on or off, but every time the lamp was turned on, it was turned off, and *vice versa.*

So the lamp cannot be either on or off—which is self-contradictory. Thomson suggests a second illustration: suppose there were a machine operating in the same way as described above which recorded the decimal expansion of π and a second machine that records the parity of the numbers written down by use of a dial that registers 0 or 1. At the end of two minutes, what would the dial read?

Black and Thomson's articles drew sharp criticism. Richard Taylor charged Black with a 'self-inconsistent notion of "an infinite collection" viz., that of a collection which . . . both has and has not a last member'.[5] For Beta could move the marble infinitely many times in the allotted time and the fact that the marble should be in its original tray after an infinite number of transpositions is not remarkable. Black assumes that there must be an end to all counting, a last member of the collection, but this is not so. This assumes Beta must reach an 'infinitieth' number. But it may move the marble infinitely many times and still be ready to count some more. No 'infinitieth' operation need be accomplished. In the Beta-Gamma arrangement Black again assumes there must be an 'infinitieth' number of moves that must be completed. According to Taylor, an infinite number of tasks could certainly be performed if each successive task took half the time of its predecessor. J. Watling also criticised Black on similar grounds.[6] He argues that to finish a number of tasks is not do do a last task, but simply to do them all. The difficulty is not that Black assumes a last task, as Taylor charges, but that he assumes that performing all of the tasks entails performing a last one; since the infinite has no last member, then were this assumption true, it would be impossible to complete an infinite number of tasks. But Taylor is correct in pointing out that one can do all the tasks without doing a last one; hence, a super-task could be completed. The way to finish an infinite number of tasks is to start and not stop after any finite number. The problem with the Hercules illustration is not that completing an infinite series is impossible, but that here one cannot stop without having logical incompatibilities. Three things may prevent completion of an infinite task: (1) not enough time; (2) no chance of stopping without logical incompatibilities, and (3) if every act requires the performance of a next. But an infinite sequence of acts such as Achilles performs can be completed. If his race can be described by saying he travels $\frac{1}{2} + \frac{1}{4} + \frac{1}{8} + \ldots$, then since the sum of this series is 1, Achilles can finish his course. The point is that all the tasks may be completed without a last one's having been performed.

Paul Benacerraf criticised Thompson's argument because whether the lamp is on or off at the first instant after the completion of the super-task is irrelevant to the possibility of the task's being performed.[7] It is only true of instants before this that the lamp was turned off after being turned on and *vice versa*. The point is that the limit of the series is not in the series, just as the limit of the series $\frac{1}{2}$, $\frac{1}{4}$, $\frac{1}{8}$, ... is not in the series. Therefore, what occurs in the series of off-on switchings does not entail that the lamp is on or off when the instant after the series is completed is reached. What Thomson has done is to confuse the instant $\omega + 1$ with an 'ωth' instant and ask what is the state of the lamp. But the condition of the lamp at $\omega + 1$ cannot be deduced from any sequence of operations in the ω type series. Benacerraf goes on to argue that we can imagine a situation in which all the points in an ω type series have been occupied by a thing, but the $\omega + 1$ point is never occupied because the thing ceases to exist the instant the ω type series is completed. Thomson would have to show a logical connection between $\omega + 1$ and the ω type series in order to prove that the condition of the lamp at $\omega + 1$ is a logical consequence to the ω type series. As for the π machine, the problem here is that it attempts to assign a value to the 'ωth' member of the decimalisation of π, but π has no 'ωth' digit at all. Therefore, Thomson fails to show that a completed infinite series of tasks is impossible. Adolf Grünbaum urges the same considerations.[8] Thomson assumes it to be a matter of logic that the description of a sequence of acts of order type ω must be determinate with respect to the character of the outcome at $\omega + 1$. The fallacy is that he is trying to deduce a conclusion about the state of affairs at an instant following a progression from information pertaining only to states of affairs within the progression. With regard to Black's machines, the discontinuity that results from their operation can be eliminated by having the distance between the trays also shrink in a convergent process as the marbles are moved.[9] Thus, at the end of four minutes, the centres of mass of all the marbles shifted by Alpha will be to the right of the line where the trays touch, and the centre of mass of Beta's single marble will rest on the line of contact between the trays. But at any rate, the deduction that the marble could not be in the right-hand tray is fallacious because, as in the case of Thompson's lamp, one is trying to deduce the state of affairs at $\omega + 1$ from information that applies only to events in the ω type series itself.

Under the force of objections such as these Black and Thomson surrendered their case. Black confesses that he erred in not making the distances crossed by the marbles as they are moved converge along with the time allotted for each transposition.[10] If every physical magnitude connected with a hypothetical process converged, then no discontinuity would result at the process's end. Otherwise a bouncing ball would never come to rest in a finite time! Thomson admits that his argument was 'worthless' because of the fallacy of considering the lamp's state at $\omega + 1$ to be deducible from information in the series itself.[11]

Thomson and Black gave up too easily. It always seems a bit dangerous to attempt to resuscitate an argument pronounced dead by even its original exponents, but in this case the risk seems to be worth it. Before we make the attempt, however, it is important to realise that the failure of Black and Thomson to show the impossibility of completing an infinite number of tasks does not prove that such a performance is possible. Critics of Black and Thomson grant that the possibility of completing an infinite series of tasks has not been demonstrated. Bearing this in mind, we believe that Black and Thomson pointed in the right direction for showing the absurdity of completing a super-task, though they did not make it clear why such a task is impossible. The reason a super-task cannot be performed is because it would involve the performance of an 'infinitieth' task, which is absurd. This can be made evident by a consideration of Benacerraf and Grünbaum's objection that the state of the lamp or position of the marble at $\omega + 1$ is not a *logical* consequence of the rules governing the events in the ω type series. This objection is certainly true in the mathematical realm. But in the *real* world, the state of the lamp at $\omega + 1$ will be determined by the state of the lamp at the prior instant, which would be the 'infinitieth' moment in the series.[12] Benacerraf is wrong in asserting that Thomson must show that the lamp at $\omega + 1$ is *logically* determined by the states of the lamp in the ω type series. What Thomson must show is that the state of the lamp at $\omega + 1$ is *causally* determined by the states of the lamp in the ω type series. Benacerraf's fallacy is the one so often committed in discussions of this sort, that of assimilating the real world to the mathematical realm. In the mathematical realm, there are no such relations as causal relations; only logical implications operate. So while it is true that in the realm of abstract mathematical entities $\omega + 1$ is not determined by an 'ωth' moment, it must be so in the real world of things. In the mathematical realm there can be no 'infinitieth' member in a set with the ordinal number ω; as we said earlier, ω is not the terminus of the series, but stands outside of and above the whole series, informing us as to how it is ordered. Thus, in a set $\{1, 2, 3, \ldots, 1, 2, 3, \ldots\}$ the second number one is in no way connected with what has gone before; it is not a logical consequence of the ω type series. But in the real world, there must be an 'infinitieth' event which contains the necessary and sufficient conditions for the existence of the $\omega + 1$ event. The lamp's being on or off at any instant is *causally* determined by the event of the prior instant. If the lamp is on at $\omega + 1$ then it was on at the 'ωth' instant since no more switchings were made after that. But being on at the 'ωth' moment means the lamp was off at the immediately prior instant. Such an instant must exist since we are talking about a series each of whose members is causally connected throughout. Benacerraf's argument works only if there is no 'infinitieth' moment and no 'infinitieth' switching of the lamp. But there must be such because the states of the lamp are causally connected. Only for atomists such as the *mutakallimūn* or occasionalists such as Malebranche could Benacerraf's argument work. He constantly appeals to mathematical examples to prove his case, but these are irrelevant, since physical events are strung together in causal series, not atomically separated like mathematical points on a line or fractions converging toward a limit. Of course in a series like $\frac{1}{2}, \frac{3}{4}, \frac{7}{8}, \ldots$ the number one is not a logical consequence of the series; but in the real world, there must be an immediate predecessor to the event corresponding to one, otherwise the event 'one' would not occur. As John Wisdom nicely observes, the mathematical argument fails when it comes to the dots, or the 'and so on'.[13] Even if the lamp were to vanish at $\omega + 1$, we may still ask what was its state at the 'ωth' instant. For such an instant is necessary if the existence of the lamp at $\omega + 1$ is only possible, not actual; that is to say, it is possible for the lamp not to vanish, and even this possibility requires the existence of an 'infinitieth' event in the series. Besides, as we shall see further, if the lamp vanished at $\omega + 1$, and there was no 'ωth' event, then we could not say an actually infinite number of events had occurred. But the overriding point is that Benacerraf's objection only works if we assimilate the real world to the realm of mathematical entities where causal relations give way to logical implications. The same analysis applies to the Beta machine. Granting that the marble will come to rest on the line of contact between the two converging trays, it is clear that in the real world its position at $\omega + 1$ will be the result of an 'infinitieth' transposition which supplied the determinate conditions fixing its position at $\omega + 1$. The real absurdity involved in an infinity machine, then, is that it would necessitate the performance of an 'infinitieth' task, which is impossible.

To make this clearer, let us return to Black's Alpha machine. If Alpha actually transferred a definite and distinct infinite collection of marbles one by one, then it must have transferred a last marble, which would be the 'infinitieth' member of the collection. Watling's suggestion that the machine could complete all the tasks without performing a last task is nonsensical.[14] For in the present case the only way of completing all the tasks is by completing each task one by one. Thus, to complete all the tasks a last task would have to be performed. Although Watling rather glibly informs us that '... the way to finish an infinite number is to start and not stop after any finite number', he does not explain how this can be done successively.[15] All he shows is that an infinite number of finite additions would equal an infinite sum.[16] But this is unremarkable. All it amounts to saying is what is a common tenet of set theory, that a denumerable number of finite sets forms a set that is itself denumerable. But the question is, could such a set be *formed* by successive addition? And here, set theory contains another tenet which states that the answer is no: a finite set added to another finite set is always a finite set.[17] An actually infinite set is made up of an infinite number of finite sets, but it is never formed by adding these finite sets together. Watling's suggestion is of no help at all in explaining how to form an actual infinite by successive addition. To do so would necessitate adding an 'infinitieth' element, which is absurd. Nor can any sense be made of Taylor's contention that Beta can move the marble infinitely many times without making an 'infinitieth' move. For to have completed an infinite number of definite and distinct moves in succession is to have completed every single one of them. Therefore, to have completed infinitely many moves would be to have performed a last move, an 'infinitieth' move. This is not to say that an actual infinite has an 'infinitieth' member. We could speak abstractly of the infinite set of all marbles or the infinite set of all moves without supposing an 'infinitieth' member, but to try to instantiate these abstract entities in reality one at a time would be impossible, for then one would reach an instant in which the last possible entity was translated into reality, and this would be the 'infinitieth' member of the set. As long as one is proceeding one at a time, and instantiates one marble the first minute, the next marble in a half-minute, the next marble in a quarter-minute, and so on, then to complete the super-task one must instantiate an 'infinitieth' marble—otherwise the task is not complete.[18]

To make the necessity of an 'infinitieth' marble even clearer, let us introduce an innovation to Black's Alpha machine. Suppose the tray full of marbles to be transferred ascends as it goes away from the machine so that the marbles will roll down as each one at the bottom is taken and transferred. And suppose the empty tray ready to receive the marbles descends as it recedes into the distance so that the marbles will roll down it as it gradually fills up. Before the machine starts we can see the first marble at the bottom of the left-hand tray ready to be transferred. In the next four minutes the infinity of marbles is moved. And now what do we see? Lying at the top of the right-hand tray is the last, the 'infinitieth' marble to be transferred.

Suppose now we invent an infinity machine of our own—a machine that counts the marbles as Alpha moves them. What will be the number registering on the machine after the four minutes of transpositions are complete? Clearly, no such number is possible, since it could always be increased by one. It would not do to say the machine registered ω or $\aleph_0$, since these have no immediate predecessors as do marbles. Nor would it do any good to say with Benacerraf that the number machine and everything else vanished at $\omega + 1$. For the number machine counted all the marbles, such that when all the marbles were transferred the machine had counted up the total number, the end of the process of transfers and the end of the computation are simultaneous. So even if the machine vanishes at $\omega + 1$ so that we cannot read the 'infinitieth' number, the machine still recorded it, and God knows what it is.[19]

But forget Alpha altogether. Suppose our number machine looks something like the odometer of a car, having an infinite number of window slots in which numbers can appear. The machine counts '1' in the first minute and so on. At the end of four minutes it will have recorded the 'infinitieth' number. We could never read this number, for it would be infinitely long, stretching away into the distance. But we can look at the last few digits at our end. Will the 'infinitieth' number be odd or even? Either is absurd, for it could always be increased by one. It is therefore impossible to have an 'infinitieth' number. Hence, such a machine could not exist. More than that, this proves that *no infinity machine could exist.* For any infinity machine could be hooked up to our number machine, which would count each task it performs. If the machine performs an infinite number of tasks one at a time, then our counter will register an 'infinitieth' number, which is impossible. Therefore, all infinity machines are impossible.

Therefore, it is impossible to form an actual infinite by successive addition. Those who believe that infinity machines are possible are trying to transform a potential infinite into an actual infinite by counting. And this obviously cannot be done, as the two are conceptually distinct. An actual infinite is a determinate and completed totality: a potential infinite can be increased *limitlessly*—no matter how much one adds, one can never arrive at an actual infinity. This becomes even more obvious when one returns to the normal rate of events in the world. For what the above arguments prove is not just the impossibility of performing an infinite number of tasks in a finite time, but the impossibility of performing them at all. As Black observes, '. . . if some cosmic bully were to say "Here is an infinite collection; go ahead and count it," only logical confusion could lead me to mutter "Too difficult; not enough time".'[20] Even given *infinite* time, the super-task could not be performed.[21]

Thus, if we were to come upon a man who tells us that he has been transferring marbles from one tray to another from eternity past and that he is now finishing this super-task, we will know him to be a liar. For (1) then he would have completed an actual infinite by successive addition, which is impossible because you can always add one more, and (2) as we saw with Tristram Shandy, the man's task would have always been done, and hence never been done, which is contrary to our seeing him doing it now. This goes to show that the temporal series of past events cannot be an actual infinite. If it were, it would correspond to the second version of the Dichotomy paradox, where to be at any point, Achilles must, in Black's words, 'have travelled along the series of points from the infinitely distant and *open* "end". . . . This is an even more astounding feat than the one he accomplishes in winning the race against the tortoise.'[22] For the set of all past events to have been both formed by successive addition and to be an actual infinite is thus absurd.

NOTES

1. My summaries are taken from Wesley C. Salmon, Introduction to *Zeno's Paradoxes*, ed. Wesley C. Salmon (Indianapolis and New York: Bobbs–Merrill Co., 1970), pp. 8–10.

2. Modern discussions of the paradoxes grow out of a suggestion by Russell that purely physical limitations aside, a person could count all the natural numbers if he counted the first in one minute, the second in a half-minute, the third in a quarter-minute, and so on. At the end of two minutes all the numbers would be counted. Bertrand Russell, 'The Limits of Empiricism', *Proceedings of the Aristotelian Society* 36 (1935–6): 143–4.

The concept of infinity machines stems from a comment by Hermann Weyl that the divisibility of the number continuum is potential only, for otherwise one could construct a machine that could complete an infinite number of acts of decision in a finite time, which Weyl apparently regarded as self-evidently ridiculous. (Hermann Weyl, *Philosophy of Mathematics and Natural Science*, rev. ed., trans. Olaf Helmer [Princeton: Princeton University Press, 1949], p. 42.)

3. Max Black, 'Achilles and the Tortoise', *Analysis* 11 (1950–51): 91–101.

4. J. F. Thomson, 'Tasks and Super-Tasks', *Analysis* 15 (1954–55): 1–13.

5. Richard Taylor, 'Mr. Black on Temporal Paradoxes', *Analysis* 12 (1951–52): 30.

6. J. Watling, 'The Sum of an Infinite Series', *Analysis* 13 (1952–53): 39–46.

7. Paul Benacerraf, 'Tasks, Super-Tasks, and the Modern Eleatics', in *Paradoxes*, ed. Salmon, pp. 103–29.

8. Adolf Grünbaum, 'Modern Science and Zeno's Paradoxes of Motion', in *The Philosophy of Time*, ed. Richard M. Gale (London and Melbourne: Macmillan, 1968), pp. 477–90. Grünbaum lays primary emphasis on kinematic objections to infinity machines, but these are not strictly relevant to our discussion.

9. Ibid., pp. 490–3.

10. Max Black, 'Is Achilles Still Running?' in *Problems of Analysis*, by Max Black (London: Routledge & Kegan Paul), p. 115.

11. James Thomson, 'Comments on Professor Benacerraf's Paper', in *Paradoxes*, ed. Salmon, p. 130.

12. Bostock argues correctly that the absurdity involved in this case is not a logical absurdity; rather the problem is that the final state at $\omega + 1$ is completely *uncaused*. A curve plotting the sequence of operations would be discontinuous, and the state $\omega + 1$ could not be connected to prior states on the curve. This is 'repugnant to our idea of causality in nature' and involves 'a discontinuity in nature'. (David Bostock, 'Aristotle, Zeno, and the Potential Infinite', *Proceedings of the Aristotelian Society* 73 [1972–73]: 49–51.) Actually, the true problem is a dilemma: either there is an infinitieth member in the ω type series or there is a discontinuity in nature and the state of $\omega + 1$ is uncaused. Proponents of infinity machines may take their pick. We shall show, however, that it is the first horn of the dilemma that disqualifies all infinity machines. Bostock unfortunately fails to see this and assimilates the physical to the mathematical world in his article by employing Black's example of the bouncing ball. For a real ball is never perfectly resilient and so never bounces an infinite number of times before coming to rest.

13. J. O. Wisdom, 'Why Achilles Does Not Fail to Catch the Tortoise', *Mind* 50 (1941): 72. Of all the various writers, Wisdom most clearly discerns the assimilation of the physical to the mathematical world as the root of the difficulty. Thus, he argues that mathematical points have no counterpart in the physical world, that a physical distance cannot be really geometrically divided, and that there are not an infinite number of physical points in a finite distance. Therefore Achilles is not required to complete an actually infinite number of tasks. (Ibid., pp. 61, 71; J. O. Wisdom, 'Achilles on a Physical racecourse', *Analysis* 12 [1951–52]: 69–70. See also Hermann Weyl, *The Open World* [New Haven, Conn.: Yale University Press, 1932], p. 59; Antonio Moreno, 'Calculus and Infinitesimals: A Philosophical Evaluation', *Angelicum* 52 [1975]: 243.) Taylor rejoins that no such assimilation of the physical to the mathematical takes place. It is just a plain fact that to cover a whole distance you must first cover a part, and this can go on *ad infinitum*. Therefore, in traversing a distance Achilles performs infinitely many tasks. (Richard Taylor, 'Mr. Wisdom on Temporal Paradoxes', *Analysis* 13 [1952–53]: 15–17.) But Taylor misses the point that this cannot go on *ad infinitum*: there really are physically minimum distances that can only be conceptually divisible. That Taylor continues to assimilate the physical to the mathematical is evident in his remark that Wisdom's reasoning means there cannot be an infinite number of fractions, all having some size, packed

in between zero and one. Does Taylor imagine the 'size' of a fraction to be like the 'size' of a physical object?

14. See Eugene TeHennepe, 'Language Reform and Philosophical Imperialism: Another Round with Zeno', *Analysis* 23 (1962–63): 44, 47–8.

15. Watling, 'Sum', p. 40.

16. Ibid., p. 45.

17. Alexander Abian, *The Theory of Sets and Transfinite Arithmetic* (Philadelphia and London: W. B. Saunders Co., 1965), p. 249.

18. This is essentially the point made by Charles S. Chihara, 'On the Possibility of Completing an Infinite Process', *Philosophical Review* 74 (1965): 74–87. See also A. P. Ushenko, 'Zeno's Paradoxes', *Mind* 55 (1946): 156.

19. In fact, to forestall Grünbaum's inevitable kinematic objections to our number machine, we may replace it with an infinite mind which counts the marbles as they are moved. This person would know the 'infinitieth' number of the last marble to be moved.

20. Black, 'Achilles and the Tortoise', p. 96. Black later changed his mind. He says that at best he has only proved that an infinite number of tasks cannot be performed *in a finite time*.

> . . . nothing in the original essay could show that there is anything absurd in the notion of an immortal (with all time at his disposal) continuing to shift marbles *ad infinitum*. (For now there is no end to the series of acts and so no question about the final location of the marble.) (Black, 'Is Achilles Still Running?' p. 116.)

Black fails to see that in such a potentially infinite series, an infinity of marbles would never be moved. But if the immortal were working from eternity, the series would have an end, and the question of the marble's final location would have to be raised.

21. In a brief but very confused article Fred I. Dretske argues that if George begins to count and never stops then he will count to infinity. For if he never quits he will count all the finite numbers, and since these are infinite in number, he will count to infinity. Dretske makes the qualification that George will never *have* counted to infinity because there will always be numbers left to count, but only that he *will* count to infinity. But what if George has been counting from eternity past? Dretske is rather baffled here: it does not seem to make sense, and it means that George has *always* been finished—we can never find him finishing. Also George will never count $\aleph_0$, because $\aleph_0$ is not a member of the natural numbers. Finally, Dretske confesses George will never reach the limit toward which he is aspiring. (Fred I. Dretske, 'Counting to Infinity', *Analysis* 25 [1964–65]: 99–101.) Dretske capitalises on ambiguous use of terms. George will never arrive at infinity; therefore the set of all numbers counted will not be an actual infinite. He will never count $\aleph_0$, but if he never does that, he will not count to an actual infinity. In what sense then is George going to count 'to infinity?'—only in the sense that he will count 'forever', or 'without limit'. Besides, if George will count to infinity, then if he has been counting from infinity, he will have finished. Dretske is right that this makes no sense, but he fails to see that if George has always been finished, then

he was never actually counting, which is contradictory to the hypothesis. This goes to show that the notion of an actually infinite temporal series of events is absurd. George will count forever only because the future, unlike the past, spawns a potential infinite.

22. Black, 'Achilles and the Tortoise', p. 94.

APPENDIX 2
The *Kalām* Cosmological Argument and the Thesis of Kant's First Antinomy

A second body of literature relevant to our argument that the universe had a beginning because an actual infinite cannot be formed by successive addition is that which has grown up around the thesis of Kant's first antinomy, which argues that the world must be finite in time and space. Although the finitude of the universe in space need not concern us, Kant's proof that the world had a beginning in time is very much like ours: Kant wants to prove that 'the world has a beginning in time', and he writes,

> If we assume that the world has no beginning in time, then up to every given moment an eternity has elapsed and there has passed away in the world an infinite series of successive states of things. Now the infinity of a series consists in the fact that it can never be completed through successive synthesis. It thus follows that it is impossible for an infinite world-series to have passed away, and that a beginning of the world is therefore a necessary condition of the world's existence.[1]

In his observations on the first antinomy, Kant attempts to clarify his concept of the infinite. He rejects the definition of the infinite as a magnitude that cannot be added to.[2] Instead, the true transcendental concept of infinitude is a quantum that cannot be enumerated by successive synthesis of units.[3]

This quantum would satisfy the mathematical definition of infinite as well, since it would contain a quantity of given units greater than any number.

In this proof it is not altogether clear whether Kant is arguing concerning the temporal series of events or concerning temporal states of the universe apart from events. In the first case, he would not have proved an absolute beginning of the universe, but only a relative beginning of events; in the second case, he would run into the problem that temporal states could each be instantaneous moments of time, so that an infinite number could elapse between any two points in time. As we examine the antinomy more closely, it becomes evident that Kant is not arguing for a beginning of time itself, but for a beginning of the universe *in* time.[4] Kant here conceives of time in an absolute, Newtonian sense as a continuum in which events exist, but which itself exists independently of events. This is even more evident in the antithesis, where he speaks of time's still existing prior to the beginning of the world. Such a view of time seems to imply that in the thesis Kant is speaking of temporal states as determined by the series of events. The states of time are differentiated by the events occurring in time. Kant is thus arguing that there cannot be an infinite regress of temporal states because there cannot be an infinite regress of events. But why not? The reason seems to be that before the present event/state can occur, there must elapse an infinite number of prior events/states one by one (successively). Hence, an infinite series of events would have to be enumerated by successive synthesis. To illustrate: imagine a set labelled 'the class of all events'. As each event in the world's history takes place, it becomes a member of that class. For the present event to occur, an infinite number of prior events would have had to occur, if the world had no beginning. But then the class of all events would be an actually infinite set formed by successive addition, which is absurd. Therefore, the world must have had a beginning.

According to A. C. Ewing, the principle common to the thesis in each antinomy is that the conditioned presupposes all its conditions, and the common pattern of argument is:

The conditioned can only arise when its conditions are complete.

If they are infinite they can never be complete.
∴ They cannot be infinite.[5]

The problem of the thesis concerns the notion of the *completed*
infinite, not just the notion of the infinite. As Ewing points
out, that is why there is no antinomy about future events,
since this series may never be completed nor is it the condition
of the present event.[6]

Kant's argument for the beginning of the universe has come
under a continual barrage of criticism. Norman Kemp Smith
argues that if the infinite is that which can never be completed,
then the correct conclusion of the argument is that the temporal
series is always completed, always actually infinite, and that
no point or event is nearer to the beginning or end than
any other.[7] We may select any point from which to start a
regress, but because the series is actually infinite, the regress
will never be completed. Thus, there is no justification for
saying at any point the series has completed itself. The series
is 'coming out of an inexhaustible past and passing into an
equally inexhaustible future'.[8] Time is by nature infinite, alike
in its past and future, and the present is 'a transition from
the infinite through the infinite to the infinite'.[9]

> That we cannot comprehend how, from an infinitude that
> has no beginning, the present should ever have been reached,
> is no sufficient reason for denying what by the very nature
> of time we are compelled to accept as a correct description
> of the situation which is being analysed.[10]

What holds of time also holds of events in time. If time is
infinite, no proof can be derived from it to prove the world
had a beginning in time. Moreover, the reference to successive
synthesis gives a 'needlessly subjectivist colouring' to the proof.[11]
Finally, the proof limits itself to past time only, which is misleading.

Russell's notorious critique of the Kantian proof charges Kant
with a definitional mistake of infinity.[12] The notion of infinity
is primarily a property of classes and only derivatively applicable
to series. And classes are given all at once by virtue of the
defining property for membership; no completion or successive
synthesis is required. Russell, like Kemp Smith, sees in this

a 'reference to mind by which all Kant's philosophy was infected'.[13] Second, all Kant proves is that an infinite series cannot be completed by successive synthesis in a finite time—which only goes to show that if the world had no beginning it must have existed for infinite time. Why did Kant make this elementary blunder? According to Russell, Kant imagined the series of events starting at the present and going back into the past and tried to grasp these in a successive synthesis in the reverse order to that in which they had occurred. Naturally he could not do this, for so considered the series has no end. But the series of events up to the present has an end, right now. 'Owing to the inveterate subjectivism of his mental habits', Kant confused the two series, identifying the mental series which has no end with the physical series which has an end but no beginning, and thus he was led to attribute validity to 'a singularly flimsy piece of fallacious reasoning'.[14] Later Russell remarks that Kant believed it was harder for the past to be infinite than for the future to be so because the past is completed and nothing infinite can be completed.[15] Russell muses that there is no sense in this, and that Kant must have believed it because he was thinking of the infinite as the 'unended'. But, of course, the future has one end and is 'precisely on a level with the past'.[16]

Elsewhere Russell attacks Kant's thesis as failing to understand the use of the class concept.[17] Kant supposes that the events preceding a given event ought to be definable by extension, which, if their number is infinite, is obviously not the case. Russell here thinks that by successive synthesis Kant means enumeration, which is, he admits, *practically* impossible for an infinite series. But the class may still be definable, and the question then is whether the class is finite or infinite. And there is nothing self-contradictory about an infinite class. Russell observes that Kant regards the previous events as causes of the later ones and that the cause is supposed to be logically prior to the effect; so stated, he admits, 'this argument would, I think, be valid'.[18] But, he adds, we shall find later that cause and effect are on the same logical level. Therefore, the thesis of the first antinomy must be rejected as false.

One very typical objection to Kant's argument is that the fact that the series of events has an end does not mean that it is therefore finite. Thus, G. E. Moore urges that just because the series has an end in the present does not mean it is finite; 'all that we mean by calling it infinite is that it has no end in the other direction or, in other words, no beginning.'[19] More recently, P. F. Strawson writes that the fact that the series has a final member only means that it either has or has not a first member; the second alternative is correct, and the series is infinite.[20] Kant was deceived by comparing the series with counting; to count one must have a beginning, but in this series there is no beginning.

C. D. Broad dislikes Kant's definition of the infinite:

It drags in a reference to an operation to be performed by someone in a sequence of steps, and it defines the infinity of a quantum in terms of the impossibility of completing that operation in any time, however long.[21]

That the time factor is extraneous is seen from the fact that no *number* of units of finite length could span an infinite line even if the measuring rod of that length were to be instantaneously applied to the line and there was no interval between successive measurements. The problem with Kant's argument is that Kant treats time like space. To have successive synthesis in space is to apply a measuring rod successively along its co-existent parts. But with time succession is intrinsic to the process. Kant, however, imagines time to be extended, and starting from the present he seeks to apply extrinsic synthesis of the units backwards. But such a picture of time is untenable because then we could ask how fast the events are flowing by, which is meaningless. At any rate, the result of such measurement might be that for any finite number, there was already a world before that.

R. G. Swinburne revives Aquinas's response to the proponents of *kalām* in order to discredit Kant's thesis.[22] In considering a series, we normally suppose a first member identified and then proceed to examine the other members or the sum. In this case a completed infinity does seem impossible. What if one has a series with a last member, but no first member? Swinburne admits that it is dubious whether such a series makes sense, but if it could exist, then the impossibility of a completed infinite series is no longer obvious. If, as seems more natural, we consider the series to be a series of causes, not effects, and if we begin at the present as the first member of the series, then we may regress back and back, and the series would have no last member and would therefore not be a completed infinite.

P. J. Zwart argues that the two questions of whether the series of events has a beginning and whether it has an end are clearly equivalent such that if one of the alternatives is possible, then the other is as well.[23] He therefore argues that Kant assumed in advance what he set out to prove, that there was a first event.[24] For an infinite number of past events is impossible only if there was a first event—this would mean there is no latest event, which is manifestly untrue. Kant assumes there was a first event, sees there is a latest event, and concludes the series of events is finite. But when we say past time is infinite, this means that when we go back in the series of events, starting from now, we never reach its beginning. In the same way the infinity of the future should be defined as the fact that the series of future events has no last member. In fact, observes Zwart, Kant would have to prove that there will be a last event as well as a first to prove that time is finite. The situation is completely symmetrical: the present event is an event somewhere in a series of events which has neither beginning nor end.

The weakness of these objections is quite amazing, considering the stature of their proponents. Norman Kemp Smith has done exactly what Broad accuses Kant of doing, namely, spatialising time. He obviously conceives of time as somehow stretched out like a line, infinite in both directions. No wonder he cannot understand why Kant concerns himself entirely with the past! For Kemp Smith the past and the future coexist and the series of events is somehow moving through it. Smith has succeeded in eliminating entirely the successive nature of time so stressed by Broad. In other words, time and the events in it are like an actual infinite; the whole class of events and moments are given simultaneously, as Russell would say. Conceived in this way, Kemp Smith's objections are absolutely correct: if one is landed in a Cantorian infinite set at any point, then a regress or progress will be infinite and uncompletable. This would be like dropping into the set {. . . −3, −2, −1, 0, 1, 2, 3, . . .} and trying to reach a beginning or end. In such a case, successive synthesis would be irrelevant, since all the members coexist. And it would be true that at any point, the series is always complete and always infinite. But, of course, such a picture is a crude caricature of time. For events in time, unlike events in space, exist serially, and the events of the future are simply events that have not happened yet. Therefore, we do stand at one end of a series that is constantly being completed; the collection of all past events. Every new event completes and increases the size of this collection. It is a collection, in other words, being formed by successive addition or, to use Kant's phrase, successive synthesis. When the temporal series of events is so understood, Kemp Smith's assertion that it is *always* infinite reveals the very absurdity of an infinite temporal regress of events. For if the series or collection of events is *always* infinite, it cannot have been formed by successive addition. It would be just given at some point, which is absurd, being contrary to the nature of time. For though God could create the universe *ex nihilo* with the appearance of age, even He could not create the world *ex nihilo* actually having a past, to say nothing of an infinite past. But this is the only way a series of events could be formed, if it is to be *always* actually infinite. If it is formed by successive addition, it will have to be a potential infinite. This is the same problem we encountered with Tristram Shandy and again with Zeno, for at any spot on the series of past events an infinity of past events has already transpired. There is thus a surd, given infinite collection of events in the series, which is a self-contradiction because the series occurs sequentially in time. But we have strayed from Kant's argument. He argues that the present event could never exist because it can occur only when all its determinate conditions are given. But if the series of past events is infinite, all the conditions would never be given. For it is impossible to complete an infinite series (of conditions) by successive addition. Notice that Kemp Smith is impotent to explain how the present event could occur; he even admits it is incomprehensible. But he asserts that the nature of time requires that the series of events be infinite. We shall show later that this is plainly false.

Russell's objections are fairly easily disposed of. First, there is no definitional error involved in speaking of a series as infinite. Such a series is one that has an actually infinite number of members. Even should we speak primarily of classes as infinite or finite, we may speak of the class of all the members of a series as actually infinite. But while the abstract class may be given all at once, the *series* is not: it is sequentially instantiated in the real world. Therefore, completion by successive synthesis is required of a temporal series. Far from smacking of subjectivism, Kant's reference to successive synthesis concerns the real way in which a temporal series comes to exist. Second, we have already seen that the time factor has nothing to do with the completion of an infinite collection by successive addition. Since it is impossible to form an infinite in this manner, the series of past events could not be infinite. As for Russell's analysis of why Kant committed his alleged error, it is Russell, not Kant, who is confused. For when we consider the temporal series mentally, we form a regress in time, which is infinite:

$$\text{Present} \text{ — — — — — — — — — —} \rightarrow \text{Past}$$
$$0, 1, 2, 3, 4, 5, \cdots$$

Russell asserts that while this series is infinite and has no end, the real series of events is happening forward and has an end. But this is precisely the problem. For the real series of events, if infinite, would thus be an infinite completed by successive addition:

$$\text{Past} \text{ — — — — — — — — — —} \rightarrow \text{Present}$$
$$\cdots -5, -4, -3, -2, -1, 0$$

It would be as though someone writing from eternity were to claim to have just finished writing down the negative number series, ending at zero. As Black observed in discussing the second version of the Dichotomy paradox, this sort of series, as exemplified in the series of real events, is even more inconceivable than the open-ended series, such as we have in the mental regress. The very fact that the series has an end but no beginning is what makes it so absurd. For it means that we have formed an infinite collection by successive addition, which is impossible. (It also raises the problems discussed in Zeno's paradoxes.) If the series had a beginning, but no end, then we could rightly conceive of it as a potential infinite, as we do the future:

$$\text{Any given point} \text{ — — — — — —} \rightarrow \text{Future}$$
$$0, 1, 2, 3, 4, 5, \cdots$$

But this description is inapplicable to the temporal series of past events, which is *actual*, not potential as is the future. Far from untangling the absurdity of an infinite temporal regress of events, Russell only tightens the knot.[25] Russell's confusion thus becomes clearly apparent when he asserts that the future is precisely on a par with the past, and since the future can be infinite, so can the past. This *non sequitur* results either from regarding the past as a potential infinite or the future as an actual infinite.[26] There is no absurdity in holding that the universe began to exist and will continue forever, since at any point the series of events will always be finite and increasing. But it is in many ways absurd that the universe had no beginning and that the series of events is already actually infinite.

Pamela Huby crushes Russell's second set of objections to Kant's thesis.[27] She points out first that Kant says nothing about whether the events preceding a given event ought to be definable by extension; Russell's comment is therefore wholly beside the point. Second, Russell himself vitiates his argument on the logical parity of cause and effect, for when one turns to part seven of Russell's book, he argues that it is 'no longer possible' to place 'cause and effect on the same logical level', which is precisely what he said he was going to prove.[28] What Russell does do is formulate a substitute for cause and effect, by which conclusions about a third state of the universe can be drawn from knowledge about two other states. But the third state is still on a logical level different from the others, and since it may temporally precede the other two, it is not what we normally mean by 'effect'. The whole discussion seems rather far removed from the argument of Kant's antinomy. Moreover, we might ask what the *logical* priority of cause to effect has to do with *temporal* priority; Kant argues that the present event could not arise until all its temporally prior conditions had arisen. Logical priority has no part in the argument, and since it would be absurd to deny that events in a temporal series are not temporally prior to each other, Kant's analysis appears to be sound. Finally, we might note that enumeration of an infinite series is not just practically impossible, if by that Russell means that we do not have enough time, for it is of the nature of the actual infinite that it cannot be formed by successive addition. And we agree with Russell that there is nothing self-contradictory about an infinite class; it is the formation of an actual infinite collection by successive addition that we and Kant question.

The objection of Moore and Strawson is remarkable in its irrelevance to Kant's reasoning. Kant was not so naive as to think that because the series of events has one end it must be finite. The point is that if the series is infinite, it has been formed by successive synthesis, which is impossible. It must therefore be finite. The argument need not even allude to counting as Strawson implies; the temporal series is by nature successively formed and cannot therefore be infinite. The issue of counting arises when the argument's detractors attempt to rebut this reasoning by numbering the series of events backwards in a misguided effort to prove that it can be infinite. Moore himself admits that the objection does not strike at the heart of Kant's reasoning and that a 'real difficulty' remains here which he is unable to resolve.[29] But, he asks, are we entitled to conclude from this Kant's 'obviously false' conclusion that nothing exists in time, that there is no such thing as time?[30] Certainly not; but we would be forced to this conclusion only if Kant's antithesis were cogent, which it is not. But his thesis is cogent, and therefore we must conclude that the temporal series of events is finite and had a beginning.

Broad's objections to Kant's definition of infinite fail to reckon with the real and temporal character of the series in question. Because the discussion concerns a real series that is formed by successive synthesis, it is of vital importance to know that one characteristic of the infinite is that it cannot be completed by successive synthesis. Broad's example of the measuring rod only shows that in an infinite line there is no *finite* number of segments of equal length. But the question we are concerned with is whether such a line could be *formed* by successive additions of equal segments. That is why this particular feature of the infinite is of such interest to Kant. The charge that Kant has spatialised time is foundationless. The intrinsic successive nature of the temporal process is vital to Kant's thesis. Broad also commits Russell's error of confusing the mental regress of events with the progress of the physical series: it is Broad, not Kant, who seeks to measure from the present backwards. Thus, Broad measures from the present back into time (as though the series came to be formed that way!) and concludes that for every finite number of time segments, there was a world before that. But this only proves that if the series of past events is an actual infinite, then it is actually infinite. The question is, how can an actual infinite come to be *formed* by successive addition? Broad never answers this question, which lies at the heart of Kant's proof.

Swinburne commits a by now familiar error. He admits that it seems impossible to complete an infinite by starting at its beginning. He admits that it is dubious that a series with no beginning but an end makes sense. Since the temporal regress of events is precisely this last sort of series, he suggests that we mentally renumber the series by beginning at the present and regressing backwards. In this way, he asserts, the series is no longer a completed infinite. Swinburne not only confuses the mental series with the real series, but he advocates doing so. Can he seriously believe that by *mentally* beginning at the present and regressing in time, the real series itself is somehow transformed from a series with no beginning but an end into a series with a beginning but no end? He fails to grasp the fact that how we mentally conceive the series does not in any way affect the ontological character of the series as one with no beginning but an end, or in other words, as an actual infinite formed by successive addition. His doubts about the sense of this are well justified.

Zwart's analysis is shot through with misunderstandings. Like Kemp Smith, he, too, obviously conceives of the series of events as laid out on a line with the future as real as the past. But future events are not like past events, for they have never happened. Kant has no burden at all to prove that there must be a last event, since if he proves there is a first event, the number of subsequent events is at all times finite. Nor is Kant's argument a *principio principi*: the reason the series of events cannot be infinite is because an infinite cannot be completed by successive synthesis. Kant is not so stupid as to presuppose a first event. Finally, Zwart also propounds the error of confusing the mental conception of the series with the progressive instantiation of the series.

But we should not give the impression that all philosophers have opposed Kant's thesis. In fact, some have supported Kant's argument in the thesis of the first antinomy. G. J. Whitrow argues not only that Kant's thesis is valid, but also that modern mathematical theories of the infinite cannot refute Kant's thesis because whereas Kant's argument is concerned with temporal concepts, modern set theory has been purged of all reference to time.[31] He cautions that Cantor's infinite sets are only 'creations of our thinking' and the '. . . extension of the Cantorian infinite to the temporal realm . . . is inapplicable'.[32] Drawing a comparison between Zeno's Dichotomy and Kant's antinomy, he comments,

> It is interesting to compare and contrast Zeno's Dichotomy and Achilles paradoxes with Kant's argument that up to the present there cannot have been an infinite number of successive states of things, because such an infinite series can never be completed through successive *synthesis*. . . . In the cases considered by Zeno the infinite series of successive acts is a purely conceptual one resulting from our method of *analysis*, whereas in Kant's case the infinite series is presumed *ex hypothesi* to have actually occurred.[33]

This is an insight rarely shared by other philosophers expounding either Zeno or Kant. In a later work, Whitrow argues even more vigorously for the cogency of Kant's thesis.[34] If the universe had no beginning, then at least one temporal chain of events had no beginning. (By temporal chain of events is meant a sequence of discrete physical occurrences that has the usual properties of discrete chronological order.) If E is an event in this chain, there is an important difference between an infinite past and an infinite future for E; one is actual and the other potential. That the future is a potential infinite means that (1) for any future event in E there will be future events and (2) any event in the future of E is separated from E by a finite number of intermediate events. On the other hand, the past is actual. Whitrow points out that when we try to think back over the series of past events, our train of thought yields only a potential infinite; but this process does not correspond to the actual successive occurrence of these events. Therefore, if the past events are infinite, they constitute an actual infinite. Consequently, if the chain of events prior to E is infinite, then there must be an event O that is separated from E by an infinite number of intermediate events. If not, then the number of events separating E from any event O would be finite, and thus the past would be only a potential infinite, which is impossible. But an infinite number of intermediate events raises two problems: (1) if E is an infinite number of events from O, then with regard to O the notion of the future as a potential infinite is destroyed, since both O and E do occur; (2) when in the temporal chain between O and E does the total number of events that have occurred since O become infinite instead of finite? Whitrow concludes that the idea of an elapsed infinity of events presents an insoluble problem and that time and the universe had a beginning.[35]

Stuart Hackett has also argued in favour of the Kantian thesis in the context of a cosmological argument.[36] He begins his proof with any existent that is an effect, that is, an existence whose character and being are determined by antecedent and contemporaneous existences external to itself. These existences are themselves effects or not, and so on. Either this series of effects and causes is infinite or not. But an infinite number of successive causes and effects is rationally inconceivable, since no series of particular and determinate entities could ever add up to infinity. But if the series is not infinite, it must end in a cause which is self-contained, a being that contains within itself the conditions of its determinate character. Hackett contends that the mathematical infinite expressed in the natural numbers series is a potential infinite only which approaches infinity by reason of the fact that no definite limit is assigned to the series.[37] If there were an eternal spirit writing from eternity, it would not even have begun to write down all the natural numbers, since an infinity would always remain between the highest number it had written and infinity. He concludes, therefore, that Kant has argued soundly in his thesis that the world has had a beginning in time.

In an article provocatively titled 'Kant or Cantor?' Huby also argues in favour of Kant's thesis.[38] Unfortunately, her argument primarily concerns the finitude of space. She contends that Cantor's mathematical theories do not necessarily have a counterpart in reality; indeed, the paradoxes would be so great if they did that it is most reasonable to conclude that reality is finite in time and space. With specific regard to time, she suggests a possible argument that the number of elapsed finite periods of time would have to be finite because of the paradoxes of an actual infinite in reality.[39]

We are not alone, then, in regarding Kant's argument as a cogent proof that the temporal series of events is finite. But, of course, Kant's argument was part of an antinomy, and he also argued in support of the antithesis. The refutation of Kant's antithesis may be found on pages 149–51, where I discuss the nature of the cause of the universe.

NOTES

1. Immanuel Kant, *Immanuel Kant's 'Critique of Pure Reason'*, trans. Norman Kemp Smith (London: Macmillan & Co., 1929), p. 396.

2. Ibid., p. 397.

3. Ibid., p. 399–401.

4. Al-Azm agrees: 'The thesis of the first antinomy asserts the finitude of the world series in time and not of the temporal container itself.' (Sadik J. al-Azm, *The Origins of Kant's Arguments in the Antinomies* [Oxford: Clarendon Press, 1972], p. 42.)

5. A. C. Ewing, *A Short Commentary to Kant's 'Critique of Pure Reason'*, 2d ed. (London: Methuen & Co., 1950), p. 209.

6. Ibid., p. 210. See Kant's relevant comments in Kant, *Critique*, p. 387.

7. Norman Kemp Smith, *A Commentary to Kant's 'Critique of Pure Reason'* (London: Macmillan & Co., 1918), pp. 483–4.

8. Ibid., p. 484.

9. Ibid.

10. Ibid.

11. Ibid.

12. Bertrand Russell, *Our Knowledge of the External World*, 2d ed. (New York: W. W. Norton & Co., 1929), p. 170.

13. Ibid., p. 171.

14. Ibid.

15. Ibid., p. 195.

16. Ibid.

17. Bertrand Russell, *The Principles of Mathematics*, 2d ed. (London: George Allen & Unwin, 1937), p. 459.

18. Ibid.

19. George Edward Moore, *Some Main Problems of Philosophy*, Muirhead Library of Philosophy (London: George Allen & Unwin, 1953; New York: Macmillan Co., 1953), p. 180.

20. P. F. Strawson, *Bounds of Sense* (London: Methuen & Co., 1966), p. 176.

21. C. D. Broad, 'Kant's Mathematical Antinomies', *Proceedings of the Aristotelian Society* 40 (1955): 3.

22. R. G. Swinburne, 'The Beginning of the Universe', *The Aristotelian Society* 40 (1966): 131–2; R. G. Swinburne, *Space and Time* (London: Macmillan, 1968), pp. 298–9. Whether Swinburne accurately represents Aquinas is a moot point. On Aquinas's doctrine, see E. Bertola, 'Tommaso d'Aquino

e il Problema dell' eternità del Mondo,' *Revista di Filosofia Neo-Scolastica* 66 (1974): 312–55. For an analysis of Aquinas's debate with Bonaventure on this point see Francis J. Kovach, 'The Question of the Eternity of the World in St. Bonaventure and St. Thomas—a Critical Analysis', *Southwestern Journal of Philosophy* 5 (1974): 141–72. Kovach declares Bonaventure the winner. See also Lucien Roy, 'Note philosophique sur l'idée de commencement dans la création', *Sciences Ecclesiastiques* 2 (1949): 223. He also pronounces Aquinas's reply inadequate.

23. P. J. Zwart, *About Time* (Amsterdam and Oxford: North Holland Publishing Co., 1976), p. 238.

24. Ibid., pp. 242–3.

25. James Thomson is also guilty of Russell's mistake when he suggests we regard the series of past events as an ω type series with the earlier and later reversed: . . . , 4, 3, 2, 1. He charges Kant with replacing the proposition that the world did not have a beginning with the proposition that the world had a beginning infinitely remote in time. (*Encyclopedia of Philosophy*, s.v. 'Infinity in Mathematics and Logic', by James Thomson.) It is only our mental conception of the series that can be enumerated as Thomson specifies; the series itself is a series of order type *ω, the order type of the negative numbers. Kant does not in any way imply an infinitely distant beginning. It is only because a beginningless series is so rationally inconceivable that we think such a beginning is entailed in Kant's argument about successive synthesis. We cannot conceive of a series that is both formed successively and yet actually infinite; the idea is so absurd that we surreptitiously slip in a starting-point to get the infinite series going. Thus, we cannot conceive of anyone writing down all the negative numbers from eternity past so that he ends at −1. So we think of him starting at an infinitely distant number and proceeding thence. This is illegitimate, of course, and the inconceivability of such a counting serves to confirm Kant's argument. For if the series of past events is actually infinite, then such a counting has, in fact, been accomplished.

26. J. J. C. Smart makes the same error. Though he correctly characterises the past series of events as an *ω type series, he fails to see that this series is actually infinite, while the future is only potentially so. He argues that Kant embraces the myth of the passage of things through time; Kant thinks of the world as having come to its present state through a series of past events, so that an infinite succession would have to be completed. Otherwise, he would have been just as puzzled about the infinite future as the infinite past. There is 'perfect symmetry', between the two. (*Encyclopedia of Philosophy*, s.v. 'Time', by J. J. C. Smart.) Smart's charge of the myth of passage would apply to some forms of the *kalām* argument (Saadia's, in particular), but it is not implied by Kant's thesis. Kant is not arguing that existence flows through time to the present event, but that the present event will not occur until its determinate conditions are present and that if these conditions are infinite in number, then they can never be completely given by successive synthesis. Nor is the myth implied in our argument that an actual infinite cannot be formed by successive addition. The reason Kant is not puzzled by the future is that the series of events from any point toward the future is a potential infinite only.

27. Pamela M. Huby, 'Kant or Cantor? That the Universe, if Real, Must be Finite in Both Space and Time', *Philosophy* 46 (1971): 121-3.

28. Russell, *Principles*, p. 496.

29. Moore, *Problems*, pp. 180–1. Moore admits himself powerless to refute Kant's reasoning. (Ibid., pp. 198–200.)

30. Ibid., pp. 180–1.

31. G. J. Whitrow, *The Natural Philosophy of Time* (London and Edinburgh: Thomas Nelson & Sons, 1961), pp. 31-2. Elsewhere he elaborates,

> The modern theory of infinity . . . is essentially a *static* theory of infinite sets. Similarly, the modern theory of the variable . . . is again a static theory, for the variable is no longer regarded by pure mathematicians as representing a progressive passage through all the values of an interval but the disjunctive assumption of any one of the values in the interval. Thus the acceptance of the modern theory of the continuum cannot be invoked as a valid argument automatically disposing of Kant's antinomies . . . , since this theory has been developed by specifically omitting all previous intuitive reference to the concept of time. (G. J. Whitrow, 'The Age of the Universe', *British Journal for the Philosophy of Science* 5 [1954-55]: 217.)

32. Ibid., p. 148.

33. Ibid., p. 152.

34. G. J. Whitrow, 'Time and the Universe', in *The Voices of Time*, ed. J. T. Fraser (London: Penguin Press, 1968), pp. 565-8.

35. Dr Whitrow has informed me that a debate between Karl Popper and Whitrow on the cogency of Kant's reasoning will be published in the near future. (See G. J. Whitrow, 'On the Impossibility of an Infinite Past', *British Journal for the Philosophy of Science* 29 [1978]: 39-45 and Karl Popper, 'On the Possibility of an Infinite Past: A Reply to Whitrow', *British Journal for the Philosophy of Science* 29 [1978]: 47-8. Popper's critique argues that while the *set* of all past events is actually infinite, the *series* of past events is potentially infinite. This again commits the mistake of confusing the mental regress of counting with the progressive formation of the series. For the series of past events to be a potential infinite, it would have to be finite and growing in a 'backwards' direction.)

36. Stuart C. Hackett, *The Resurrection of Theism* (Chicago: Moody Press, 1957), pp. 194-5.

37. Ibid., p. 294.

38. Huby, 'Kant or Cantor?' pp. 121-32.

39. W. H. Newton-Smith effectively criticised her argument for the finitude of the universe in space (W. H. Newton-Smith, 'Armchair Cosmology', *Philosophy* 47 [1972]: 64-5), as did N. W. Boyce (N. W. Boyce, 'A Priori Knowledge and Cosmology', *Philosophy* 47 [1972]: 67). But their rather facile arguments that there are no *logical* paradoxes in set theory or that it is *logically* possible for the universe to have an infinite age amount to nothing, for, as she rejoins, logical possibility does not imply real possibility. (Pamela M. Huby,

'Cosmology and Infinity', *Philosophy* 48 [1973]: 186.) Neither of her critics understand the notion of potential infinity, and Boyce commits the fallacy of equating our mental conception of an infinite regress with the real series of events.

Index

Printed in Poland
by Amazon Fulfillment
Poland Sp. z o.o., Wrocław

65873763R00128